D0204544

ETHIOPIA AND THE RED SEA

By the same author:

Ethiopia, the Era of the Princes
Oil, Power and Politics

ETHIOPIA AND THE RED SEA

The rise and decline of the Solomonic dynasty and Muslim–European rivalry in the region

MORDECHAI ABIR

Institute of Asian and African Studies
Hebrew University of Jerusalem

FRANK CASS

First Published 1980 in Great Britain by
FRANK CASS AND COMPANY LIMITED
Gainsborough House, Gainsborough Road,
London, E11 1RS, England

and in the United States of America by
FRANK CASS AND COMPANY LIMITED
c/o Biblio Distribution Centre
81 Adams Drive, P.O. Box 327, Totowa, N.J. 07511

British Library Cataloguing in Publication Data

Abir Mordechai
  Ethiopia and the Red Sea.
  1. Ethiopia – History – To 1490
  2. Ethiopia – History – 1490–1889
  I. Title
  963'.02   DT383

ISBN 0-7146-3164-7

*Typeset by Saildean Ltd.,
Printed in Great Britain by*
Biddles Ltd, Guildford, Surrey

To Rutha
who helped to write this and my other books
and to Ronit who stood by us in difficult days.

Contents

Maps

Preface

This book is partly the outcome of research for the chapter called 'Ethiopia and the Horn of Africa' (from the middle of the sixteenth century until the middle of the eighteenth century), published in the fourth volume of the *Cambridge History of Africa*. The extensive research conducted for several summers between 1967 and 1971 for a forty-page chapter left me with substantial material, most of which I was unable to use, and a strong feeling that I had not done justice to the subject which I discussed. The period covered by my chapter (justly prescribed by the editor because of the need for uniformity in the volume) did not, moreover, correspond with what I later came to feel was a more suitable and cohesive and exceedingly important time-framework in the history of the Horn, beginning with the rise of the Solomonic dynasty (1270). I also felt that not enough attention was devoted by me and by earlier authors who dealt with the Horn of Africa to the correlation between events in that region and those in other countries of the Red Sea basin (and Europe), or to the impact of economic phenomena on their political, social and commercial development since the beginning of the second millenium A.D.

Mistakenly believing that I already had most of the material for the second half of the book in hand and with my appetite whetted to acquire additional knowledge about the earlier period, I began to plan a book which would cover the history of the Horn of Africa and the Red Sea from the rise of the Solomonic dynasty in the thirteenth century to its final decline.

Another incentive to write such a book was a course which I taught at the Hebrew University of Jerusalem in 1973/4 called

'Islam and Christianity in the Red Sea area'. Notwithstanding the multi-volume, outdated and, to some extent, inaccurate, superficial but still monumental work of Albert Kammerer, *La Mer Rouge, l'Abyssinie et l'Arabie. . . .*, I could not find books with a comprehensive approach to the subject which might help my students, other than my own research. Hardly any of the texts which I used appreciated the interrelation between the lands of the Red Sea basin, the meeting and confrontation of Islam and Christianity with the semitic and African cultures in the region, and the commercial importance of the Red Sea not just as an international waterway but for the socio-economic and political development of the countries around it and for 'power politics' of this period. Forced to refer to numerous works which related at best to one region and which in many cases were chronologies which ignored environmental and socio-economic factors, I concluded that a book with a comprehensive approach to the subject focused on the history of the Horn was badly needed.

When researching the chapter for the *Cambridge History of Africa*, I had already found to my distress that I was 'pioneering' a period relatively neglected by historians of the Horn due to misconceptions concerning its importance and the scarcity of source material (with the outstanding exception of the Portuguese and the Jesuit period in Ethiopia – mainly the first decades of the seventeenth century – which resulted in enormous but, to a great extent, repetitious data). My difficulties concerning source material for the earlier period of the Solomonic dynasty were even more acute because apart from laconic royal chronicles, mostly of doubtful quality, and the limited contributions of Muslim scholars mainly interested in the expansion of Islam and trade, the area of the Horn was in that period largely *terra incognita*.

A welcome surprise was an excellent Ph.D. thesis written by Dr. Taddesse Tamrat called 'Church and State in Ethiopia 1270-1527' (in fact it ends with the latter part of Zara Yaeqob's reign in the mid-fifteenth century; presented to London University in 1968, Dr. Tamrat's work was published under the same title by the Clarendon Press, Oxford, in 1972). Undoubtedly, this dissertation was an important addition to the background material which I had been collecting because, using many primary sources, Dr. Tamrat emphasizes the role of the Ethiopian church and monastic orders in the spiritual and political evolution of Solomonic Ethiopia. Despite the bias and inhibitions of the writer and the fact that through expediency he focused his attention mainly on the reigns of two or three important emperors in the fourteenth and fifteenth centuries, Dr. Tamrat's work is a most important and original contribution to our understanding of relations between the development of the Ethiopian church and the Ethiopian polity.

When in London in 1970 I met my friend and former colleague Dr. Merid Wolde Aregay, who was working on a Ph.D. thesis called 'Southern Ethiopia and the Christian Kingdom 1508-1708'. Dr. Wolde Aregay, who needed my help in certain matters, generously reciprocated by putting at my disposal copies of a few documents which he had found in the Portuguese and other archives. Moreover, when planning this book several years later, I consulted his thesis (London University, 1971). The thoroughness of his research, his originality and meticulous attempt to reconstruct Galla history since the beginning of the sixteenth century merit special praise. Although I disagree with many of his conclusions concerning developments in the Horn, his reticence in regard to the national church and similar matters, and his relative disregard of the correlation between the economic and political history of the Indian Ocean and the Red Sea and that of the Horn, his thesis is undoubtedly a most important contribution to our knowledge of the latter region, especially in the 'Portuguese-Jesuit period'. It was also a valuable addition to the sources which I already had.

If anything, Tamrat's and Wolde Aregay's works further convinced me of the need for a book on the history of the Horn and the Red Sea with a comprehensive approach. They also convinced me that the period from the eve of the rise of the Solomonic kingdom in the thirteenth century to its contraction and the beginning of its rapid decline and developments in the Red Sea in the same period, made a fascinating and inseparable historical context. A history of the people of the region in this period, taking into account the correlation between the countries of the Red Sea basin, their economic history as well as religious and cultural dynamics and relation to 'power politics' in the region is, it seems, badly needed. My book, although focusing on the history of the Horn, attempts to do exactly that.

When mentioning Ethiopian and Arab names, terms, titles and words I have used the most common transliteration, deleting, for convenience sake, whenever possible, the diacritical marks. Names, terms and words commonly used in European languages and books are spelt in their accepted form even if this deviates from the correct transliteration.

Finally I owe thanks to Dr Victor Low for his help in editing my English.

JERUSALEM   MARCH 1980

Introduction

An important waterway for international trade, the Red Sea is about 2000 kms. long and generally between 200-300 kms. wide. In its southern part the Arabian peninsula approaches the Horn of Africa to a distance of about 25 kms., creating the straits of Bab al-Mandab which connect the Red Sea with the Indian Ocean. The significance of this expanse of water resembling a long canal is that it projects northwards through the Gulf of Suez nearly as far as the Mediterranean and through Hijaz and the Gulf of Eilat towards the heart of the Middle East. Hence, the Red Sea became of old a major artery for international trade between the Far East, Europe and the Muslim empires of the Middle East. This transit trade benefitted the population and governments of the region who participated in it, but it also helped develop the export of local products, especially luxury items produced in the Horn of Africa. It was only to be expected that such trade activities would generate cultural and economic influences and enhance relations between the different peoples of the Red Sea basin.

Immigrants from South Arabia who reached the Horn during the first millenium B.C. introduced influences which created the semito-Cushitic cultural synthesis and probably accelerated the process of state-building. But population movement was not restricted to one direction only; tribes and conquering armies coming from the Horn established themselves in southwestern Arabia and took part in the cultural and political evolution of the area. Cultural crossfertilisation and political contacts were also developed by merchants from the Mediterranean countries and Arabian visitors to Ethiopia, while their counterparts from the

Horn of Africa travelled to or settled in the commercial centres of the Middle East.

Christianity was implanted in northern Ethiopia as early as the fourth century A.D. It became a factor of immense importance in the cultural and political evolution of the Axumite, Zagwe and Solomonic empires. Dependent on the See of Alexandria, the Ethiopian church maintained contacts with the Christian communities of the Nile Valley and the churches of the east and was the cause of the special relations between Ethiopia and Egypt.

Islam had already reached the Ethiopian coast from its birthplace in Hijaz in the seventh century. Closely related to trade activities, it slowly advanced into the highlands, competing in the coming centuries with Christianity for hegemony in the Horn of Africa. Although at first it made little headway, it provided a link between the peoples of the Horn and those of the Middle East and the Muslim world as a whole. As elsewhere, its pragmatism and flexibility at a time when the Red Sea trade flourished and a growing number of Ulama arrived from Arabia, proved an immense advantage for its success among the people of the Horn of Africa.

The close correlation between the countries of the Red Sea basin and socio-political and cultural development in the Horn is evident. Indeed, positioned as it is near the entrance of the Red Sea, being the source of most of the Nile waters and considered an important producer of luxurious trade goods, the Horn of Africa, especially after the arrival of the Portuguese in the Indian Ocean at the end of the fifteenth century, attracted the attention of its neighbours in no proportion to its true importance. In fact the Portuguese believed that they could deprive the Muslim world of an important source of its power by blocking the flow of trade through the Red Sea and diverting the Nile waters from Egypt with the help of Ethiopia.

The topography, climate and ecology of the different parts of the Horn are most varied. The Ethiopian plateau which rises in places to a height of about four kms. has in most areas ample rainfall and is ideal for the development of agriculture. In the north, nevertheless, some parts of Tigre are relatively arid and the rugged mountain ranges of the northern 'Falasha provinces' are far less suitable for cultivation than other areas of the highlands. The greater part of the plateau, however, is relatively level tableland dotted with flat-topped mountains called *amba*s and bisected by deep gorges, rivers and valleys. The Ethiopian Rift Valley and its chain of lakes, moreover, separate the central Sidama highlands from the eastern verges of the plateau. In the south where rainfall can reach 80 inches per annum the vegetation is lush and similar to some extent to the Equatorial forest zone. Further south, the plateau falls gradually towards the deserts of Northern Kenya and the area resembles in part the Savannah of the sub-Saharan belt, or becomes a desert.

In contrast to the pleasant climate and fertility of the highlands the torrid coastal plain of the Red Sea is among the most difficult arid regions in the world. This plain widens substantially when it approaches the Harar-Chercher plateau and penetrates the highlands for some distance along the Awash valley. The fertile Chercher-Harar highland projects towards the east and gently descends in the direction of the northern Somali coast. Its southern slopes, the Ogaden, is crisscrossed by numerous valleys and dry-river beds which join the Webi Shebeli and the Juba. While the main river-valleys are suitable for limited cultivation, the majority of the territory is ideal for pastoralism.

The ancient inhabitants of the plateau, of Negroid stock, were submerged in pre-history by Cushitic immigrants and their remnants found refuge in the less accessible peripheral areas of the plateau. The 'new' Cushitic population became in most cases agriculturalists and live today in most of the highlands alongside the Galla who immigrated into the area from the sixteenth century.

The number of immigrants from the Arabian Peninsula who settled in the Horn was relatively small. But their impact on the culture, languages and political structure of the Cushitic societies which absorbed them was deep and lasting. In northern Ethiopia the peoples later known as Tigrean and Amhara were those most affected by this process. But the Axumite (Ethiopian) culture was far from being Semitic and has many specific Cushitic traits (for convenience these groups will be called henceforth semitised). Other Arabian immigrants who crossed the Bab al-Mandab and settled among the Cushites of the Harar-Chercher plateau produced the semitised culture of the Adare of Harar, the Harle cultivators and the Warjih pastoralists of the region. The latter penetrated from the Harari highlands into parts of eastern Showa and later served as a vehicle for the expansion of south Arabian cultural influences and Islam into the area.

Some parts of Eritrea and the deserts and Savannah of the southern, southeastern and eastern Horn are inhabited by Hamitic (for convenience the non-semitised Cushitic pastoralists will be called henceforth Hamitic) pastoralists belonging to different groups. These may have moved into the less hospitable sections of the Horn after the first wave of Cushitic migrants, or may have been driven into areas of southern and southeastern Ethiopia at a later stage by the temporary expansion of the Bantu people in that direction in the first millenium A.D. Coming from the north, the Beja people caused the decline of Axum and the transfer of its centre southwards in the sixth century. This early migration of pastoralists demonstrates the impact that such movements could have on developments in the plateau. Other groups, such as the Somali, Afar, and later the Galla, made their first appearance in the history of the Horn only in the early decades of the second millenium A.D. This did not mean that they had not lived in the region before but rather that they were insufficiently important to be mentioned by historians (on their migration see below).

A watershed of peoples, with divergent climatic conditions, cultures and many physical barriers and natural fortresses, the Horn of Africa was conducive to the development of different societies which evolved their own languages and socio-political institutions. The establishment of a cohesive polity over a large area of the plateau was, therefore, a major achievement. To unite the Horn or most of it, with its pastoralist population, into one political entity was a virtually impossible undertaking.

The introduction of semitic influences and their fusion with the local Cushitic customs, as well as the development of commercial activities in the region, undoubtedly accelerated the process of state-building and of integration in certain areas. The role of the semito-Cushitic groups as a link between the population of the Horn, its coast and the Red Sea basin was extremely important and led to the expansion of the former at the expense of the latter. Enhanced by the wish to monopolise trade this trend was quickened by the introduction in the fourth century of Christianity in the northern plateau and Islam in the seventh century among the peoples of the coast and the verges of the highlands. Religion became, thereafter, an integral part of the ideology of the Solomonic kingdom and of its Islamic counterparts.

The integrative forces were always frustrated by strong centrifugal elements in the Horn. This paradox is typical of the history of
the region, especially since the second millenium A.D. This book
will attempt, among other things, to analyse and explain this
phenomenon which was typical both of the Christian kingdom and
of the Muslim principalities. It will also examine why the
Solomonic monarchs were unable to exploit the national church
with its roots in the African soil and why the Muslim sultanates did
not benefit from the well-known advantages of Islam in Africa and
elsewhere in the world.

Because they had literate classes and were visited by foreigners
who wrote about their societies and history, the Christian monarchy and to some extent the Muslim sultanates dominate the
history of the region. The majority of the people of the Horn,
illiterate until modern times, were virtually ignored. Thus, although
the great Galla migration from the sixteenth century and the
evolution of Galla society and culture thereafter should have had
precedence in the history of the Horn, they were neglected by most
historians. The author has attempted in this book to rectify this
shortcoming, as far as possible, without 'manufacturing' history
lacking a foundation.

Ahmad Grañ's Jihad is undoubtedly a milestone in relations
between the Christian semitised-Cushitic sedentary elements and
the Muslim mercantile and pastoralist societies. To understand the
polarisation of relations between Muslims and Christians and the
conditions which paved the way for the success of the Galla
migration and the failure of the Ethiopians to assimilate them, it is
imperative to study the first centuries of the Solomonic kingdom,
its institutions and national church. These are additional reasons
why the obvious starting point for this study is the establishment of
the new dynasty by Yekuno Amlak in 1270.

Although the short concluding chapter of the book takes the
story up to the mid-eighteenth century, the detailed study termin-
ates with the reign of Emperor Fasilidas (r. 1632-1667). This date
was chosen because it marks the end of the revolutionary attempt
by his father to revive the Ethiopian kingdom by modernising it
through Westernisation and conversion to Catholicism. No serious
effort to re-establish the power of the Solomonic monarchy in its
'traditional' borders was undertaken thereafter. Moreover, the
backlash created by the attempt to convert Ethiopia to Catholicism

caused it to turn away from Western Christianity and isolate itself voluntarily from the spiritual and technical revolution which Europe underwent in this period.

The rise of Fasilidas also marks the acceptance of the greatly reduced political borders of Ethiopia caused by the Galla migration. It had been the custom of the Solomonic emperors and royal camp to move from one province to another according to necessity and circumstances. In addition to the strategic-military importance of the presence of the monarch and his followers in peripheral parts of a rapidly expanding kingdom, this phenomenon served as an important integrative factor for an empire suffering from lack of cohesion and homogeneity. The establishment of a permanent capital by Fasilidas in Gondar amounted to a final acceptance of the new realities and opened a new era in Ethiopian history. The palaces built in Gondar gradually came to resemble the 'golden cages' of the Ottoman sultans in Istanbul and led to the final decline of the authority of the monarch and the semitised-Cushitic society and to the rise of Galla power.

The Horn of Africa became marginally involved in the struggle between Western Christianity and Islam from the time of the Crusaders. The increasingly bitter struggle between Europe and the Muslims culminated, as far as Ethiopia was concerned, in the appearance of the Portuguese in the Red Sea at the beginning of the sixteenth century attempting to block the passage of the Far East trade to the Muslim world. This dramatic development coincided, however, with the virtual conquest of most of the Red Sea basin by the Ottomans after 1517. In the coming period, relations between Ethiopia and its Muslim neighbours underwent a substantial upheaval. This development was influenced by the arrival of the Portuguese and Jesuits in Ethiopia, who, in addition to taking part in power politics, became directly and indirectly involved in the country's socio-political and cultural affairs. The expulsion of the Jesuits from Ethiopia and the Ottomans from Yemen in the 1630s marked the virtual termination of the impact of foreign powers on political and cultural dynamics in the region. But it also opened an era of continuous stagnation in the Horn and the Red Sea which ended only in the nineteenth century.

CHAPTER I

Economic and Political Background

Trade and Politics in the Red Sea to 1500

The contribution of the lucrative Far East trade to the prosperity of the Middle East and to the economy of parts of the Arabian Peninsula goes back to the period before the advent of Christianity. Some early sources and archaeological finds furnish fragmented information about the pattern of this trade, which reached the Middle East by way of the Persian Gulf and the Red Sea. Flourishing trading metropolises such as Adulis, Sheba and Kataban, Hormuz and Kuwait and trading colonies established by Greek, Roman, Arab, Persian, Indian and other merchants along the coasts of the Red Sea and the Persian Gulf bear evidence of the prosperity of this trade.[1]

The development of maritime technology and navigation in the Indian Ocean was relatively slow, and until about the turn of the first millenium A.D. shipping in this region was basically coastal. Nevertheless, its contribution to the expansion of the Far East trade with the Mediterranean and indirectly to developments in the region was considerable. Undoubtedly, the rise of Islam was affected by changes in the patterns of the caravan routes in the Arabian Peninsula related to the international trade. The rise of the Muslim empire, which theoretically united all the territory from India to the Iberian Peninsula, was a major factor contributing to the rapid expansion of the Far East trade in the coming centuries.

Composed of luxury items such as gems, ivory, and above all spices, the Far East trade shifted its centre of gravity to the Persian Gulf when the centre of the Muslim empire moved from Damascus to Mesopotamia in the middle of the eighth century, because the Red Sea countries were convulsed, during this period, by migrations

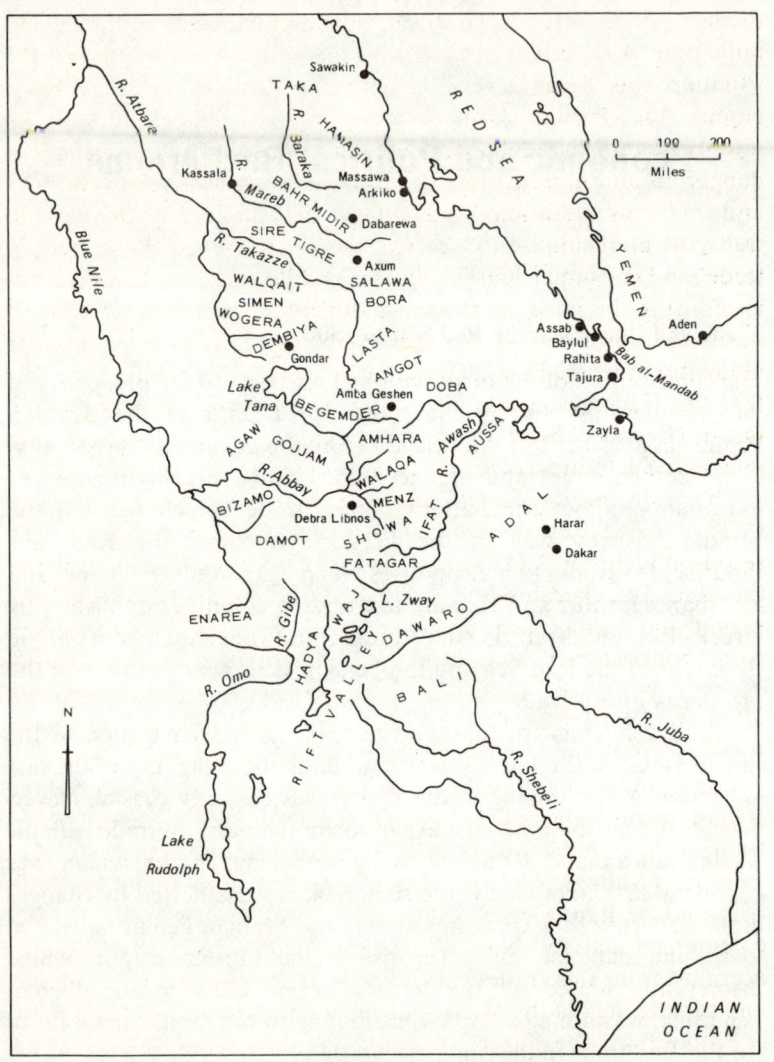

THE HORN OF AFRICA AT THE BEGINNING OF THE SIXTEENTH CENTURY
Principalities, Provinces and Major Landmarks

and internal wars. The Abbasid empire prospered due to international trade and the wealth of Golden Baghdad became the theme of many legends. However, already by the end of the second millenium A.D. it was evident that the wheel had turned and the situation was being reversed. With the decline of the Abbasid empire the Persian Gulf became infested with pirates, who interfered with the seaborne trade, and transport by this route was dangerous and more costly. The Red Sea route was relatively safer and had the additional advantage of enabling merchants to transport merchandise by sea to ports far nearer to the centres of trade, and consumer markets in the Middle East and Europe, thus minimising the need for the more difficult, expensive and dangerous land transportation. This advantage more than offset additional taxation incurred in Yemen and Egypt[2], not to mention the fact that the Hajj season was always an occasion for an international fair in Hijaz because many pilgrims combined the pilgrimage with mercantile activities *(Hajj Wa-Hidja)*.

The main trading centres and ports along the Red Sea and the Gulf of Aden were already flourishing by the beginning of the second millenium A.D.[3] Aden itself, situated near the entrance of the Red Sea, became the unrivalled trading metropolis of the region and a major entrepôt for Far East and African trade. A cosmopolitan town, its population was composed mainly of merchants from Arabia, the Horn of Africa, Egypt and from countries all around the Indian Ocean. Many merchants settled in the town for a few years and others arrived in this port every season.[4]

Cognizant of the growing importance of the Red Sea trade, the Italian towns (above all Venice) began to participate in it by transporting merchandise from Egypt's Mediterranean ports to Europe. Although excluded from direct involvement in the Red Sea and Indian Ocean trade, they prospered thanks to this commercial activity. Nevertheless, the major part of the benefits accruing from this trade went to Red Sea and oriental merchants and to the rulers of the Muslim countries, notably Egypt.[5]

Profits from the Far East trade were so enormous that it was commonly believed in Europe that this trade was a pillar of the economy of the Muslim world and the source of its strength and military power. A naval expedition launched by the Crusaders in 1183 from Eilat into the Red Sea was partly motivated by the wish to undermine the Muslim economy. According to Salah ad-Din's chronicler, the Qadi al-Fadhl, the Christian flotilla not only attacked Muslim shipping in the northern part of the sea, but also beyond Bab al-Mandab.[6] Ironically, the Crusaders greatly contributed to the expansion of the Red Sea trade and the rise in the revenues of Ayyubid and later of the Mamluk rulers of Egypt. The tens of thousands of Crusaders and pilgrims returning to Europe from the Holy Land who had acquired a taste for eastern luxuries were responsible, to a great extent, for the rapid expansion of the use of spices among the upper classes in Europe and a considerably expanded market for exotic oriental products in general.

The continuous development of the Red Sea trade since the opening of the first millenium A.D. had a substantial impact on political dynamics in the countries of the Red Sea basin. Salah ad-Din was determined to establish his authority in the region even before the abortive maritime adventure of the Crusaders. By 1172 an Ayyubid dynasty ruled most of Yemen and its capitals were Zabid and Aden. Soon afterwards, however, this dynasty was replaced by the Rassulids and though their authority in Yemen's highlands was even more precarious than that of the Ayyubids, they revived the traditional rivalry between Yemen and Egypt over the control of Hijaz and the trade of the Red Sea.

The most fertile and populous part of the Arabian Peninsula, Yemen, was a focus of cultural and political fermentation long before the rise of Islam. All this, notwithstanding its geo-physical characteristics, enhanced the preservation of its fiercely individualistic tribalist society, and it was a haven for sects of heterodox Islam and other minorities. The numerous dynasties and principalities which sprang up in Yemen opposed any attempt at centralisation, and often assumed theological difference as their cause.

The south and the Tihama coast, with its population of mixed blood (closely related to Ethiopia), are considered predominantly Sunni, but in reality the latter was the home of many tribes who adhered to heterodox Islam, including several Shi'i sects. The central plateau and parts of the north, the stronghold of the Zaydis, had strong Isma'ili (Shi'ite) enclaves and were periodically swept by Kharijite movements. Religious upheavals, led by Shi'i or Khariji Imams, other puritan leaders or adventurers of different sorts, were, therefore, a most common phenomenon in Yemen's history. Indeed, regionalist orientation, and paradoxically also movements for greater unification and cohesiveness, were often translated into religious terms. Invariably such a state of affairs was not conducive to the development of greater cohesion and of a strong centralised authority in the country. All this, however, did not affect the commercial importance of Yemen, although it may have impeded its development.

Traditionally Indian Ocean shipping did not sail beyond the port of Aden. Merchandise from the Far East was unloaded in this port-town and after paying local taxes it was reloaded on the smaller, flat-bottomed boats coming from Egypt, Hijaz and Yemen. While in Aden, Far East merchants met and traded with their local counterparts or with merchants from Arabia, the Middle East and the Horn of Africa. Contemporary Muslim historiographers such as Al-Mas'udi, Al-Idrisi and Qalqashandi[7] claim that until the fifteenth century Indian Ocean captains did not sail into the Red Sea because they were unable to navigate their heavy boats through the shallow straits of Bab al-Mandab. It is far more likely, however, that the true cause for this arrangement was economic, as Aden's and Yemen's rulers were unwilling to lose the rich revenues from the transit trade.

Very much aware of the benefits of trade, Egypt's rulers, despite their merciless war against the Crusaders, encouraged European merchants, especially from the Italian towns, to trade with Egypt. But, dissatisfied with their share of the trade, sultans such as Baybars (r. 1260-1277) and An-Nasir Muhammad b. Qala'un (r. 1293-1294, 1298-1308, 1309-1340) were determined to bring the merchants of the Far East directly into ports under their control. Facilities for shipping and trade were provided in Suez, At-Tor and Jedda and Egyptian merchants (many of them Jews) were instructed to invite their counterparts from the Far East to trade in Egypt and its Red Sea ports. At the end of the thirteenth century, during the reign of Sultan Qala'un, Aden's rulers, it seems, attempted to prevent the establishment of direct relations between Egypt and the Far East, but abandoned such efforts in the face of Egyptian threats to conquer Yemen.[8] Thus, by the fourteenth century it was already quite common for Indian and other Far East merchants to accompany their merchandise to Egypt as passengers of ships belonging to the Red Sea.

The first half of the fourteenth century, during the long reign of An-Nasir Muhammad b. Qala'un, was one of the most prosperous and outstanding periods in Egyptian history. In this period the Mamluks gradually consolidated their control over Hijaz and extended their influence in Sudan to the Red Sea coast.[9] But the bitter struggle for power between the Bahri and Burji Mamluks in Egypt in the second half of the century[10] interrupted the aggressive, economically oriented policy of Egypt's sultans and postponed additional measures to overcome the obstructions of Yemen's rulers in the context of the rivalry over the control of the Red Sea trade.

After their final victory over the Bahris at the turn of the fourteenth century, the Burjis strengthened their hold over Hijaz and consolidated their control on the Sudanese coast nearly as far as Sawakin.[11] Significantly, in the 1420's the first Indian captain sailed through Bab al-Mandab directly to Suez and Jeddah. When Aden's rulers threatened to take reprisals against such captains, Egypt's sultan Al-Malik al-Ashraf Barsbay began in 1428 to prepare a maritime expedition against Yemen. Aden's master realistically reconciled himself to the new situation and refrained from interfering with ships trading with Egypt. Even so Barsbay and his successors launched economic warfare against Aden in order to undermine its commercial importance. They levied taxes on merchandise reshipped from Aden and penalised merchants trading with this port. But the Egyptians could not overcome the objective attractions of Aden as a convenient half-way port, an established trading centre with stable government and an important emporium of the Horn and the Persian Gulf commerce. Finally the Egyptians gave up the campaign and were satisfied with the new *status quo* which left them with the lion's share of the revenues of the Red Sea trade.[12]

Aden continued to prosper as the major entrepôt and trading centre in the region, despite the loss of its previous monopoly. Even at the beginning of the sixteenth century following the arrival of the Portuguese in the Indian Ocean, it continued to flourish as a safe haven for shipping going into the Red Sea. Ironically, the decline of the town began with its bombardment in 1516 by the Mamluk fleet, organised to save the Indian Ocean trade from the Christians. The final blow to its importance, from which Aden did not recover until the nineteenth century, was dealt by its conquest by the Ottomans in 1538.

Trade, Islam and Christianity in the Horn of Africa until the rise of the Solomonic Dynasty

The Horn of Africa was known of old for its luxury products such as gold, ivory, precious skins, incense and slaves. Some of the earliest trading expeditions, sent by the Pharaohs, are thought to have gone to the area of present-day Ethiopia and Somalia, and colonies of foreign merchants, Greek, Egyptian, Arab and possibly Indian are reported along the Ethiopian coast as early as the end of the first millenium B.C. The lucrative character of some of Ethiopia's products, and the secrecy surrounding transactions in such merchandise, were the cause of the myth concerning the size and value of this trade. In reality the less glamorous but voluminous exportation of Ethiopian foodstuffs to Arabia, carried by inconsequential merchants, may have been more important than the trade in luxury products.[13] However, slaves more than anything else contributed to the fame of Abyssinia's commerce and dominated it throughout history.

Young *Habsha*[14] males were always sought in the markets by the rulers of Arabia, the Persian Gulf and India, who trained them as soldiers for their armies. In addition to their warlike qualities, the Abyssinian slaves were reputed for their loyalty. Therefore, many were brought up and educated in the houses of their masters and later became their trusted servants, guards or commercial representatives. Known for their beauty and sensuality young *Habsha* females, suitable as concubines, were highly prized and considered superior to all other female slaves with the exception of white concubines imported from the Caucasus. Consequently, the demand for them in the slave markets of the Muslim world was nearly insatiable.

The sources of most of the Horn of Africa's luxury products as well as of the majority of the Abyssinian slaves were the southern and western parts of Ethiopia. Thus, caravan trade in Ethiopia, which transported the produce of the interior to the coast and northwards to Egypt, began to develop already in earliest times. The 'city states' of northern Ethiopia, including Axum, probably owed their rise, to a large extent, to their being important centres of trade or in control of a major route of the extensive caravan trade, which went through northern Ethiopia to Adulis on the coast[15] or to Dongola or Egypt. The rise of the coastal and the Harar-

Chercher principalities should also be attributed to their involvement in the caravan trade of the highlands. All this notwithstanding, the trade of the Horn of Africa was only a minor branch of the international trade going through the Red Sea, especially when the latter had developed its full volume by the beginning of the second millenium A.D. Developments in the Red Sea and especially in Yemen were, however, closely related to the economic and political dynamics in Ethiopia.[16]

An important feature of Ethiopia's economy since the decline of Axum was the absence of coined money and the use of gold, iron and above all salt as the principal means of exchange.[17] Salt, essential for human beings and the rearing of animals, was lacking on the plateau. It was to be expected, therefore, that it would be imported from the nearest and most accessible source. Moreover, Ethiopia's salt trade was distinguished by the fact that from the Arho salt plains at the foot of the Tigrean escarpments salt bars could be hewn to a specific shape and measurement, called *amoleh*, accepted almost throughout the plateau as currency and considered far more valuable than an equivalent quantity of salt in other forms (or from deposits in the Dankali desert).[18]

The *amoleh* from Arho[19] and salt chips and powder from this source and from Lake Asal (not far from Jibuti) were an important incentive for the development of coastal caravan trade with the plateau. The *amoleh* were transported to the verges of Tigre, where they were given their final shape and taxed; from thence they were transported by numerous caravans, on thousands of porters and beasts of burden through the network of trade routes to every major market as far as the remotest parts of the plateau.[20]

The most important overland trade route to Ethiopia by the second millenium A.D. was the one from Egypt along the Red Sea coast through the Bogos and Marya territories, the area of the Beja pastoralists of present-day Eritrea, across the river Mareb into Tigre to Amhara or to the heart of the Zagwe kingdom in Lasta. Another route from Egypt was along the Nile to the Christian kingdoms of Nubia (Dongola) and Alwa (Sennar) and from there through Chellega and Begemder to the northern markets of Ethiopia.[21] Merchants who preferred the sea to the land route landed at Sawakin or Massawa and from there reached the plateau by way of Hamasen to Tigre and Amhara. It seems that Angot and the eastern part of Amhara were then, and remained until the nineteenth century, important centres of the caravan trade. Here, the trade routes forked. The main highway (in use until the end of the Solomonic period) led, along the eastern part of Showa, to the southern plateau. Not less important, but not as well known because of circumstances, was the route through Amhara to Gojjam and from there to Damot and the other Sidama kingdoms of the Gibe river basin in southwestern Ethiopia, a major source of Ethiopia's most lucrative products.

The terminals of the caravan routes between the Arabised-Muslim coastal principalities and the highlands by the tenth century were a number of small ports[22] on the Afar and northern Somali coast. These, and semitised communities established on the Harar-Chercher plateau, were of old the centres of slave trade and Muslim propagation in the region.[23] One of the oldest trade routes from the coast was the one across the Awash to eastern Showa. The Muslim principalities established on the eastern escarpment since the end of the first millenium A.D. became the centres of the caravan trade with the kingdom of Damot and western Ethiopia. Another branch of the coastal trade route complex went through the Harari plateau to Dawaro, the most important of a number of new Muslim principalities in the region of the Rift Valley lakes of Ethiopia. From Dawaro the caravan route continued to the south, mainly through Hadya and to the southwestern kingdoms which were a major source of luxury items.[24]

There is a clear correlation between the expansion of semitic influences from Arabia to northern Ethiopia and the Chercher-Harar plateau and the development of the main avenues of the network of the caravan trade in the Horn of Africa. Once the influence of the semitic immigrants produced the 'Ethiopian' culture,[25] which was a synthesis between the imported culture and the local Cushitic one, the new culture was diffused in the north along the major trade routes. From the northern Somali coast, the Adare (Harar) cultural synthesis had spread into the Chercher-Harar plateau. This correlation became even more apparent later on in regard to the expansion of Christianity and Islam in the region.

The impact of the Muslim mercantile penetration on the Sidama Cushitic population was twofold. On the one hand, a number of Muslim sultanates emerged, or existing principalities converted to Islam. Although it is doubtful whether the new religion penetrated beyond the ruling circles in these sultanates, Islam facilitated the contact with Muslim caravan merchants and may have also contributed to greater cohesiveness of the heterogeneous population of the region. On the other hand, new developments were partly responsible for the growth and expansion, even before the Zagwe period, of several pagan Sidama kingdoms, such as Damot and Enarea.[26] Instead of merely serving as middlemen in the lucrative trade between south-west and east, the rulers of these kingdoms gradually extended their borders to include the sources of trade, markets and routes between the interior and the coast. In the process they may have exerted pressure upon the Christian areas in Showa, but they also blocked the expansion of Muslim hegemony in the Showan plateau.

Ethiopia was not considered part of *Dar al-Harb* and thus was not subject to Jihad, because, according to the Muslim tradition, the Ethiopian king had granted refuge to the persecuted followers of the Prophet. Although just across the sea from Arabia, Islam made little headway in the Ethiopian plateau until the fall of the Axumite kingdom, and the process of islamisation of the coastal pastoralist tribes was still far from complete at the end of the tenth century. Muslim communities gradually emerged, however, in different parts of northern Ethiopia, mainly along caravan routes, and these became caravan stations or centres of trade in their area. The Muslim trading principalities which gradually developed along the Ethiopian-Somali coast remained divided and of little consequence. In fact these principalities, including Zayla, were tributary to the Christian kingdom until its final collapse.[27] Nevertheless, some minor trading sultanates were already established by the Arabs and coastal Muslims on the eastern verges of the Showan escarpments by the tenth century. Such, for instance, was the Makhzumite sultanate of Showa.[28]

The Christian kingdom's relations, mainly commercial ones, with neighbouring Arab countries and especially with Yemen, were on the whole friendly. In addition to the usual Ethiopian products thousands of slaves were exported annually to this country. The offspring of these slaves became an important factor in the composition of Yemen's population and *Habsha* slave-soldiers even produced dynasties such as the Banu Najah of Zabid (1022-1150), which took an active role in Yemen's politics.

Ethiopian society, made up of nobles, soldiers, priests and

agriculturists, maintained old taboos concerning mercantile activities and handicraft. Thus, trade in the Ethiopian region during the Axumite period was left, invariably, to foreigners. Byzantine merchants were replaced, however, after the seventh century by Arab, Jewish, Armenian and Ethiopian Muslims. The latter became increasingly more important as Ethiopia's caravan trade continued to develop. Slaves were an important component of Ethiopia's commerce. Yet although slavery was an accepted institution in Christian society, Christians were not supposed to trade in slaves. Consequently Muslims had an important advantage over their Christian rivals. The Muslim merchants, moreover, enjoyed hospitality and co-operation in Muslim communities along the caravan routes and were also welcomed in trading centres on the Uthiopian coast and in the Arab world. Thus, just before the final collapse of Axum, Muslim Ethiopian merchants and their Arab counterparts practically monopolised the trade in the Horn. Their export and import activities involved travel to and from Aden, Zabid, Jeddah, Suez, Cairo, Damascus, Baghdad and even Persia.[29]

Commonly called in a later period Jabartis,[30] Ethiopian Muslims generally enjoyed religious toleration and were economically and culturally better off than the average Ethiopian. Respected for piousness and Muslim scholarship in the Muslim countries, Jabartis established a college *(riwaq)* in Al-Azhar, the mosque of Al-Madina and the great Umayyid mosque of Damascus.[31] Being literate, well travelled and connected in the Red Sea countries, their services were often used by Ethiopian kings of different dynasties in trade and for diplomatic missions to neighbouring Muslim rulers.

It was not Muslim pressure but rather that of the pagan kingdom of Damot and its Agaw-Falasha allies which probably caused the final downfall of the Axumite kingdom at the end of the tenth century.[32] For more than a century, just as the trade of the Red Sea underwent a striking revival, Christian Ethiopia remained in a state of complete chaos. During this period the Fatimid dynasty, which had established itself in Egypt, tried to consolidate its hegemony in the Red Sea, partly through religious (Shi'i) propagandists *(Du'a)*, extremely active in Yemen. In this period of the decline of the Christian kingdom and church, Islam had begun its rapid expansion in the Horn of Africa and made some progress even among the coastal pastoralists.[33]

An obvious correlation exists between the final triumph of the Red Sea trade route and the new political and economic dynamism in the Horn of Africa from the beginning of the second millenium A.D. The intensification of mercantile activities in Aden and the Red Sea ports and the influx of many foreign merchants inevitably led to a substantial growth in the demand for Ethiopian products. The trading communities and principalities of the plateau immediately responded to this challenge. Jabartis in the north expanded their activities, despite political instability, and organised trading caravans which penetrated deeper into the interior and on their return sold the products of the interior to the many foreign merchants, especially from Aden and Yemen, who traded in the area.[34]

Even more dramatic was the impact of developments in the Red Sea on the Muslim principalities of eastern Showa and the Harari plateau. The collapse of Axum at the end of the tenth century created a political and cultural vacuum in central and southern Ethiopia and left the field open to the Muslim sultanates. The increased demand for Ethiopian products gave new momentum to the development of the Muslim principalities, the backbone of whose economy, if not their *raison d'être*, was trade. Many caravans from such sultanates, accompanied by Arab and other merchants, penetrated through Showa westwards to Damot, the most important political and commercial centre in the region, and southwards, through the Cushitic Sidama kingdoms, possibly as far as the kingdom of Kaffa, in search of additional exportable merchandise. The devout Muslim merchants who brought prosperity to the ruling classes of the pagan Sidama principalities had a considerable cultural impact on at least these ruling classes, if not their subjects, and caused them to adopt Islam.[35] This commercial and religio-cultural expansionism of the coastal Muslims was also accompanied by an important political process.

The Makhzumite kingdom on the periphery of eastern Showa gradually expanded from the end of the tenth century, despite local opposition, while other Muslim trading principalities were being established on the eastern escarpments of Showa and on the Harari plateau. Yet, although occasionally they utilised religio-cultural affinities to expand political influence, the Muslim sultanates, due to their character and mercantile rivalry, remained disunited and in many cases hostile to one another, and thus were unable to produce a significant political-military power in the region. Hence, by the thirteenth century, when a new Christian power emerged in the north, it was able to nullify most of their gains.

Free from Christian domination from the end of the tenth century, Zayla developed in the coming centuries as a most important centre of trade and the diffusion of Islam. In addition to its relations with Muslim principalities, established in eastern Showa between the eleventh and thirteenth centuries, other Muslim commercial-political entities, drawing their strength from Zayla, were established in the same period along the Harari plateau, as far as, and beyond, the Rift Valley lakes. Politically and historically the most important, however, was the sultanate of Ifat in eastern Showa.

Ifat emerged in 1277,[36] when the Makhzumite sultanate was in its last stages of disintegration. Its founder, Wali Asma,[37] claimed descent from the tribe of Quraysh,[38] defeated his Makhzumite counterpart in 1285 and annexed his territories. Shortly afterwards he also gained the submission of all the other small Muslim trading principalities, spreading to the eastern escarpments of Showa as far as Adal.[39] Driven by ambition and economic motivations, Ifat's rulers began to expand their government westwards and inevitably clashed with powerful Damot and the local Christian and pagan principalities. While Ifat was attempting to establish its hegemony in the Showan region, other Muslim political entities such as Dawaro, Fatagar, Bali and the Sidama kingdom of Hadya consolidated their power in the south.

The expansion of Islam beyond its old borders created a sort of Muslim commonwealth, which embraced most of southern and central Ethiopia and was undoubtedly conducive to trading activities. It also produced a chain of sultanates stretching from northeastern Showa southwards all the way to the Rift Valley lakes. Nevertheless, this process by itself was insufficient to overcome rivalries and produce a strong political entity which could later stand up to the expanding Solomonic state.

Islam, imported into the central and southern plateaux in the twelfth and thirteenth centuries, was a byproduct of trade activities. Its agents, mainly the inhabitants of the coast, were very often themselves nominal Muslims, whose beliefs were influenced by Hamitic-Cushitic cultural features. The impact of such an Islam was invariably quite superficial, a common phenomenon in the process of Islamic expansion in Africa. But early, corrupt and superficial Islam, in other areas, was gradually replaced by a more fundamental Islam, due to the teaching of foreign and local Ulama, who arrived, or returned from, centres of Islamic scholarship, and by the impact of the Hajj. However, Islam in Ethiopia's central and southern plateaux, the eastern escarpments notwithstanding, was not allowed to enjoy a sufficient time-span for consolidation. When these areas were conquered by the Solomonic kings in the first half of the fourteenth century, the process of islamisation there was only partially successful and many of the new converts found it prudent to adopt the religion of the new rulers.

Despite the collapse of the Axumite empire, the Christian and semitised-Cushitic cultural heritage of Axum was sustained, during the chaotic period of the eleventh century, by the Christian inhabitants of northern Ethiopia and the assimilated Cushitic population of Amhara and parts of Showa. Ironically, the Agaw-Zagwe dynasty of Lasta and Wag, which in 1137 'usurped' the power of the Axumite monarchs[40] and which may have previously led the opposition to Axumite political and cultural expansion, became the vehicle by which Christianity and the cultural synthesis of the Axumite empire, with additional Agaw pagan elements, penetrated Agaw provinces to the west and north-west of Lasta. Indeed, in their efforts to become accepted by their northern subjects and to gain legitimacy, the Zagwe kings, now the champions of Christianity and the Ethiopian culture, tried to strengthen relations with the Alexandrian church and even fabricated a dynastic relation to the Axumite dynasty.[41] However, despite their efforts and military pressure on the northern provinces, they were never truly recognised by the population and nobility of the Axumite kingdom.[42]

Although at first unsuccessful, the Zagwe gained the support of the See of Alexandria. The Zagwe kings were not only pious, but successfully expanded their rule in Agaw-inhabited areas and reconquered and colonised territories north of the Mareb river already overrun by the pagan Beja in the sixth and seventh centuries.[43] The political orientation of the Zagwe kingdom was evidently towards the north and while Amhara, to the south of Lasta, became a peripheral province, the Christian principalities in Showa were generally left to themselves.

It is to be assumed that echoes of the Crusades filtered into Ethiopia, but there is no evidence as to their impact. The Zagwe continued to cultivate trade and political relations with Egypt even after they gained the recognition of the Alexandrian church.[44] Isolated and dependent on the See of Alexandria, the Ethiopian church was not associated by the Muslims with the inimical western Christianity. Hence, when he reconquered Jerusalem in 1189 Salah ad-Din granted the Ethiopians special privileges in the holy places and Ethiopian pilgrims en route to Jerusalem were not molested.[45]

The prosperity in the Red Sea basin was bound to affect the Zagwe kingdom once it had consolidated its hold over the northern provinces.[46] Luxuries imported into the country and the beautiful churches built in Roha and elsewhere in this period were a byproduct of such development.

Relations with Egypt continued to develop during the reign of the Ayyubid dynasty and the beginning of the Mamluk period. The Zagwe kings even attempted to exploit them, unsuccessfully, to intercede on behalf of Egypt's persecuted Copts. Muslim Ethiopian merchants were instrumental in developing such relations, and enjoyed the traditional toleration shown to Muslims in Ethiopia, notwithstanding a poll tax levied upon them by the Christian authorities. Because the Zagwe could not control the pastoralists of the coast, many of whom were still pagan, merchants going to Egypt and Yemen preferred the land route through Tigre, the Eritrean plateau and along the Red Sea coast or the secondary route from Lasta through Begemder to the Christian kingdom of Alwa (Sennar). The increased foreign trade and prosperity attracted many Copts to Ethiopia and led to a cultural and spiritual renaissance, which the country enjoyed during part of the Zagwe period.

In addition to their victories over the Falasha in the northwest[47] the Zagwe rulers unsuccessfully attempted, at least on one occasion, to challenge the powerful kingdom of Damot in the west. But they remained, on the whole, indifferent to developments south of Amhara. Thus the political and cultural vacuum created by the fall of Axum was exploited unhindered by the Muslim sultanates in the east during the twelfth and thirteenth centuries.

NOTES

1. Schoff, W. H. (trans. and ed.), *The Periplus of the Erythrean Sea*, New York, 1912. Compiled about the first century A. D. or the middle of the second century, but based on earlier material, this book is in a sense a guide to the merchant-mariner interested in the trade of the Red Sea, parts of the Indian Ocean and the Persian Gulf, On archaeological finds in Kuwait see: Freeth, Zahra and Winstone, Victor, *Kuwait Prospect and Reality*, London, 1972, pp. 26-8.

2. Neushtadt, D., 'Kavim letoldot hakalkala shel hayehudim veyishuvam bemitsrayim beyemei habenayim', *Zion* (Hebrew), 1937, p. 217, according to Yaqut; Heyd, W., *Histoire de Commerce du Levant au Moyen Age*, Leipzig, 1865, Vol. I, pp. 378-9.

3. Heyd, Vol. I, pp. 378-9, according to Al-Idrisi.

4. On the size and importance of Aden's Jewish community at the turn of the first millenium A.D., see: Neushtadt, D., and Goitein, S. D., (ed. Ratshabi, I.), *Boyi Teyman*, perek beit: 'Negidei Eretz Teyman' (Hebrew), Tel Aviv, tav sheen kaf vav. On Aden's importance in the mediaeval period – Serjeant, R. B., *The Portuguese off the South Arabian Coast*, Oxford, 1963, pp. 3-4, 138.

5. Neushtadt, 'Kavim', p. 219.

6. Newbold, D., 'The Crusaders in the Red Sea and Sudan', *Sudan Notes and Records*, Vol. 26, part 2, 1945, pp. 123-227. This bold venture of Renauld d'Chatillion ended in a disaster when he tried to attack al-Madina in Hijaz.

7. Heyd, Vol. I, pp. 378-9; Vol. II, pp. 449-508.

8. Heyd, Vol. I, pp. 425-6; Wiet, G., 'Les Marchands d'épices sous les sultans Mamlouks', *Cahiers d'histoire d'Egypte*, 1955. Yemen's Rasulid ruler forbade the trade of spices with Egypt until its sultans stopped the construction of a fleet to be used against his country. There were several Egyptian attempts, one in 1307, to conquer Yemen. On a campaign by Sultan An-Nasir Muhammad b. Qala'un see: Wiet, 'Les Marchands', p. 93.

9. Wiet, G., *L'Egypte Arabe 642-1517*, Paris, 1937, pp. 489-96; Yûsuf Fadl Hasan, *The Arabs and the Sudan*, Edinburgh, 1967, pp. 78-9.

10. 1340-1382: final decline of Bahris and many puppet sultans.

11. Yûsuf Fadl Hasan, pp. 78-9.

12. Sylvester de Sacy, A. I., *Christomathie Arabe*, Paris, 1826-27, Vol. II, p. 54; Heyd, Vol. I, pp. 378-9; Vol. II, pp. 444-508; Neushtadt, 'Kavim', p. 217; Adler, E. N., *Jewish Travellers*, London, 1930, pp. 246-7; Abir, M., 'Trade and Christian-Muslim relations in post-mediaeval Ethiopia'. A paper submitted to the International Conference of Ethiopian Studies, Chicago, April 1978.

13. Andrea Corsali, Letter to Duke Giuliano de Medici, in Ramusio, G. B., *Delle Navigationi e viaggi*, Venice, 1563, Vol. I, pp. 183, 186.

14. A term used by Arabs for Abyssinian slaves.

15. In a later period the coast between Massawa and Sawakin.

16. Heyd, Vol. I, pp. 444-6; Serjeant, p. 23; Adler, *Jewish Travellers*, p. 276; pp. 60-1, according to Benjamin Metudela – on Jewish Adeni merchants in Ethiopia at the end of the 12th century. On Aden's trade relations with Christian Ethiopia – Abir, International Conference. On Jewish merchants from Aden trading in Zayla – Taddesse Tamrat, *Church and State in Ethiopia 1270-1527*, Oxford, 1972, p. 66.

17. Pankhurst, R., *An Introduction to the Economic History of Ethiopia*, London, 1961, p. 260. This was a common phenomenon in Africa. See below, p. 141, on the contribution to Afar's economy.

18. Abir, M., 'Salt, Trade and Politics in Ethiopia in the "Zamana Masafent" ', *Journal of Ethiopian Studies*, Vol. IV, No.2, 1966 (abridged version in Z. A. and J. M. Konczacki, *An Economic History of Tropical Africa*, Vol. 1, London, Frank Cass, 1977). On the Arho salt mines – Le Grand, J., *Voyages historiques d'Abyssinie du R. P. Jérôme Lobo*, Paris, 1728, pp. 58-60.

19. An important Tigrean officer with the title *Balgada* was responsible for the protection of the mining and transportation of the salt blocks to Tigre – Alvarez, F., *The Prester John of the Indies* (ed. Beckingham; C. F. and Huntingford, G. W. B), Cambridge, 1961, Vol. I, pp. 171-2.

20. The damage incurred on the way was enormous. In Enarea, where *amoleh* were exchanged at a premium for all commodities, including gold, only about a third of the *amoleh* originally shipped from Tigre arrived because a third was taken in tribute, and another third was damaged along the road – Almeida in Beckingham, C. F. and Huntingford, G. W. B., *Some Records of Ethiopia 1569-1646*, London, 1954, pp. 42-5.

21. The importance of this route resurfaced since the 16th century – Ludolphus J., (trans. Gent, J. P.), *A New History of Ethiopia*, London, 1864, p. 394; Thévenot, Jean de, *Voyages de M. de Thévenot tant en Europe qu'en Asie & en Afrique*, Paris, 1689, Vol. I, p. 237. Of the many Jews from Aden who took the Nile route see: Benjamin Metudela in Adler, *Jewish Travellers*, pp. 60-1.

22. Ibn Fadl Allah al-Umari, *Masalik el Absar fi Mamalik el Amsar*, Paris, 1927, p. 4, 'the country of Zayla'.

23. Ibn Batuta, *Rihla*, Cairo, 1939, Vol. I, pp. 285-6.

24. Al-Umari, pp. 4, 19; Ahmad ibn 'Ali ibn 'Abd al-Kadir Al-Maqrizi, *Historia regnum Islamicum in Abyssinia* (ed. Rinck, F. T.), Leiden, 1790, pp. 11-5; Alvarez, Vol. I, pp. 182-7, 193; Suriano, F., *Il Trattato di Terra Santa E dell' Oriente* (ed. Glubovich, G.), Milano, 1900, pp. 84-5. On the Zagwe route see also: Tamrat, pp. 81-3.

25. 'Ethiopian' culture is a term usually used to denote the outcome of the synthesis between the Cushitic culture of northern Ethiopia and southern Arabian influences. Eastern Christianity has been a major component of this culture since the 4th century and its proponents, mainly the Amhara and Tigrean peoples, speak languages belonging to the Semitic group. Since the rise of the Solomonic dynasty the term Ethiopian or Ethiopia came to be closely associated with the Solomonic kingdom.

26. See below, pp. 161-3.

27. Al-Idrisi in the 10th century calls these Muslim communities 'the *dhimmis* of the Abyssinians' – Trimingham, J. S., *Islam in Ethiopia*, London, 1965, p. 80.

28. On this subject see: Cerulli, E., 'Il sultanato dello Schioa nel secolo XIII', *Rassegna di Studi Etiopici*, Vol. I, 1941, pp. 5-41.

29. According to Alvarez (Vol. II, p. 442) all the big trade, excluding that in foodstuffs, was in Muslim hands.

30. After a Muslim district of Jabara or Jabarta in eastern Showa.

31. Al-Umari, pp. 2-3, 7, 16; Ibn Batuta, *Rihla*, Vol. I, p. 73; Perruchon, J., 'Notes sur l'Histoire d'Ethiopie. Le règne de Lebna-Dengel', *Revue Sémitique*, I, 1893, pp. 77-8; Maqrizi, p. 15.

32. Conti Rossini, C., *Storia d'Etiopia*, Milan, 1928, Vol. I, pp. 285-6. Also below on Falasha pp. 158-60.

33. Adler, *Jewish Travellers*, Benjamin Metudela, pp. 30-1.

34. On Egyptian caravans with many Jewish Adeni merchants entering Ethiopia from Sudan – Adler, *Jewish Travellers*, Benjamin Metudela, p. 30. On Jewish merchants at the beginning of the Zagwe period in Amhara – Tamrat, p. 66.

35. Maqrizi, pp. 3-4; Al-Umari, pp. 3, 16, 10; Tamrat, pp. 52-3, 85-9.

36. Just after the rise of the Solomonic dynasty.

37. Corrupted to Walasma or Walashma in Ethiopian and Arab sources, respectively.

38. Maqrizi, p. 17; Cerulli, E. 'Documenti Arabi per la storia dell' Etiopia', *Rendiconti della Reale Accademia dei Lincei,* ser. 6, Vol. IV, 1931, p. 43 and 'Il sultanato', p. 15.

39. Trimingham, p. 59, according to Abu'l-Fida. Quoted by Al-Umari (p. 4). Ifat controlled Zayla.

40 An Agaw dynasty, the Zagwe were not completely accepted by the Ethiopian semitised population. Sources from the post-Zagwe period and even modern writers tended to ignore the Zagwe, and when mentioning them described them as usurpers to the throne of Ethiopia. The Solomonic rulers, however, were as much usurpers of that throne as the Zagwe.

41. Trimingham, p. 56, according to Abu Salih, *The Churches and Monasteries of Egypt and some Neighbouring Countries* (trans. Evett and Butler), Oxford, 1895, pp. 288-90.

42. On the resistance to the Agaw-Zagwe dynasty see: Tamrat, pp. 59-66. The above assertion should be accepted with reservation because most sources concerning the period date from the new Solomonic era.

43. Trimingham, p. 55.

44. On a letter and presents sent to the Fatimid Khalifa al-Adid, received in 1173 by Salah ad-Din see: Conti Rossini, *Storia d'Etiopia,* p. 336 (according to Maqrizi).

45. Trimingham, p. 56. On relations between the Zagwe kings and Rome see: Wansleben, J. M., *A Brief Account of the Rebellions and Bloodshed Occasioned by the Anti-Christian Practices of the Jesuits and the Popish Emissaries in the Empire of Ethiopia,* London, 1679, pp. 5-6; Kammerer, A., *La Mer Rouge, l'Abyssinie et l'Arabie depuis l'antiquité,* Cairo, 1952. Vol. III, pp. 3-4; de la Roncière, C. G. B., *La découverte de l'Afrique au moyen age, Cartographes et explorateurs,* Cairo, 1925-27, Vol. V, pp. 67-8.

46. Abu Salih, *The Churches and Monasteries of Egypt,* p. 296.

47. On the expansion of Christianity to the area of Lake Tana, Tamrat, p. 190. On Falasha, below pp. 158-60.

CHAPTER II

Ethiopia's Foreign Relations to 1500

The Solomonic Monarchs, the Horn's Muslims and Egypt

The Christian districts in Showa, an important centre of caravan trade, probably benefitted to some extent from the prosperity generated by commerce.[1] Isolated and beyond the borders of Zagwe interest, they became a refuge for political and religious malcontents from the Zagwe kingdom, but were also under constant pressure from their neighbours. Following the decline of their power about the middle of the thirteenth century, the Zagwe kings lost control of the northern provinces. In the general chaos which ensued, Christianity suffered a reverse and Islam gained ground at its expense. All this probably made the Showan and Amhara Christians an ideal infrastructure for the 'revivalist' political-cultural movement led by Yekuno Amlak, which in 1270 overthrew the last of the Zagwe rulers.

Yekuno Amlak came from a Showan family. His bid for power was supported by the Amhara-Showan Christians. Once established, the new monarch was bound to take up the cause of the Showan Christians and become involved in the multi-sided struggle for the predominancy in Showa. Moreover, the rise of the new Solomonic dynasty was undoubtedly related to the intensification of trade in the Red Sea, which influenced the economic and political dynamics in the Horn of Africa. The Solomonic rulers were also in a better position to comprehend the importance of the control of trade and its sources in the south.

No longer satisfied with the crumbs accruing from the revenues of caravan trade in northern Ethiopia, Yekuno Amlak and his heirs renewed the southward-oriented policy of the Axumite kingdom.

Confrontation with the Muslim and pagan principalities in the region was inevitable because such a policy was on a collision course with the Muslim east-west axis. Moreover, Ifat and the other eastern Muslim principalities, whose economic backbone was trade, were determined not to relinquish their hegemony, or influence, in the central and southern plateaux. All this notwithstanding, the motivation of the Solomonic monarchs was purely politico-economic. Consequently, they were even supported by Showan, Amhara and northern Muslim trading communities, who stood to benefit if the Christian kingdom gained control over the trade routes and markets of the south.[2] This seemingly ambivalent relationship between the Solomonic monarchs and the Muslims of the Horn was a natural outcome of the clash of interest between Ethiopian Muslim merchants and those of the eastern sultanates, as well as the lack of a religious motivation in these early wars. However, once Christian Ethiopia succeeded in conquering the Muslim and pagan Cushite-Sidama kingdoms, an extension of Ethiopian defence infrastructure and administrative borders to the eastern escarpment became necessary in order to protect the kingdom from local Muslim rulers and the coastal pastoralists. Indeed, this area was also needed as a springboard against the coastal and Harari principalities and to ensure the passage of Ethiopian trade to the coast and Arabia by way of Zayla. The ground was thus prepared for the future bitterness in the relationship between Muslims and Christians in the region.

In 1272, shortly after coming to power, Yekuno Amlak sent an embassy to Egypt to request an *abun* from Sultan Baybars. A patriarch was essential to maintain the existence of the Ethiopian church but the Solomonic monarch also wished to have one in order to gain legitimacy and to unite his Christian subjects. The claim of the Amhara noble to descent from the kings of Axum did not impress the Tigriña-speaking nobility, which considered him an upstart,[3] and Yekuno Amlak was constantly occupied in campaigns to establish some authority over the northern provinces. It took the new dynasty more than fifty years to accomplish this in northern Ethiopia and overcome local resistance.

Muslim merchants served as Yekuno Amlak's emissaries to Sultan Baybars.[4] In his letter, moreover, Yekuno Amlak informed the Egyptian sultan that 'he protected all the Muslims within his territories'. Obviously he was not referring just to his subjects, but also to the many foreign merchants, Egyptian, Yemeni and others, who were trading in Ethiopia. Co-operation with Muslim Ethiopian merchants and the protection of foreign merchants was a pillar of Yekuno Amlak's policy as it was during the reign of his heirs. This amicable relationship should be dissociated from the bitter wars conducted against the Muslim sultanates in Showa and elsewhere, motivated by politico-economic factors.[5]

Baybars disregarded the pleas of the Ethiopian monarch for an *abun*, either because of the breach of etiquette or because of policy considerations. Determined to do away with the Christian threat to Egypt, Baybars was engaged in the conquest of the Crusaders' last strongholds in the Holy Land, but he also directed a campaign aimed at destroying the Christian kingdom of Nubia. Possibly an outcome of the anti-Egyptian orientation of the crusades, this campaign was also due to Baybars' sensitivity to commercial development[6] and because the Egyptian sultan wished to stop the incessant Nubian raids on upper Egypt and on trade caravans. Be that as it may, Baybars exploited the opportunity to consolidate Egypt's control over, and strengthen the safety of, the important trade route along the Red Sea from Qus to Aydab and Sawakin.

Despairing of getting an *abun* from Egypt, Yekuno Amlak appointed Syrian Jacobite priests as heads of the national church. These priests caused endless dogmatic controversies in a church already torn by disagreement and rather enhanced the disunity of the country.[7] Partly because of the political decline of Christian Ethiopia, new monastic orders, called after their founders, Tekla Haymanot of Showa (d. 1313) and Ewostatewos of Seraye (d. 1352), emerged at this time in Ethiopia. These monastic orders, however, added controversies and tensions to an already problematic situation.[8]

After Yekuno Amlak's death in 1285 Christian Ethiopia, still far from being united and with relatively fluid borders, was constantly convulsed by a struggle for succession in the ruling dynasty. Following the death of Yekuno Amlak's son, Yagba Siyon, in 1294 five kings emerged in less than five years. During this period of chaos, the nobility of Tigre reasserted its autonomy, the Agaw were in rebellion and the Showan Christians came under growing pressure from the rulers of Ifat.[9] Some stability was established during the reign of Widim Ra'ad (r. 1299-1314), but the kingdom was put on firmer foundations only after his son Amda Siyon came to power.

Amda Siyon (r. 1314-1344) was the first Solomonic king able to disengage himself from wars of succession and internal struggles and to mobilise the resources of the Christian kingdom for a policy of rapid territorial expansion. Motivated by political-economic considerations, this expansionist policy, in addition to achieving political power, was aimed at gaining control over the trade routes between the sources of trade and their outlets on the coast. The monarch's attitude was that wherever unable to establish direct control over conquered territories, he would temporarily be satisfied with coercing their rulers to recognise his overlordship and pay him tribute. Such territorial expansion and the considerable increment of his revenues enabled him to build and organise a powerful army, which in the second stage was utilised to break the resistance of his opponents and establish his authority in all the territories which he conquered.[10]

Not satisfied just with revenues from taxation and tribute, this farsighted ruler became intensively involved in the Red Sea and foreign trade. With the co-operation of the loyal highland-Muslim trading communities he was able to develop a trading empire. Royal caravans constantly travelled from the interior to the trade outlets on the coast and his Muslim representatives (*wakils*) traded on the king's behalf in all the capitals and markets of the Middle East as far as Iraq.[11] On their return the caravans carried imported luxuries for the monarch and his court or to be used to reward his army commanders and loyal followers.[12]

Already in 1316/7 Amda Siyon succeeded in conquering the rich pagan kingdom of Damot. From here he gradually extended his authority to the important source of Ethiopian trade in the Gibe and Omo river basins. The southward expansionism of Amda Siyon was on a collision course with the east-west axis which the Muslims, led by the Walasma dynasty, had contrived to build since the last decades of the thirteenth century. Once he had crushed the opposition of Ifat, Amda Siyon succeeded in overcoming the resistance of the disunited southern Muslim kingdoms and princi-palities with relative ease, but his authority over them remained, for a time, nominal. With the central, western and southern plateaux subdued, Amda Siyon turned to the northern provinces.

Control of the northern Christian provinces was symbolic for the

Christian king. Indeed, the reassertion of royal power in this area, beyond its political implications, was essential for his economic policy which necessitated the control of the northern trade-route complex and of the maritime outlet to the Red Sea. By 1325 Amda Siyon's army consolidated his hold over the coast around Massawa after establishing his authority in the north. Notwithstanding his military victories and the reforms that he introduced in the local 'feudal' administrative system, the king prudently accepted realities and compromised with the hereditary rulers, whom he incorporated in his administration.[13] Amda Siyon also believed, it seems, that in the unavoidable confrontation with the Muslim-pagan coalition he would need all the support that he could get.

Once the affairs of the north were settled, Amda Siyon turned again to the south. The conquest in 1330 of Hadya, the centre of Muslim influence and resistance in this area, led to the submission of all the other Sidama principalities in the south. Thereafter royal administration was established in the area, which lost its previous orientation to the Muslim sultanates.[14] This blow to the economic foundations of the Muslim coastal complex, the king realised, was far too serious not to produce reaction. The only way to safeguard his achievements was to secure the eastern flank of his kingdom from Muslim attack. Walasma Sabr ad-Din, moreover, constantly interfered with royal caravans and was in a position to block the important trade route to Zayla altogether.

In 1332 the royal army launched an attack against the united army of the Muslim rulers of the eastern sultanates. The Muslims were completely routed and Ifat and its satellites, essential for caravan trade with the coast, were annexed to the kingdom. Although local Muslim nobles were still appointed by the king as their governors, they were gradually garrisoned by royal regiments.[15] Amda Siyon was now in full control of all the trade routes and sources of trade of the Ethiopian region.

Amda Siyon's victory of 1332 was inconclusive. Led by the Walasma dynasty, the struggle against Ethiopia continued for more than a century; it was later carried on from a new centre in Adal, south of Ifat. Yet, despite their bitterness, the Muslim rulers of the eastern sultanates were still unable to unite and produce a force capable of seriously challenging the power of the Ethiopian kingdom, whereas their Muslim subjects, tired of war, on some occasions even refused to fight the Ethiopian monarch.

The rise of Amda Siyon to power coincided with the final collapse of the Christian kingdom of Dongola (Nubia) and the decline of the Christian kingdom of Alwa (Sennar). It also coincided with the long and successful reign of Sultan an-Nasir Muhammad b. Qala'un in the first half of the fourteenth century in Egypt.[16] In 1325, about the time that his armies reached the Red Sea, Amda Siyon despatched an embassy to Egypt, requesting Sultan an-Nasir to send an *abun* to Ethiopia. On this occasion the self-confident Amda Siyon informed an-Nasir that unless he adopted a more tolerant policy towards his Christian subjects, he, Amda Siyon, was in a position to disrupt Egypt's trade with the Horn, and the flow of the Nile, and to retaliate against his numerous Muslim subjects.[17]

Following Amda Siyon's victory of 1332 a delegation from coastal and eastern Ethiopia's sultanates reached Egypt[18] and requested an-Nasir to intercede with Amda Siyon on behalf of eastern Ethiopia's Muslims. As a result of this mission the Coptic patriarch was coerced to implore Amda Siyon to ameliorate his treatment of his Muslim vassals.[19] It is clear, however, that Amda Siyon's policy was not to persecute Muslims *per se* but was the outcome of military and economic expediency. The fact remains that he was loyally served by many Muslims and in addition to taxes and tributes he only expected the conquered Muslim communities to recognise his supreme authority.[20]

An interesting inter-dependence between Egypt and Ethiopia began to emerge in the fourteenth century. Many Egyptian and Arab merchants traded in Ethiopia and enjoyed the protection of its rulers, and Ethiopian merchandise, among others, contributed to Egypt's prosperity. The Ethiopian rulers again became a political factor in the area, and they ruled numerous Muslims who considered Egypt's sultan their patron.

On the other hand, the very existence of the Ethiopian church depended on the availability of an Egyptian *abun*.[21] The Ethiopian monarch became, to a degree, also dependent on Egypt's goodwill, through his intensive commercial activities related to markets controlled by Egypt. The Egyptian sultan's control of Ethiopia's northern outlet also had political implications. Moreover, the assumed patronage of Ethiopia over Egypt's Copts could be, and was, occasionally used against them in relation to the politics of the Horn, the Red Sea, or other matters. But generally speaking, the horizons of the Ethiopian rulers now stretched well beyond the limits of the Ethiopian plateau, and it was not long before they began to view their relations with their neighbours in the context of those with the Muslim world as a whole and their affinity and duties to Christianity. This theoretically interesting relationship assumed a new dimension due to Christian Europe's increasing interest in the Red Sea trade and Ethiopia.

Ethiopia, the Red Sea and Christian Europe – early contacts

News of Amda Siyon's victories aroused the interest of Europe's rulers. By this time it was generally assumed that the revenue derived from the Indian Ocean trade was the backbone of the Muslim, especially Egypt's, economy and power, and plans were hatched in Europe to undermine it. The strength of Christian Ethiopia, strategically situated south of Egypt and near the Indian Ocean, was greatly exaggerated. Some European monarchs began to contemplate an anti-Muslim Christian alliance in which Ethiopia was assigned a major role. Interested in Ethiopia's conversion to Catholicism, the Pope also became involved in the attempt to develop relations with the Solomonic rulers.[22]

Notwithstanding the prohibition on Europeans to trade beyond Egypt, a few Italian merchants and adventurers reached the Red Sea and Ethiopia in the fourteenth century. They, and emissaries from European rulers, were instrumental in encouraging the Ethiopian monarchs to initiate, on their part, relations with Europe. Probably informed of this development by Jabarti merchants, the Mamluk sultans of Egypt became apprehensive by this turn of events. With Red Sea trade having a most beneficial impact on their country and just when Islam had triumphed in Sudan, Egypt's rulers believed that despite the Crusades a junction between European and Ethiopian interests could prove most detrimental to their interests. The abortive crusade of the king of Cyprus against Egypt in 1365[23] only served to increase Egypt's concern regarding a possible linkage between Ethiopia and the Europeans.

The persecution of the Copts during the reign of Sultan al-Malik al-Salih (r. 1351-1354) was intensified and culminated in the arrest in 1352 of Patriarch Marcos. Muslim historians attribute this development to excessive demonstration of wealth by the *Dhimmis* and their insolence towards the Muslims[24]. But it is also possible that these persecutions were triggered off by the complaints of the Muslim population of Ifat and its neighbours, who were heavily punished by Negus Sayfa Ar'ad (r. 1344-1371) after they rebelled against him, following his succession in 1344 and their complaint to Egypt's ruler.

Hearing of the detention of Patriarch Marcos, Sayfa Ar'ad imprisoned all the Egyptian merchants in his kingdom, allegedly pillaged Egyptian caravans and his army ravaged the territory as far as, and beyond, the confines of Egypt.[25] Sultan al-Malik al-Salih (1361) promptly released Patriarch Marcos, after the latter had agreed to implore Sayfa Ar'ad to renew his amicable relations with Egypt. But the persecution of the Copts was resumed, on a larger scale, following the crusade of the king of Cyprus against Egypt mentioned above.

The death of Amda Siyon and the succession of his son Sayfa Ar'ad in 1344 gave rise to renewed attempts of the Muslim sultanates, led by the Walasma dynasty, to reassert their independence and influence. Despite occasional successes, this uneven struggle always ended with the defeat of the Muslims. To gain essential strategic depth, one of the Walasma's descendants, Haq ad-Din, transferred the centre of his government in the 1360's south of Ifat to the area of Adal. From there he began to attack Ethiopia, but was killed in 1373-4 during the reign of Niwaya Maryam, Sayfa Ar'ad's son.

The rise to power in 1386/7 of Walasma Sa'ad ad-Din II, considered by Muslim and other historians the most aggressive of his dynasty[26], is described as the culmination of the Walasma dynasty's struggle against Ethiopia. In reality Sa'ad ad-Din was not an important ruler nor an able general or strategist. Operating during the reign of Negus Dawit (r. 1380-1412), his hit-and-run raids and occasional successes were of local importance, conceived with no real objective in mind and in the final analysis they did more harm to the Muslim cause than benefit. They hardened the determination of the Ethiopian ruler to crush Muslim resistance on the eastern escarpments, assured their trade outlet to the Somali coast and accelerated Christian colonisation of the area.

A number of well-coordinated campaigns organised by the Ethiopian monarch led to the total defeat of Sa'ad ad-Din. Chased by Dawit's army as far as Zayla, he was killed there in 1402.[27] However, the death of Sa'ad ad-Din did not terminate the struggle with the Walasma dynasty. His sons, who escaped to Yemen, returned to the Harari plateau, assumed the title of Sultans of Adal and renewed the struggle against Ethiopia from Dakar, to the southeast of Harar. Though of relatively little consequence, the war with Adal exasperated the Ethiopian monarchs and both Dawit's sons, Tewodros (r. 1412-1413) and Ishaq (r. 1413-1430), it seems, died in campaigns against the Adalite and coastal Muslims.[28]

The endless bitter wars with the Muslims gave rise to what amounted to religious persecution in the provinces bordering on the eastern escarpments. Attempting to terminate the troublesome problem of the eastern sultanates, the Ethiopian rulers began to colonise the areas with Christians and garrison it with *Chewa* regiments. Indeed, even forced conversion occasionally took place in an attempt to uproot the Muslim population. Negus Ishaq, who used similar methods against the Falasha in the north, implemented this policy in the east in order to secure Ethiopia's outlets to the coast. The outcome of this uneven struggle was that the Muslims lost their influence in the whole of eastern Showa, Fatagar and Dawaro, where Islam nearly disappeared and direct Ethiopian rule was instituted.

The correlation between the treatment of the Copts in Egypt and the pressure exerted on the Muslim population of the eastern principalities since the reign of Sayfa Ar'ad is quite evident and may have influenced Ethio-Egyptian relations in other fields. It is obvious that the Walasma dynasty received support from Yemen's rulers, but the weak Bahri puppet sultans probably just exploited the power they had over Egypt's Copts and the Ethiopian church, through the appointment of an *abun* to exert pressure on the Ethiopian monarch in relation to the Muslims of the Horn. Such a policy sometimes backfired because the Ethiopian rulers, whose confidence and arrogance were bolstered by their successes, rather than decrease the pressure on the eastern sultanates, increased it and occasionally even took action against Egyptian merchants and Egyptian-controlled territories.[29]

Friendly relations between Egypt and Ethiopia were temporarily restored during the reign of Sultan Barquq (r. 1382-1398),[30] possibly because he stopped the persecution of the Copts or because Negus Dawit was still preoccupied with internal matters.[31]

The claim of Ethiopian sources that Negus Dawit already contemplated the liberation of the Holy Land seems presumptuous.

Nevertheless, interested in developing his relations with Christian Europe and in European technology, he had sent a Florentine, Antonio Bartolli, in 1392[32] at the head of an embassy to several European rulers. Moreover, the fact that Dawit granted asylum to many Bahri refugees at the end of the fourteenth and the beginning of the fifteenth century indicates to what extent he chose to interfere in Egypt's internal affairs.[33]

Their power and the access which they gained to the Red Sea encouraged Ethiopian monarchs to expand the sphere of their interest beyond the limits of the Ethiopian plateau to Red Sea politics and Christian-Muslim relations. An incentive for this new trend was the incessant wars with their Muslim neighbours which made them aware of the emotional and political ties between the latter and the Muslim world with its vast resources. Having taken to themselves the patronage of the Egyptian Copts, they had also become automatically involved in a conflict with Egypt, which took upon itself the protection of the Horn Muslim sultanates.[34] European attempts to form an anti-Muslim alliance with them helped inflate the Ethiopian monarchs' self-confidence and whetted their appetite to become involved in 'power politics'.[35]

It seems that insufficient weight has been given to the Ethiopian Judaic connections and the seriousness with which Ethiopian monarchs in the fourteenth and fifteenth centuries regarded their role as heirs of Solomon and that of the Ethiopians as being the Lord's 'chosen people'. A strong emotional connection to the Holy Land is a central theme in many Ethiopian traditions and led to the establishment of the Ethiopian community in Jerusalem and a continuous interest in the Holy Land.

The Burji Mamluks who ruled Egypt from the end of the fourteenth century were more active in developing Egypt's commerce and hegemony in the Red Sea than their predecessors had been. Notwithstanding increased exactions from foreign merchants, the Italian towns were encouraged in their efforts to trade with Egypt. Indeed, the Burji sultans took steps to break the monopoly which Yemen's rulers maintained on shipping from the Far East and their control of the trade of the Horn and East Africa.[36]

Evident from the increasing quantities of luxurious merchandise in transit through Egypt, the prosperity of the Red Sea trade made Europe acutely aware of the importance of this trade to Muslim economy and power. Ironically this development facilitated the endeavours of some Europeans to reach the Indian Ocean and Ethiopia. It also encouraged Ethiopia's monarchs to intensify their destructive wars against the coastal and Harari principalities, to ensure the safety of their maritime outlets and ability to participate in Red Sea politics.

The short period of instability after Dawit's death, followed by that of his elder son Tewodros, which enabled discontented elements to rebel or, in the case of Adal, to overthrow Solomonic authority and to mount an offensive against Ethiopia, came quickly to an end with the rise of Negus Ishaq. Even more aggressive, determined and able than his father, Ishaq quickly re-established his authority over all the kingdom and further expanded the borders of Ethiopian administration in the Falasha and Agaw provinces of the north[37] and northwest.[38] The rebellious Muslims were also heavily punished in several campaigns and control of the coast was strengthened when the army reached the Red Sea on several occasions.[39]

Another group of Mamluk refugees under their Turkish chief Altenbugha (At-Tabungha) reached Ethiopia in the 1420s. These helped Ishaq to organise and train his army and taught the Ethiopians the art of horsemanship. They introduced to Ethiopia the use of naphtha and built an arsenal which produced swords, spears, coats of mail and other weapons, which were usually smuggled to Ethiopia because of Muslim prohibition on their exportation to that country. Among the many Christian refugees from Egypt was the distinguished Fakhr ad-Dawla, who helped the Negus in reforming his administrative and financial system.[40] The large Egyptian 'diaspora' may have informed Ishaq of the weakness of Egypt and could have incited him to take action against Sultan Barsbay (r. 1422-1438).

Ethiopia's external political involvements and increasing commitment to the Christian cause, in the wider sense, greatly increased during the reign of Dawit's second son Ishaq. The closing of the church of the Holy Sepulchre in Jerusalem by the Mamluks and their renewed persecution of the Copts prompted the Negus about 1424 to exact retribution against local Muslims and their mosques and organise a campaign against Egypt.[41]

Muslim sources accuse Ishaq of corresponding with European rulers in order to form a grand alliance against Islam.[42] In reality a delegation was sent to Europe by Ishaq led by a Florentine, who had lived in Ethiopia since Dawit's reign, which visited in 1427 the courts of Alphonso V of Aragon and the Duc de Berry. There may have been political aspects to this embassy but what is clear is that Ishaq requested artisans and arms. As a result of the mission some artisans, sent by the Duc de Berry, actually reached Ethiopia, but a group sent from Aragon never arrived. Prompted by his fascination with European technology, this great king despatched one of the people sent to him by the Duc de Berry back to Europe to recruit additional artisans and craftsmen. In 1432 this person was in Pera (Byzantium), recruiting artisans and builders for his master.[43]

Another adventurer, a Persian merchant called Ali Tabrizi, won the king's confidence by selling him arms and rendering him other services. On the king's request he wrote to European rulers, calling upon them to attack Egypt from the sea, while Ishaq could march upon it by land to re-establish Christianity in the Nile Valley. Tabrizi, who carried the letter to Europe, visited the courts of several rulers. On his way back, carrying a quantity of arms, he was arrested in Egypt and publicly executed. Closely watching any European attempt to reach Ethiopia, the alarmed Egyptians arrested some artisans recruited for Ishaq, who reached Egypt in 1430.[44] Unfortunately little material is available about Ishaq, but what is known about his activities indicates a desire for technical developments and to become a meaningful factor in the politics of the Red Sea, if not in Christian-Muslim relations. It is sad that the troubled days which followed Ishaq's death overclouded his achievements in reorganising his administration and army.

The death of Ishaq in 1430 and the succession of three kings within four years disrupted the kingdom's stability. The monarch's authority was challenged in different parts of the country. Among the first to exploit Ethiopia's weakness was the Walasma ruler of Adal, who attempted to regain a foothold on the eastern plateau. Considered the greatest of the Solomonic monarchs, Zara Yaeqob (r. 1434-1468) was preoccupied with re-establishing royal authority in the first years after coming to power. He was, nevertheless, aware of the inherent weakness of the military administrative system of the country and the threat to its stability due to the endemic hostility of the Muslim sultanates.[45]

While re-establishing his authority in the Horn, Zara Yaeqob moderated Ethiopia's policy concerning Egypt. In 1437/8 he wrote a friendly message to Sultan Barsbay, which was accompanied by costly presents. However, soon afterwards he was informed by Patriarch Yohannis (1428-1452) that Sultan Jaqmaq (r. 1438-1453) had reversed the tolerant policy of his predecessor towards the Copts and demolished one of their holiest shrines. The deeply religious monarch immediately wrote to Jaqmaq and strongly reprimanded him about the atrocities which he committed. Zara Yaeqob pointed out that he was able to punish his numerous Muslim subjects, who, unlike the Copts in Egypt, enjoyed full freedom, and also reminded Egypt's ruler that he controlled the sources of the Nile.

The Sultan, who took Zara Yaeqob's threats seriously, despatched an ambassador to Ethiopia, carrying a letter protesting friendship for Ethiopia in which he also agreed not to persecute the Copts, but refused to permit the building of the demolished church. Dissatisfied with the answer, Zara Yaeqob detained the ambassador for several years in Ethiopia while he campaigned against Adal. This struggle ended with the death of the last aggressive descendant of the Walasma, Sultan Badla'i, in 1445.[46] Incensed by Zara Yaeqob's behaviour and anti-Muslim policy, Jaqmaq intensified the persecution of Egypt's Copts and arrested and flogged the patriarch. Only when Zara Yaeqob returned the Egyptian ambassador was the patriarch released. Moreover, he undertook not to correspond directly with Ethiopia's ruler in the future.[47]

Constantinople was captured by the Ottoman Turks in 1453, but the Turkish advance through the Balkans towards the heartland of Christian Europe had started earlier and was temporarily halted by the advance of the Mongols and the Tartars. It led, nevertheless, to attempts by European rulers to produce a united front. This could have been one of the reasons for earlier European efforts to develop relations with Ethiopia. Be that as it may, the revival of Christian power in the Iberian Peninsula and the strong anti-Muslim sentiments of its Christian rulers in the wake of the 'reconquista' prompted them to continue their offensive against the Muslims. Spurred by religious as well as economic motivations, they became determined to gain control of what was believed to be the source of Muslim power – the Indian Ocean trade.

Information about the Red Sea, the Persian Gulf and the Indian Ocean was systematically gathered from Muslim merchants in North Africa and from Italian sources. The latter were by now surprisingly well informed about the areas beyond the Middle East and Ethiopia.[48] During the time of Henry the Navigator and his successors, Portuguese ships sailed further and further southwards along the coast of Africa with the intention of getting round this continent and reaching the Indian Ocean. Spies were also sent to the region and their reports to Lisbon were of immense importance for preparations to break into the Indian Ocean. Portuguese plans in the second part of the fifteenth century hinged on gaining the co-operation of the 'Presbiter John', who was now identified by Europeans with the Christian rulers of Ethiopia.[49] The overtures which Ethiopian kings in the fifteenth century, and especially Zara Yaeqob, made to European rulers were more than welcomed. Indeed the Europeans, who had reached the court of Ethiopia by Zara Yaeqob's time, were undoubtedly partly responsible for Ethiopian attempts to develop their relations with Europe, but they also supplied Europe with information on Ethiopia and the flourishing trade of the Red Sea.[50]

Zara Yaeqob's ruthless campaigns against Adal and the coastal pastoralists should be completely dissociated from his religious policy and attempts at administrative and military reforms.[51] If Muslims were forcibly converted in the process, it was in a way an extension of Ishaq's determined policy to uproot the Muslims from the eastern escarpments which were of immense strategic and economic importance. Generally speaking, the highland Muslims were excluded from the kingdom's coerced evangelisation drive and the monarch continued to use the services of Ethiopian Jabartis for trade and 'foreign relations'. Zara Yaeqob realised, however, that the seemingly unequal struggle of Adal and its satellites against Ethiopia was perpetuated, and had an importance far beyond its dimensions, due to the emotional, economic and political ties between the Horn's Muslims and their brethren in Arabia and elsewhere and the importance of the Red Sea trade to the economy of the Muslim world.

The Walasma dynasty spearheaded the Muslim struggle against Ethiopia for two centuries until the death of Sultan Badla'i in 1445. In this period control of the maritime outlets became increasingly important for Ethiopia's economy and politics, while Muslim resistance to Ethiopia's expansionism did not decline. Thus it became even more essential to eliminate the Muslim presence in the eastern part of the Horn. Yet victories against the Adali and pastoralist armies without colonising or garrisoning their territories were practically meaningless. The pastoralists did not constitute a target and their main forces could always evade the Ethiopians, and the cultivators and merchant communities were always able to establish new centres of power from which they renewed their activities, supported, to some extent, by nearby Muslim countries with which they had territorial continuity. Moreover, in so far as the permanent settlements were an easier target, Ethiopian campaigns in the fifteenth century indirectly helped enhance the power of the pastoralist element, mainly the Somalis, which had been on the rise since the twelfth century.[52]

After his victory over Adal (1445) and the increasingly strained relations with Egypt's ruler, Zara Yaeqob took up more actively the European-oriented policy of his predecessors. This orthodox monarch and his priestly administrators must have been aware of the Ottoman threat to Europe, culminating in the fall of Constantinople (1453). A representative of Zara Yaeqob is said to have participated in the abortive council of Florence which met between 1439 and 1441 A.D. to try to heal the break between Rome and Constantinople.[53] Zara Yaeqob, like his predecessors, toyed with the idea of an anti-Muslim Christian alliance, but his immediate objective in developing relations with European rulers was to obtain their aid in the fields of military technology and craftsmanship.

Pietro Rambulo, a Sicilian who had reached Ethiopia at the beginning of the fifteenth century and was later sent to India to trade in the king's name, was despatched to Europe in 1450 at the head of an Ethiopian delegation. His visits to the courts of the Pope and the king of Aragon resulted in the arrival in Ethiopia of a number of artisans and a papal delegate. The Aragonian embassies, which left for Ethiopia, carried a letter requesting the Ethiopian ruler to divert the Nile from its course and to attack Egypt in order to support an Aragonian crusade to the Holy Land.[54]

Despite the growing exactions of the Mamluks, Egypt's prosperity in the middle of the fifteenth century was at its height. Egyptian merchants, Muslim and Jewish, increased their trading activities in the Red Sea, the Indian Ocean and Ethiopia and partly contributed to this prosperity. In control of Syria, the Mamluks had strengthened their hold over Hijaz and the Sudanese coast[55] and gradually improved their relations with the Tahirid dynasty of Aden and Zabid. Naturally, the renewed communications between Ethiopia and Europe caused consternation in Egypt. The Mamluks, whose newly established hegemony over the Red Sea proved extremely profitable, feared the impact, economic and political, of a junction between European and Ethiopian interests. Moreover, the devastating defeat inflicted by Zara Yaeqob upon Adal nullified, it seemed, its function as a counter-balance to Ethiopian power in the Horn.

Somewhat worried about Zara Yaeqob's policy in the Red Sea, the Mamluks hoped to exploit their improved relations with the Tahirids of Yemen and their common interests to counter if necessary any Ethiopian move in this region. However, the growing instability in Ethiopia and Zara Yaeqob's death in 1468 dispelled such fears. This event also marked the beginning of the end of Ethiopia's power and ability to influence regional politics.

Ba'eda Maryam (r. 1468-1478) succeeded his father, Zara Yaeqob, after a short struggle for power among the court functionaries. He lacked the ability, vision and ambition, as well as ruthlessness, which contributed to his father's greatness. He was probably chosen by the nobility to succeed his father[56] for just this reason. Real power during his reign was in the hands of influential officials from Showa and Amhara who supported his succession. Foremost among them was Bitwadad Amda Michael, who had gained considerable authority under Zara Yaeqob. Most of Zara Yaeqob's reforms were abolished and full privileges and authority were restored to the dispossessed nobles who soon subverted the authority of the monarch. No longer restrained, the church and the monastic orders returned to their traditional rivalries, which were further aggravated by the arrival in Ethiopia of Egyptian-Syrian and even European priests. On several occasions the leaders of the church were the most active in inciting the population against the authority of the monarch and participated in plots against him.[57]

Following his rise to power, Ba'eda Maryam received a delegation which brought the customary tribute from Muhammad ibn Badla'i (r. 1445-1471), who on his succession accepted Ethiopian overlordship.[58] Stability on the Adali border enabled the monarch to deal with a Falasha uprising and even to consolidate and further expand Ethiopian administration in their provinces.[59] The Doba pastoralists on the verge of Angot, who constantly interfered with the main trade route along the eastern escarpments, were also punished for erupting once again into the highlands and an attempt was made to proselytise them.[60] However, this period of grace at the beginning of Ba'eda Maryam's reign was relatively short.

Led by Zayla's governor, Othman, Adali amirs disregarded their sultan, and after 1471 renewed their raids on Ethiopia's southeastern provinces. Amda Michael continued to prove his worthiness and the royal army led by him completely defeated the Adali army, taking prisoner many of their amirs. This victory against Adal, like previous ones, was not conclusive and two Ethiopian armies which operated against the rebellious Afar and Adal in 1473/4 were annihilated. This debacle signified the end of Ethiopian military supremacy. A defensive strategy, conducted by Amda Michael and based on the province of Fatagar, although generally successful, tended to enhance the aggressiveness of the Adali-Somali and Dankali amirs. It also led to the intermittent closure of the trade routes to the coast, because of the intensified activity of the pastoralist elements on the coastal plains and the Chercher-Harar plateau.[61] Consequently Ethiopian armies penetrated Adal nearly as far as Zayla,[62] but the Muslims avoided a headlong clash and resorted to guerilla tactics which were very effective against the cumbersome Ethiopian armies.

It is likely that Ishaq's and Zara Yaeqob's resounding victories over Adal and its pastoralist allies actually produced a paradoxical effect on the coastal Muslims. Sheer exasperation and desperation produced the tenacity of the struggle of the Adali and coastal amirs against Ethiopia and laid the foundations for closer co-operation between the merchant and agriculturist communities and the pastoralists, who were fighting among themselves for control of the region. Their frustration was increasingly channelled into religious expression by leaders who ignored the authority of the Walasma sultans and took the title Imam, when leading the struggle against Christian Ethiopia.

Even when their military power and political importance declined Ifat and Adal, it seems, played a decisive role in shaping the history of the Horn of Africa. Their quixotic but persistent struggle against the Ethiopian kingdom in the fourteenth and fifteenth centuries gained them respect and sympathy in the Muslim world. Despite the loss of most of the eastern escarpments, their enduring resistance was, to some extent, responsible for keeping Islam alive in the eastern part of the Horn, and for stopping the Ethiopians from expanding into the Harari plateau and implanting their authority on the coast. Above all, however, the unceasing and exhausting Muslim campaigns against Ethiopia were partly responsible for the inability of the more able among the Solomonic monarchs to divert their attention to the acute internal problems of their kingdom and to implement the badly needed consolidation of their achievements.

A relatively substantial part of Ethiopia's resources, military and financial, were exhausted in the fruitless wars with the Muslims and could not be utilised for consolidating the authority of the monarchy in the heartland of the kingdom and establishing it in other parts of the country. The monarchs were also unable to implement badly needed reforms and thus remained dependent on the traditional feudal administration. Therefore, although numerically and politically inconsequential, the Muslim sultanates and pastoralists, from the middle of the fourteenth century, played an important role in the historical dynamics in the area by preventing the Solomonic monarchs from establishing a stronger and more cohesive framework for their vast kingdom. Had the great Solomonic monarchs, until Zara Yaeqob, been free from Muslim pressure, it is possible that the history of the Horn would have evolved in a very different way during the dramatic developments in the region in the sixteenth century.

Ba'eda Maryam, who renewed the special relationship which had existed between the 'Amhara' monarchy[63] and the church, allied with the order of Tekla Haymanot. At the suggestion of this element, an embassy was sent to Egypt, carrying costly presents and protestations of friendship to Egypt's ruler, to request from him two *abuns*. The delegation was received by the Mamluk ruler, who granted the Ethiopian request.[64] This move signified the beginning of a reconciliation between Egypt and Ethiopia. The rapprochement between the two countries became even more evident during the reign of Ba'eda Maryam's young son Eskender (r. 1478-1494). In 1481/2 another Ethiopian embassy was received by Sultan Qa'itbay, who despatched the *abun*s promised by his predecessor and granted the Ethiopian church several concessions in Jerusalem.[65]

Queen Mother Illeni, Zara Yaeqob's *itege*,[66] with the help of some powerful courtiers, succeeded about 1484 in overthrowing Amda Michael's power and became the power behind the throne in the coming thirty years.[67] The daughter of Dawaro's Muslim ruler, Illeni was baptised only when she married Zara Yaeqob. She had first-hand knowledge about the internal relations of the eastern Muslim sultanates and between the principalities of the Horn and the Muslim world with its immense resources. Having watched her husband's failure to reform the institutions of his heterogeneous kingdom, she was also cognizant of the internal weakness and the strong centrifugal forces which threatened the decentralised kingdom surrounded by Muslim countries. To preserve the shaky framework of the kingdom, Illeni accepted a policy of compromise with the nobility and appeasement towards the Muslim neighbours of Ethiopia. The goodwill and co-operation of the latter was also needed to develop Ethiopia's caravan trade. Matrimonial arrangements with the ruling families of Adal and the other Muslim sultanates were made, therefore, and the tribute due from them was overlooked in order to strengthen their friendship, in the hope that this would lead to the cessation of raids against Ethiopia and erode the anti-Ethiopian front.[68] This policy was maintained, in the face of growing pressure from the coastal pastoralists and the Adali amirs, throughout the reigns of Eskender, his son Amda Siyon II (a child who ruled six months), Na'od, Ba'eda Maryam's second son (r. 1498-1508), and in the first years of Na'od's younger son, Libna Dingil (r. 1508-1540). In reality this policy completely misfired. The internal weakness of the kingdom and the lack of strong leadership only encouraged the coastal elements to increase their pressure on the border provinces of the plateau.

It is ironical that just when Christian Europe's interest in Ethiopia and Portugal's involvement in the Indian Ocean reached a peak, the Ethiopian monarchy was no longer interested in developing its relations with Europe or in an anti-Muslim alliance. Indeed, despite the fact that the struggle with the Adalis did not diminish, and even when the Portuguese arrived in the Indian Ocean at the end of the fifteenth century, Ethiopia's rulers continued to attempt to foster relations with the Muslim countries of the Red Sea and especially with Egypt. European envoys, adventurers and priests, who arrived in Ethiopia in the last decades of the fifteenth century, were coolly received and were ignored by the Ethiopian monarchs. Paradoxically Europe's growing aggressiveness caused the Muslim rulers of the Red Sea to become even more concerned and apprehensive about a possible alliance between Europe and

Ethiopia in this period, especially in view of the decline of Mamluk power.[69]

The change in Ethiopia's attitude to its neighbours was related to the decline in the power of the monarchy. A figurehead, the monarch no longer formed a policy and the nobles, who controlled the administration, were uninterested in foreign affairs, but concerned rather to fortify their own position. The heads of the church and the order of Tekla Haymanot, once again in favour, supported the rapprochement with Egypt and viewed with apprehension the arrival of the Catholic emissaries and the possible influence of relations with European countries.[70]

Only in 1509, more than a decade after the arrival of the Portuguese in the Indian Ocean, did Illeni decide to send an ambassador to Portugal to ask for help. This step, recommended by Pero de Covilhão since 1494, undoubtedly influenced by the arrival at the Ethiopian court of messengers of the Portuguese Admiral[71] and the total defeat of the Mamluk fleet off Diu in 1508, was taken only after her policy of appeasement proved a complete failure. Be that as it may, Illeni's indecisive and ambivalent policy and the fact that she contributed to the victory of the centrifugal forces in the kingdom, accelerated the decline of the power of Ethiopia in the most crucial period in the history of the region.

NOTES

1. Cerulli, 'Il sultanato', p. 10.
2. Tamrat, pp. 127-8; Haberland, E. von, 'The influence of the Christian-Ethiopian Empire on Southern Ethiopia', *Journal of Semitic Studies*, 1964, No. 1 – on the Sidama kingdoms and early clashes between the Solomonic monarchs and Muslim Hadya.
3. Tamrat, pp. 67-8.
4. Politically naive, he had asked Yemen's ruler Al-Malik al-Muzaffar (r. 1250-1295) to forward his letter and to intercede on his behalf with Baybars at a time when bitter economic competition existed between the two rulers (Tamrat, pp. 70-1; Wiet, G. 'Les Relations Egypto-Abyssines sous les Sultans Mamlouks', *Bulletin de l'Association des Amis des Eglises et de l'Art Coptes*, Cairo, 1938, p. 117). But this incident, nevertheless, is indicative of Ethiopia's economic orientation.
5. Yagba Siyon's letter (c. 1290), in which he refers to his father's inimical policy towards the Muslims, is wrongly interpreted by Tamrat (pp. 126-7). The same applies to f.n. 4, p. 126, concerning a drawing in an Ethiopian manuscript of Yekuno Amlak surrounded by Muslim ambassadors and servants.
6. See his relations with the Italian city-states and efforts in the Red Sea to break Yemen's monopoly of shipping.

7. Wiet, 'Les Relations', pp. 117-22.
8. On this subject see below. Also Tamrat, Chapter VI, pp. 206-47.
9. On attacks of coastal pastoralists and a 'Jihad' led by Shaykh Muhammad abu 'Abdallah in 1299 – Tamrat, pp. 130-1.
10. On this army see below pp. 46-51.
11. Al-Umari, p. 3; Huntingford, G. W. B., *The Glorious Victories of Amda Seyon King of Ethiopia*, Oxford, 1965, p. 67.
12. On co-operation between Ethiopian kings and Muslim rulers to guarantee the safety of trading caravans – Ramusio, Vol. I, p. 186, letter from Andrea Corsali (16 June 1517) to Lorenzo de Medici.
13. See below, text.
14. On revival of this orientation and autonomy see below, pp. 149-50.
15. Maqrizi, pp. 18-9; Al-Umari, p. 2; 'Documenti Arabi', p. 44.
16. See above, text.
17. The belief that Ethiopia could interfere with the flow of the Nile even led a Zagwe ruler to use this argument – Wiet, 'Les Relations', pp. 115-16, 117-23, 132-4.
18. Abdallah al-Zayla'i and his colleagues stayed in Egypt 1332-1338 and were Al-Umari's main source on the Horn, later copied and expanded by Maqrizi.
19. Al-Umari, pp. 2-3.
20. Tamrat, p. 85.
21. See below p. 59.
22. De la Roncière, Vol. V, p. 67; Kammerer (1952), Vol. III, pp. 3-4; Serjeant, pp. 3-4.
23. During the reign of Al-Malik al-Salih.
24. Perruchon, *Sémitique*, 1893, pp. 77-8, 176; Bruce, J., *Travels to Discover the Source of the Nile in the Years 1768, 1769, 1770, 1771, 1772, and 1773*, Edinburgh, 1790, Vol. IV, p. 96.
25. Maqrizi, according to Quatremère, E., *Mémoires géographiques et historiques sur l'Egypte et sur quelques contrées voisines*, Paris, 1811, Vol. II, pp. 276-77; Schefer, C., *Le Voyage d'Outre Mer de Bertrandon de la Brocquière*, Paris, 1892, p. 148. Reports by Muslim and Christian chroniclers about Ethiopian incursions as far as Aswan in the second half of the 14th century and the beginning of the 15th century seem exaggerated. Logistic problems notwithstanding, the concepts of contemporaries concerning borders were very vague. More likely, the peripheral areas of Sudan and its coast, under Egyptian hegemony, were raided by Ethiopian armies. These raids led to the expansion of territories in the north, inhabited by pastoralists, which paid tribute to the Ethiopian king – Wiet, 'Les Relations', p. 123; Perruchon, *Sémitique*, 1893, p. 78; Bruce, Vol. IV, p. 96; Trimingham, pp. 73-4; Alvarez, Vol. I, p. 129 – On *Bahr Nagash* raiding Nobiis, 5-6 days' march from the frontiers of the country towards Egypt. Alvarez, Vol. II, p. 450 – Sawakin border of kingdom, beyond Sawakin Egypt begins. See claims of Susinyos in 17th century, below pp. 200-4.
26. Cerulli, 'Documenti Arabi', p. 46; Maqrizi, p. 22.
27. Maqrizi, pp. 26-7. Cerulli mistakenly dates his death as 1415, during the reign of Ishaq.
28. Maqrizi, p. 39.
29. An Ethiopian army was reported near Aswan in 1381 and on several occasions in the coming century – Wiet, 'Les Relations', pp. 123-26; Maqrizi, p. 8; Trimingham, pp. 74-5; Perruchon, *Sémitique*, 1893, pp. 77-8.
30. Trimingham, p. 75.
31. In 1387 Barquq received an embassy from the Ethiopian ruler with many costly gifts.

32. According to Tamrat (p. 257) in 1402, Dawit already employed European merchants and artisans in his court.
33. After the Burjis emerged triumphant – Wiet, 'Les Relations', p. 126; Maqrizi, p. 4.
34. The many Jabartis in Cairo were the advocates of this cause.
35. Of a letter from King Henry IV from 1400 A.D. praising Dawit, of whose achievements he had heard in the Holy Land (1392-3), and suggesting a joint campaign to liberate the Holy Land – Tamrat, p. 257.
36. See above pp. 4-5.
37. On Falasha wars in Jewish sources see: Eshcoly, A. Z., *Sipur David Hareuveni* (Hebrew), Jerusalem, 1940.
38. The process of conversion and expansion in Falasha provinces of the north began in Amda Siyon's reign. Coerced conversion was used by the monarch in the case of the Falasha, whereas in the past proselytising was carried on by monastic orders. The name Falasha was probably derived from the word *Falasi,* plural *Falashotch,* meaning 'exiled', because Emperor Ishaq proclaimed that whoever did not convert would be dispossessed from his land – see below pp. 158-60.
39. According to Maqrizi (p. 2) Ethiopia's borders stretched from the Indian Ocean and Bab al-Mandab to the land of Takrur. Ishaq attempted to build his own port near Massawa – Tamrat, p. 261. According to Trimingham (p. 78) Ishaq conquered most of the rich Sidama areas in the southwest.
40. Wiet, 'Les Relations', p. 126; Maqrizi, p. 8; Trimingham, p. 75.
41. Trimingham, p. 75, f.n.4, according to Taghri-Birdi; Wiet, 'Les Relations', p. 126.
42. Maqrizi, p. 7; Tamrat, according to Taghri-Birdi, p. 201.
43. Wiet, 'Les Relations', pp. 128-9; Maqrizi, p. 8; de la Roncière, Vol. VI, pp. 115-7.
44. Maqrizi, p. 8; Wiet, 'Les Relations', pp. 127-8.
45. On his administrative and military reforms see below, text.
46. Perruchon, J., *Les Chroniques de Zar'a Ya'eqob, et de Ba'eda Maryam, rois d'Ethiopie de 1434 à 1478,* Paris, 1893, p. 58.
47. Wiet, 'Les Relations', pp. 124-5; Al-Sakhawi, *At-Tibr al-Masbuq,* Cairo, 1896, pp. 67-72; *Les Chroniques de Zar'a Ya'eqob,* pp. 57-67. It is an interesting speculation whether the attempts of one section within the Ethiopian church in this period to renounce the dependence on the Alexandrian See was not motivated, in addition to spiritual and nationalistic factors, by the increasing involvement of the church in Zara Yaeqob's administration and the wish to undermine Egypt's hold over Ethiopia through the appointment of Egyptian *abuns* and thus overcome the endemic shortage of priests which curtailed evangelical efforts.
48. The details of the map produced by Fra Mauro in 1460 are surprisingly accurate.
49. Pero de Covilhão left Lisbon in 1487, visited the Persian Gulf, India and the Red Sea and reported to Lisbon from Cairo before turning to Ethiopia, which he reached in 1494.
50. On the many Europeans at the Ethiopian court see: Suriano, p. 86; Heyd, Vol. II, pp. 508-19; Tamrat, p. 267. For how well informed Europe was of events in the Horn, see letter of 1448 from the Grand Master of Rhodes to the King of France – de la Roncière, Vol. II, p. 119.
51. See below, text.
52. Alvarez, Vol. II, pp. 409-11.
53. Trimingham, p. 76, note 2.

54. Wiet, 'Les Relations', pp. 129-30; Suriano, p. 86; Wansleben, pp. 5-6; Tamrat, pp. 264-6. While European sources are clear about these events, there is no indication about them in Ethiopian sources.
55. Serjeant, pp. 5-6.
56. See below, text.
57. Morié, L. J., *Histoire de l'Ethiopie*, Paris, 1904, Vol. II, p. 224; Suriano, p. 86; Tamrat, p. 291.
58. *Chroniques de Zar'a Ya'eqob*, pp. 131-3.
59. Chihab ed-Din Ahmed Ben Abd el-Qader (Arab Faqih), *Futuh al-Habasha - Histoire de la conquête de l'Abyssinie* (trans. and ed. Basset, R.) Paris, 1897, pp. 342-3, on the suppression of Falasha and their becoming serfs.
60. *Chroniques de Zar'a Ya'eqob*, pp. 144-6.
61. See below, text.
62. In 1493-4 Pero de Covilhão found Eskender not far from Zayla - Alvarez, Vol. II, p. 375.
63. The Solomonic dynasty was of Amhara origin and derived its power, at first, from the provinces of Showa and Amhara. It always tried to present itself, however, as being Ethiopian. The dynasty, moreover, consistently intermarried with the ruling families of the different peoples of the plateau and especially with the Tigrean nobility. Nevertheless, due to personal rivalry and jealousy, and to the traditional support which the dynasty found in the Amhara provinces, it was not uncommon that rebels and writers with regional tendencies alluded to the fact that the kingdom was dominated by the Amhara.
64. Although a long time elapsed before the *abun* reached Ethiopia.
65. Trimingham, p. 82.
66. Chief wife.
67. Alvarez, Vol. I, pp. 278-9. But not without resistance of the courtiers and opposition from the church and some monks - Tamrat, pp. 288-91. Morié, Vol. II, p. 225.
68. Trimingham, pp. 82-3; Alvarez, Vol. I, pp. 186-7, 251 - on matrimonial arrangements with Muslim rulers.
69. Wiet, 'Les Relations', pp. 130-1; Suriano, pp. 85-7; Morié, Vol. II, pp. 225-7. Pero de Covilhão, sent by King Joao of Portugal in 1487 to the Indian Ocean, reached Ethiopia in 1494, and experienced a similar treatment during the reign of Eskender - Alvarez, Vol. II, p. 375.
70. Morié, Vol. II, pp. 223-4; Suriano, pp. 84-6; Tamrat, pp. 291-2.
71. By Albuquerque or Tristão da Cunha, governor of India. Alverez, Vol. I, pp. 276-7; Whiteway R. S., *The Portuguese Expedition to Abyssinia in 1541-1543, as Narrated by Castanhoso with some Contemporary Letters, the Short Account of Bermudez, and Certain Extracts from Correa*, London, 1902, XXV, XXVI, Introduction. See below pp. 72, 111-12.

CHAPTER III

Government, Administration, Army and Church to 1500

Feudal government and military system

Not unlike other African empires, the Axumite kingdom emerged as the result of an amalgamation of a number of commercially oriented 'city states' by the most aggressive or enterprising among them. This relatively loose confederation, which served as the nucleus for later expansion, was ruled by a king who at first was considered *primus inter pares*. But little information is available about the political dynamics of this early period. Yet the titles of governors of provinces, districts and even of large villages[1] in use during the reign of the new Solomonic dynasty, and the fact that many retained hereditary rights and symbols of past status and independence,[2] are evidence of this evolutionary process. Indeed, even the title of the Ethiopian king – *Negusa Nagast*[3] – is indicative of the process which led to the rise of the monarchy of Axum.[4]

Despite its becoming the champion of Christianity and the Cushitic semitised culture of Axum, the Agaw-Zagwe dynasty, which ruled Ethiopia from 1137 to 1270, was not considered a legitimate heir of Axum.[5] Ironically the Zagwe dynasty, centred in Lasta, notwithstanding its northern-oriented policy, is to be credited with the expansion of Christianity and the semitised Ethiopian culture among the pagan Agaw and Falasha of northern and northwestern Ethiopia, areas which Axum had been unable to penetrate in the past. The Zagwe kings, moreover, established their control over, and received tribute from, rulers of the northern provinces and even reconquered areas beyond the Mareb, previously lost to pastoralist tribes. Their relationship with the province of Amhara and the northern settler communities in Showa, however, remained ambivalent and less clear.

Yekuno Amlak, a noble of Showan origin who founded the new Solomonic dynasty in 1270, claimed that he was a descendant of the Axumite dynasty. Nevertheless, many northern nobles did not welcome the upstart king. Preoccupied with the fierce struggle among several powers, including the Walasma dynasty of Ifat, over the control of Showa, Yekuno Amlak and his immediate successors inherited the traditional feudal-style relationship which existed between the Zagwe monarchs and their subordinate governors. In fact, until the reign of Amda Siyon (r. 1314-1344) the dynasty's authority was still not fully recognised in many parts of the old kingdom and foreign military colonies had to be established in the area.[6]

The struggle of the Solomonic monarchs against autonomous tendencies of subordinate governors and other centrifugal forces in their kingdom is a dominant theme in the history of mediaeval and post-mediaeval Ethiopia. The Solomonic myth, which surfaced after the rise of Yekuno Amlak to power, is a clear attempt to legitimise the new dynasty and endow it with a special status. For the same reason the Christian kings continued to observe customs relating to divine kingship, which probably had their roots in the pagan past of Axum.[7] But legitimacy, prestige and even divine standing were of little consequence in a decentralised and semi-feudal system, unless the monarch was strong, gifted, successful in war and able to curb the ambitions of the nobility. Indeed, centrifugal forces triumphed when the monarch was weak and in periods of interregnum, which the aristocracy could exploit to consolidate its position at the expense of the central authority. Yet, because the kingdom's existence was still threatened by enemies from outside, it was generally realised that weak kings and lengthy periods of interregnum could lead to bloody civil wars and harm the interests of all concerned. Therefore, measures were taken to minimise times of instability and ensure succession by an able heir, sound in mind and body.

The *Kebra Negast*,[8] compiled probably at the end of the thirteenth century and the beginning of the fourteenth, and attributed to Yekuno Amlak, endeavours to establish the legitimacy of the new dynasty, but also deals with the problem of succession. Although it clearly limits succession to the male descendants of Yekuno Amlak, it does not qualify primogeniture as a clear prerequisite for succession. Obviously, in the difficult times which the kingdom faced, a mature, experienced and, if possible, inspiring monarch was essential.[9] Therefore, unless the monarch had a mature and able offspring at the time of his death, one of his brothers could be chosen to succeed him.

To minimise the possibility of civil war, a royal prison was established in the thirteenth century at Amba Geshen.[10] Once they reached maturity all the king's sons were imprisoned there in addition to his brothers. The princes were closely guarded by many troops commanded by a trusted officer who enjoyed substantial power and revenue.

The choice of heir by the dead monarch was invariably ignored, as he was considered biased. The successor was elected by a special council, made up of the chief court officers and some important nobles, including the two *Bitwadadotch*[11], the heads of the church hierarchy, the queen mother and possibly the *Itege* – the chief wife of the departed king. Obviously in a country as heterogeneous as Ethiopia, where the king was polygamous and, for political purposes, married daughters of tributary kings and into provincial nobility, intrigues relating to succession were rife long before the monarch's demise.

Ethiopian society could be considered matrilineal. Therefore the family, or province, from which the mother of a prospective heir originated would greatly benefit if he was to succeed and nobles and military commanders from his province usually supported 'their' candidate. The final choice of the successor was the result of an intricate process of compromises and accommodations, or even of war, between coalitions formed to support different candidates. On the other hand, when quick and determined action was taken by a small group of powerful courtiers, who kept the death of the king secret, they confronted everyone with a *fait accompli* and could save the country the convulsions which usually followed the death of a king. But such a smooth succession was rare and necessitated strong leadership and the co-operation of several military commanders, including the one of Amba Geshen.[12]

Despite all the precautions mentioned above, the death of a king usually signalled a power struggle between different factions in the court, involving governors and military commanders. If, however, the new king was able and he gained increasing support after his coronation, such a struggle was short or avoided altogether. All this notwithstanding, the system of succession was open to abuses, especially by powerful officials and nobles who held key positions in the court and the administration. At the turn of the fifteenth century, for instance, several rulers were chosen not because of their merits, but rather because they were weak and accepted the tutelage of powerful administrators or were young and enabled their regents to rule in their place.

The rise of the new Solomonic dynasty was accompanied by a shift of the centre of power of the monarchy southwards and a change of policy orientation and, from the fourteenth century, by rapid expansion towards the sources of the trade in the southern and western parts of the Horn of Africa. By the middle of the century the size of the new kingdom was not only huge in relation to its core, but it had become extremely heterogeneous. In addition to the nucleus of a Christian semitised population, it now incorporated many pagans and Muslims, organised in various socio-political frameworks with different languages and cultures.

A process of gradual expansion at the side of integration and assimilation took place during the Zagwe period, especially in Agaw areas. Its success depended to a large extent on a cultural-religious assimilation of the conquered Agaw pagans and Falasha. This process was, however, insufficient to eradicate in the north historical, regional and political differences perpetuated, to a large extent, by the traditional feudal[13] military-administrative system of Ethiopia.

The new dynasty embarked upon rapid conquests at the beginning of the fourteenth century, without previously establishing a cohesive form of administration in the nucleus of their kingdom. In newly annexed areas they did not attempt to exploit evangelisation and assimilation and to produce a religious-cultural integration, either because of apathy or their preoccupation with wars. It could also be that they were not impressed with the results of the cultural-religious assimilation and integration process, or by the pace with which it was achieved.

The Solomonic monarchs based the government of their vast heterogeneous empire on military power and conquest. Faced with the pressing problems of administering and defending their extensive possessions they tended to adopt *ad hoc* solutions, exploiting in some cases the old feudal military-administrative system, in other cases local government frameworks and in others they appointed army officers, court officials and kinsmen, as governors of the new territories with full authority for the duration of their tenure. This hybrid administrative system tended to become with time increasingly detrimental to the authority of the central government and often resembled the feudal system predominant in the north.

The traditional feudal military-administrative system in Ethiopia rested on the principle that in return for royal recognition of the right of a noble family (or families) to govern a certain area, this family (or families) undertook to pay the monarch part of the taxation of the region in addition to personal tribute (*mashumya*), to maintain law and order within their governorship and, whenever called, to participate in the monarch's wars, at the head of their private army[14] or armies put under their command. Yet, although restricted to such a family (or families) this did not ensure tenure nor direct succession and the governorship could be conferred upon another member of the family, or upon another family with a claim to this position.

In theory, the traditional feudal system deprived the monarch of the authority to administer many parts of the kingdom and made him dependent on the armies of his feudal lords. However, theoretically the final master of all the land and the source of all authority, the monarch, as long as he was strong and with the help of an intricate system of checks and balances, was able to exercise his supreme power, replace hereditary governors at will, and indeed any other functionary who did not please him. This system also provided the strong monarch with a relatively wide base of support because his disunited feudal hierarchy competed for his favours and had a vested interest in the continued existence of the kingdom. Moreover, the monarch was able through his military-administrative system to mobilise large armies in a relatively short time, irrespective of logistic and economic considerations.

The vulnerability of the system emanated from the fact that it depended on the personality and power of each individual king and his ability to exploit rivalry among the provincial nobility. As the kingdom continued to grow and became progressively more heterogeneous and decentralised, control of the vast monarchy through the hybrid and traditional military administration became more difficult, and the monarch's dependence on feudal armies proved dangerous.

A clash of interests between the monarchy and the nobility was inevitable. Successful in war and occasionally free from pressure, the monarch tended to consolidate his power by strengthening the central authority and army and increasing his control of all sources of revenue. On the other hand, the feudal military-administrators, old and new, and different appointed governors wished to perpetuate the decentralised administrative system and, if possible, consolidate their autonomy by increasing their economic and military power.

In a moneyless society[15] the economic base of power was control of land, labour and other sources of revenue, mainly trade. Land, and revenue from it, meant more power and ability to maintain larger military forces. As long as the monarch was strong, the kingdom expanding and governors continued to depend on royal appointment, the king was theoretically the final master of all wealth and controlled all military power. Additional land, gained through conquest, enabled the monarch to expand his military forces and reward loyal military commanders and functionaries. However, once expansion was halted, or worse, if the size of the territories under royal control diminished due to outside pressure or the success of powerful lords in consolidating their autonomy, the kingdom's military administration became a threat to the central authority. Moreover, the correlation between military power and administration was inevitably detrimental to any attempt at administrative reorganisation and integration.

The best guarantee which the monarch had against attempts to usurp his authority and undermine his power, other than machiavellian manipulation of competing nobles, was his ability to maintain, and put in the field, a strong army. In view of the power of the many feudal armies, the royal forces by themselves, or together with the armies of loyal governors, were expected to be able to overcome any force that a rebellious governor, or governors, could muster.

It is to be expected that the army which the first Solomonic rulers had at their command was relatively small and composed of their own mercenary soldiers and followers and the armies of subordinate rulers and allies. As custom dictated, the nobility of the districts which they had occupied usually had sent sons or young relatives to be raised at the court and serve in a way as hostages. These, together with slaves acquired from specific areas who were trained as warriors, and the employment of additional mercenaries, enabled the monarchs to expand the royal bodyguard battalions.[16] Units in the royal camp were maintained by revenue in kind received from certain provinces.[17] However, important as such units were until the time of Amda Siyon, its few thousand soldiers served thereafter mainly to protect the king and his camp and for ceremonial purposes. The spearhead of the royal army were, already by the time of Amda Siyon, regiments called *Chewa*,[18] who were recruited at first from Ethiopian elements[19] and were commanded by the king's most loyal followers and kinsmen, whose title was in most cases *Ras*.[20]

Although the basic unit was the regiment, there were circumstances in which several *Chewa* regiments were put *ad hoc* under one commander or the governor of the province who, for this specific purpose, carried the title of *Azmatch*.[21] Each regiment was allocated a fief *(gult)*, whose revenues paid for its upkeep and was administered by their regimental commander, who maintained law and order in the area and controlled all the farmers-serfs who lived within the area of the fief[22]. Inasmuch as the revenues of Amda Siyon grew, additional regiments were formed and the *Chewa* became the backbone of the royal army. Moreover, the rapid annexation of territories enabled Amda Siyon and his successors to form many new *Chewa* regiments from elements among the conquered peoples, known for their warlike qualities. Devoted to the king, who pampered them, and commanded by his close friends, the new regiments were frequently stationed in border provinces or areas where the king's authority was challenged. Their mobility and armament made the *Chewa* superior to traditional forces.

Admittedly inferior, qualitatively, the armies of feudal governors[23] nevertheless made up the bulk of the monarch's forces, mobilised for major campaigns. In addition to the cost, logistic and other constraints limiting the size of the royal army, the dependence on feudal forces was also due to the problem of manpower.

The traditional class system, related to occupation, restricted mobility within Ethiopian society and the number of soldiers that it could produce. Farmers, who constituted the great majority of the population, were prohibited from joining the relatively small soldier class,[24] nor were they permitted to carry arms lest they rise against their masters, who cruelly exploited their labour and their authority over them. It is to be expected that the soldiers wished to monopolise their trade and benefit from revenue accruing from it. However, it is more likely that this state of affairs was institutionalised by the feudal nobility which needed the labour of the farmers-serfs in a country where land was plentiful and the population sparse.

The sources of manpower, other than the soldier class, available to the king were slaves and hostages, recruited to the royal bodyguard. But as the kingdom expanded, the monarchs, following Amda Siyon's example, were able to form many new *Chewa* regiments, drawing upon the reservoir of manpower of the conquered people.[25]

At first *Chewa* regiments were used as a mobile striking force, but as the kingdom expanded they were increasingly deployed to garrison frontier provinces as far as possible from their homeland, and only a few regiments were kept in the royal camp. Gradually the *Chewa* became less and less mobile, they developed strong connections with the territories where their fiefs were located and assumed the character of a territorial army.[26] The change in concept concerning the deployment of *Chewa* probably stemmed from the fact that their mobility could no longer compensate for the need to defend vast territories with long borders, especially against fast-moving pastoralists. Army units, ready at potentially dangerous areas, could at least block the enemy's first onslaught until reinforcements arrived. How correct this strategy was, was proven once the *Chewa* abandoned their defensive posture in the 16th century and were again turned into a mobile striking force. The weak Ethiopian defences collapsed under Muslim, and later Galla, pressure and the royal army was unable to stop the enemy, who overran the different parts of the plateau.[27] Moreover, as a foreign element, subordinated to the king, *Chewa* regiments were also supposed to offset the power of local governors and to suppress rebellions and attempts to defy the monarch's authority.

The reorganisation of the royal army and the gradual transformation of the *Chewa* regiments into a territorial army had begun, it seems, during Amda Siyon's reign. With his kingdom rapidly growing, the monarch was determined to reform the traditional administrative-military machinery and reorganise the royal army in order to adapt it to the new needs of the kingdom and strengthen the central authority. The battalions and regiments under the royal command were considerably strengthened, but high priority was given to organising new regiments from among the conquered people, and these were later posted to different areas. Hoping to undermine the feudal forces, Amda Siyon could not foresee, of course, the process by which this new framework would degenerate and integrate with the old military-administrative system.[28] At least during his lifetime the *Chewa* proved their worthiness by overcoming rebellions and repeatedly and soundly defeating Ifat and the Muslim pastoralists.

Chewa regiments were mainly infantry with some cavalry elements.[29] Their size was irregular, never stable and depended on the circumstances in which they were established, the origin of each unit, attrition due to battles, the extent of the fiefs granted to them and the character of the region which they garrisoned. Most regiments were composed of people of common ethnic origin and cultural and linguistic background. Undoubtedly a constraint on the size of the regiment, this made it into a more efficient fighting machine. Only offspring of the soldiers could join the regiment and, if attrition was high, the regiment could become very small. If a regiment, however, grew beyond a few thousand soldiers, it became operationally unmanageable and logistically a problem, and it would be either split, reorganised or moved to another area. The last step, as well as attempts to move regiments from tranquil areas – their 'home' for some time – because they were no longer needed there, or because of disobedience or rebellion, could lead to grave consequences and was taken only in extreme circumstances.

Efforts of the Solomonic monarchs to maintain direct control over the *Chewa* regiments became increasingly difficult due to their number and dispersion. Indeed, with time, soldiers were assimilated by the local population and their ambitious commanders married into the local nobility and began to identify with it. As they grew 'fat' and complacent, regiments became less efficient and gradually reluctant to participate, and shed their blood, in campaigns in remote territories. Others were afraid to forfeit their fief (*gult*) when absent from the area, or that while in the royal camp the monarch would transfer them to less desirable environments. In some instances they blatantly disregarded the monarch's orders and in others, being only superficially connected to Christian Ethiopia, they even deserted to the enemy.[30]

As military apparatus, meant to protect the political boundaries of the kingdom and lead attacks against its enemies, the *Chewa* were a success. As a measure to offset the power of regional lords their contribution was only temporary and partial. However, insofar as they were meant to replace the traditional and new military-administrative systems they completely failed. Indeed, in some instances the *Chewa* regiments, made up of 'foreign' elements, with little sentiment for Ethiopia's Christian semitised heritage, even aggravated the centrifugal forces which threatened the power of the monarchy. To expect that such an army would serve as an integrative force and would assimilate the pagan Cushites, a conquered people, was extremely naive.

The inability of the central authorities to undermine the power of the feudal military-administrative system was not unique to Ethiopia during this period. Especially in societies with a barter economy, any attempt to create an alternative military framework loyal to the monarchy was doomed to failure. Such a new military machinery, if dependent on revenue from the land or fiefs, was inevitably bound to produce a new military aristocracy or join the old one. In the case of a monarchy, whose base of power was an army made up of soldiers of fortune and slaves, paid by the royal treasury from revenues accruing from trade and other sources, their loyalty to the monarch, who organised this army, usually did not last beyond his lifetime. Involved in court intrigues, unless controlled by strong kings, such an army was even of greater danger to the monarchy than feudal, or territorial armies. At best its commanders turned the monarch into a puppet and formed a new military aristocracy.[31]

It was unrealistic to envisage the creation of any military-administrative organisation based on nationalist, or even religious, sentiments in mediaeval or post-mediaeval Ethiopia (as elsewhere). Indeed, most Solomonic monarchs rightly disregarded, in the circumstances, the possibility of producing a common cultural-religious infrastructure for their heterogeneous kingdom and created or developed the *Chewa* military framework. The development of this system was, in the circumstances and for its time, probably the best solution which the Solomonic monarchs could provide for the challenges, military and other, but not for assimilation and integration, which they faced.

Administration

The strong rulers of the new Solomonic dynasty in the fourteenth and first half of the fifteenth centuries were, on the whole, generally preoccupied with wars. Their approach to problems of government in newly annexed territories was of necessity empirical and depended on circumstances and existing socio-political frameworks. Whatever the degree of resemblance to the northern military-administrative system, the government of the new territories lacked the benefit of a common cultural-religious background. The personal authority of the king, recognised by his governors and to different degrees by his subjects, was the only common denominator between the heterogeneous population and it contributed to the internal weakness of the kingdom.

Probably the most logical approach to classifying the hybrid administration which emerged *post facto* in the vast territories conquered between the thirteenth and fifteenth centuries would be to divide it into three concentric circles around a core. This core consisted of the provinces of Amhara and parts of Showa, where northern colonisation, which had begun during the Axumite period, resulted by the thirteenth century in complete assimilation of their original Cushitic population. Begemder and parts of Gojjam, which gradually underwent a similar process from the thirteenth century, could be considered, at a later stage, also part of the heartland of the Amhara-dominated Solomonic kingdom.

Although there were a few districts where ancient political entities governed by hereditary dynasties retained some autonomy, nearly all of the core area of the kingdom was directly controlled by the king and administered by his representatives. Its revenue was paid to his treasury or was earmarked for the maintenance of the royal household and bodyguard battalions. The only partial limitation on the absolute power of the monarch in these provinces were the many fiefs granted to churches, monasteries, members of the royal family and some regiments. Nevertheless, if there was a semblance of centralised administration in any part of the kingdom, it was in the 'core' provinces.

The first circle, composed of the provinces of northern Ethiopia on both sides of the river Mareb and mainly inhabited by Tigriña-speaking people, was previously the heartland of the Axumite kingdom. The semi-feudal military-administrative system was firmly established here. The Solomonic king could here only appoint governors from the traditional ruling families. Although they paid tribute and were expected to render military service whenever ordered to do so, such governors held complete administrative and judicial authority in the areas under their command and the loyalty of the population went first to their lords and only through them to the monarch.

The provinces within the first circle, together with the core area of the kingdom, constituted the nucleus of Christian Ethiopia. With a common heritage, religion and culture, the population maintained a certain affinity to the kingdom. Their nobility was involved in the administration and government of the kingdom, as well as in the intrigues of the court. Immigrants from such areas extended the borders of Christianity and were the vehicle by which the 'Ethiopian' culture was diffused into newly conquered territories. But besides the marked difference between the measure of royal control over the administration of the Amhara core areas and what is loosely termed Tigre, traditional regional, cultural and linguistic differences were enhanced by the attitude of the Tigre nobles who considered themselves the true heirs of Axum, to the 'upstarts' of the Amhara-dominated core. This tension was aggravated from the end of the thirteenth century by ecclesiastic controversies which assumed regional identity.[32] Thus it is impossible to consider even the nucleus of Christian Ethiopia as one unit.[33]

The second circle, the largest part of the kingdom, was composed of territories of Cushitic agriculturalists, annexed since the beginning of the fourteenth century, in which northern colonisation and cultural assimilation remained marginal and superficial. A distinction should be made between districts closer to the heartland of the empire, where the king's authority and the degree of cultural-religious assimilation were stronger, and the other districts further removed, where the monarch's authority tended to become more ambiguous and cultural influences were hardly noticeable, if at all.

Constantly occupied with military campaigns, the Ethiopian monarchs lacked a proper government and administrative machinery which they could extend into the newly occupied territories. Their policy in the second circle was, therefore, extremely pragmatic. With communication, transportation and other services being as they were, it was in any case unrealistic to expect that any type of centralistic administration could be established in such areas. Hence, whatever 'kingdoms' or other political entities existed, their rulers, if they submitted to the king, could expect to be reappointed to their previous governments and maintain a certain amount of autonomy. As long as they paid their tribute and satisfactorily performed their other feudal duties, they could expect to retain their position. But the degree of autonomy which such rulers enjoyed depended on circumstances and their previous position. Their subjects had hardly any contacts with the monarchy or any sentiments towards it and their loyalty was exclusively to their traditional ruler. Practically the only factor which kept them, as well as their rulers, within the framework of the Ethiopian kingdom was coercion by its military power, as long as the monarchy was able to exert such power.

The majority of the territory within the second circle reverted to the king through conquest. It was divided into provinces and subdivided into districts, governed by the king's relatives, military and court officers and clergymen, as well as those who could afford to buy the appointment. Though they had substantial authority in their respective governorships, such an appointment was for a limited duration and tenure was extremely precarious. The governor administered the territory in the king's name, collected taxes and maintained law and order in the area under his command. As every administrative appointment incorporated a military function, the governor was expected to finance the cost of an army from his revenue. The size of the force of each governor was in relation to the size of his governorship and his rank. When called to render military service the district governor at the head of his army joined the army of the provincial governor. The latter, at the head of his and his district governors' armies, either led local campaigns or joined the royal army in a major war.

Most of the provinces in the second circle were *de facto* border provinces. They were heavily garrisoned by regiments (*Chewa*) whose commanders administered their substantial estates *(gult)*. With the exception of judicial authority they exercised full authority over the farmers of such a fief and thus limited the power of the governors. These regiments, as was the case in the first circle, were also supposed to offset the military power of the governors and to constitute a check on their authority. But, unlike governors who were often rotated, regimental commanders and regiments were normally kept in the same area. It was a natural process that they began to identify with the local nobility and even attempted to establish hereditary governorships in the fiefs of their regiment.

As long as the monarchy was strong, the king retained considerable authority over the administration of the second circle of the kingdom, but in the case of local hereditary rulers, and especially appointed governors, whenever and wherever confronted with disloyalty or disobedience he would exploit rival powers in the area or would activate the other governors or the regiments stationed in the province. Only rarely did he have to deal with such matters personally. Despite some exceptions, therefore, the position of governors and even of regimental commanders in areas within the second circle remained relatively precarious until the second half of the fifteenth century, although there was a tendency on their part to perpetuate their appointments and even to establish some autonomy.

The third circle was composed of all the territories beyond the limits of the king's direct control, but still considered within the political borders of Ethiopia. The Ethiopian monarch's authority in such territories was nominal and its rulers were considered autonomous, although they were expected to recognise the king's overlordship and to pay him tribute. But even such nominal authority depended on the monarch's ability to coerce such governors to obedience by repeatedly invading and ravaging their domains, if tribute was not voluntarily forthcoming.

In the north this circle included the territories of the Hamitic pastoralists and the enclaves of Negroid agriculturists, stretching as far as the plains of Sudan (an important source of horses, slaves and auxiliaries for the Ethiopian army).[34] To the west and south this circle included the Cushitic and Negroid principalities and peoples on the peripheral territories of the plateau (an important source of slaves, gold, ivory and other precious and agricultural products).[35]

The Muslim principalities around Harar and along the coast, although included in the third circle, make a separate category. Here the opposition to Ethiopian control had historical roots and was motivated by strong politico-economic and cultural factors which gradually assumed a religio-ideological dimension. It is not only that the population was Muslim, but it also represented a rival Semito-Cushitic cultural synthesis influenced by immigrants from southeastern Arabia, which after the rise of Islam considered itself superior to that of Christian Ethiopia. But whereas Ethiopia was cut off from the spiritual and material development of the

Christian world, the Semito-Cushitic cultural sphere of the south-eastern part of the Horn was closely connected to the Arab and Muslim world.

Not reconciled to the loss of their influence on the plateau, the Harar, Chercher and coastal principalities refused to accept Ethiopian overlordship and consistently attempted to re-establish their power in the highlands. Yet, until the 16th century their exasperation was insufficient to cause them to overcome their differences and create a united political-military power, able to challenge the Ethiopian military machine. On its part, Ethiopia was unable to exploit the weakness and disunity of the Muslims and establish direct control on the coast beyond the eastern escarpments. Even when the bitter and continuous wars resulted in an overwhelming Ethiopian victory, the highlanders who served in the king's army so abhorred the climate of the lowlands that they refused to settle there. Thus, at best the Ethiopian monarchs intermittently succeeded in forcing the rulers of the Muslim principalities to recognise their overlordship and pay them tribute. But their struggle against Ethiopia, drawing on the endless resources of the Arab-Muslim world, could not be stopped and they constantly tried to exploit the weakness of Ethiopian administrative and military infrastructure in the second circle.

Reform and the Ethiopian church

Amda Siyon was probably not the first Solomonic monarch who realised the inherent danger to the central authority emanating from the highly decentralised system of government. Notwithstanding the constraints which limited his power and the grave external problems which he faced, he was the first to attempt to reform it. Yet, rather than risk a headlong clash with the nobility and its allies he chose an indirect approach and tackled the problem by strengthening the system of checks and balances built into the existing administrative framework in order to undermine the sources of power of the nobility.

The political-military might of the hereditary nobility in the north and in some of the conquered areas depended on their economic power, which emanated from revenues accrued from the land which they controlled. This was evident to Amda Siyon, who attempted to diminish this source of power by granting numerous *gult*s to churches, monasteries, different appointees and other favourites. Although he did not challenge the direct authority of provincial and district traditional rulers he began the process, later developed by Zara Yaeqob, of uniting some provinces into a larger administrative unit and appointed a member of his family or a loyal follower as 'super-governor' or 'viceroy', carrying historically impressive titles.[36] Responsible directly to the monarch, such functionaries, during seasonal campaigns, were in command of all the armies of their governorates, including regiments from this area, put under their command by a royal order.[37] Although their direct authority was limited, their position enabled them to undermine the power of the hereditary governors under them, *inter alia*, by exploiting rivalries within their provinces and between one ruler and another. District administrators and functionaries were also appointed by the monarch whenever possible. Though this rival class of royal administrators did not have the power, nor the prestige, of their hereditary counterparts and could not infringe on their authority, they nevertheless constituted another step in the attempts to strengthen the centralistic administration.[38] Many of the above innovations may have been introduced by Amda Siyon, but they were only implemented by King Zara Yaeqob (r. 1431-1458) a century later. Evidently Amda Siyon's partial and hesitant attempts at reform were insufficient to undermine the established power of the traditional military-administrative system. The basic concept behind these reforms was the ancient tactic of divide and rule but, paradoxically, in the long run Amda Siyon's reforms resulted (after his death) in the strengthening of the old system when elements of the new administration gradually became absorbed by the traditional feudal class.

Although relatively little is known about their achievements, the strong kings who followed Amda Siyon may have attempted to carry on his policy. Echoes of such attempts emerge from their chronicles and from foreign, mainly Arab, sources.[39] Nevertheless, the control of the monarchy over the administrative machinery in the century following Amda Siyon's reign continued to deteriorate. The most serious and comprehensive attempt to reform Ethiopia's administration and military system as well as its church, however, took place under King Zara Yaeqob.

Until about the middle of the fifteenth century the political boundaries of the Solomonic kingdom extended far beyond the frontiers of the church and the limits of the semitised Ethiopian culture. The semblance of Christianity in newly conquered areas was dangerously superficial and usually corrupted by pagan and Muslim influences. In view of the moral and spiritual decline of the church and its grossly exaggerated involvement in ecclesiastical controversies in this period, adverse influences began to spread even in the very core of the Christian kingdom.

In view of the internal weakness of the Christian kingdom and the increasing external pressures on it, Zara Yaeqob realised the seriousness of the threat to its very existence. Moreover, cognizant of the inherent dichotomy between the interests of the feudal administrative-military machinery and the interest of the monarchy to establish a strong centralised administration in the vastly expanded kingdom, Zara Yaeqob was determined to implement far-reaching reforms, over and above those attempted by Amda Siyon, in order to undermine completely the power of the nobility.

Distrustful of the nobility and disillusioned with the performance of the *Chewa* regiments, the deeply orthodox monarch decided to use the church and its monastic orders in a two-pronged role to implement his reforms. The first and more obvious role was to provide Ethiopia with the religio-cultural infrastructure, if necessary even through compulsory proselytising, which he hoped would lead to the assimilation and integration of its heterogeneous population. The second role which he envisaged for the church was the active participation of its leadership in the centralised administrative system, which he was determined to create. Zara Yaeqob realised, however, that the church was incapable of undertaking such demanding roles before it had reformed itself and terminated the endless controversies which sapped its energy and augmented the divisive forces in the country. Farsighted and gifted as Zara Yaeqob was, he underestimated the extent of the opposition to his reforms and grossly overestimated the ability of the church to rise to the challenges which he posed it.[40]

With its roots deep in the African soil, the Ethiopian national church could have become a tremendous asset to the Solomonic kings as a vehicle for religio-cultural assimilation leading to integration, if they had wished it, had the time-span, or could exploit it. Always under pressure the monarchs may have lacked the foresight, and they may possibly have realised that their church did not possess the spiritual qualities, evangelical drive and inspiring leadership to serve as the spearhead for Christian expansionism on the plateau.

An elitist church, connected to the ruling ethno-cultural groups, the Ethiopian church preferred a sheltered existence within the boundaries of traditional Christian Ethiopia. On the whole it looked with distaste at, or at least disregarded, the masses of pagan and Muslim Cushites, despised their negroid neighbours, who became the subjects of the Ethiopian kingdom and, unlike Islam, was uninterested in proselytising them. This may have been the outcome of a 'chosen people' complex which the Ethiopian Christian culture adopted with other Judaic philosophies and which prevailed in the church. But this attitude might have also been an outcome of the basic religious tolerance of Ethiopian society and the absence of tension between the different religious communities of the kingdom.

Since the fourth century, after the Council of Chalcedon, the Ethiopian church became spiritually separated from the main body of Christianity and depended solely on the See of Alexandria. Inasmuch as Egypt was incorporated from the seventh century in the Muslim empire, Ethiopia also became physically separated from the western and eastern churches and its spiritual development was even more dominated by its relations with the Coptic church. In its turn, the latter underwent a process of decline due to its position and virtual isolation from the centres of Christian spiritual development. This adverse process, aggravated by the collapse of Christian Nubia and the impact of the Crusades, was bound to affect the Ethiopian church even more than the Egyptian one.

The *de facto* head of the Ethiopian church and, at least theoretically, its spiritual link with the Coptic church, was the *abun*. An Egyptian monk, an *abun*, was sent to Ethiopia by the Coptic patriarch after the death of his predecessor, at the request of the Ethiopian monarch, who was expected to give costly presents to Egypt's Muslim ruler. Far from being outstanding spiritual leaders or scholars, *abun*s were, at best, of mediocre quality, who sought the appointment for personal gain or, more often, were troublesome monks whom the patriarch wished to exile because, once they reached Ethiopia, *abun*s were not permitted to leave the country until their death. Naturally such a person did not contribute to the enrichment of the spiritual life of the Ethiopian church, but frequently rather aggravated the endless ecclesiastical controversies over relatively minute matters, which in addition to augmenting disunity in the country, sapped the spiritual resources and dynamics of its church.

Though the titular head of the church, the *abun* (who in most cases did not understand the language of the country) was normally in many ways just a figurehead. His most important role was to ordain priests and deacons, who were essential to maintain the organisational framework of the church, because he alone had such a power. As Ethiopia went through long periods without an *abun,* quantity and not quality were the yardsticks for ordaining new clergymen. For the same reason two *abun*s served at the same time when they could be obtained from Egypt. Endowed with vast properties by pious kings and nobles, the church became a refuge for misfits, physically and mentally and otherwise handicapped people and a horde of parasites who shunned physical labour and opted for the respected, though economically unrewarding, membership in the church organisation. Although many gifted and dedicated people were to be found in the upper echelons of the church and especially in its monastic orders, it is doubtful if, even if it wished to do so, such a church was capable of evangelising among the masses of pagans and confronting Muslim scholars who had previously settled in territories annexed by the Solomonic monarchy.

Until the time of Zara Yaeqob the Solomonic kings were indifferent to evangelisation *per se* nor did they attempt, as previously pointed out, to exploit the church to enhance the integration and cultural assimilation of the multitude of peoples of their kingdom. As in the past, the church hesistantly followed emigrant and soldier communities into new areas in order to provide them with religious services. Thus emigrant clergymen as well as heretics who prudently escaped or were exiled to the peripheries of the kingdom were instrumental in the sporadic expansion of Christianity. But, unlike previous military colonisation, *Chewa* regiments, now composed mainly of foreign elements, had a very marginal religious and cultural influence in the areas in which they were settled and were in many cases culturally assimilated by their new neighbours. The most important contribution to the limited evangelisation came, however, from the new monastic orders which arose in Ethiopia in the thirteenth century.

At first, rejected by the establishment and even persecuted by the church, leaders of the new movement escaped to remote areas among pagans. In the tradition of the monastic movement, which developed during the Zagwe period and greatly contributed to the expansion of Christianity among the Agaw-Falasha people in Gojjam and around Lake Tana, the new monastic orders established centres of learning for their followers, who satisfied their meagre needs by cultivating land in peripheral provinces. Such communities not only gained the respect of their pagan neighbours, but became dedicated to evangelising the heathen and to spreading Christianity. In the first decades of the fourteenth century one monastic order called, after its founder, Tekla Haymanot, gained recognition and was taken into the folds of the establishment. Once its importance was established its monasteries were granted substantial *gult*s for their maintenance. Gradually its leaders became increasingly powerful and they wielded considerable influence over internal politics and in the royal court.

Until the sixteenth century the order of Tekla Haymanot drew its power mainly from Amhara and Showa and was identified, in most periods, with the Solomonic dynasty and in its doctrinal attitude with the Alexandrian church. In the fourteenth and fifteenth centuries it supported, *inter alia*, the efforts of the patriarchs to cleanse the Ethiopian church from pre-Christian and Judaic influences, notably the celebration of the Jewish Sabbath as a day of rest. More pragmatic than the rival order, it attempted to adapt the dogmas of the Ethiopian church to the challenges of the dynamics of other streams of Christianity. It joined forces with the *abun*s in the second half of the fourteenth century and by the end of the century received royal sanction to abolish the (Jewish) Sabbath.[41] Its power by this time was predominant in the court and among the leading nobles of the kingdom and it seemed, for a time, that it had succeeded in completely defeating its rivals.

The order of St. Ewostatewos, drawing its power mainly from Tigre (and later from Gojjam), closely adhered to the dogmas, theories and customs evolved by the Ethiopian church throughout centuries of separate development. Obviously, it vehemently rejected any attempt to abolish the Sabbath and bitterly fought what it considered attempts to compromise the principle of the unity of Christ's nature. Although persecuted in the fourteenth century, mainly in relation to the Sabbath, it persevered and by the beginning of the fifteenth century emerged even stronger than before and achieved royal support. The guardians of the national character and independence of the Ethiopian church, its members became the favourites of the strong kings who ruled Ethiopia in the first half of the century and who were suspicious of the Egyptian Coptic church.[42]

In addition to augmenting existing centrifugal forces, the ecclesiastical controversies, which the leaders of the monastic orders inflamed, caused these orders to become introverted and to abandon their interest in evangelisation. Thus Christian Ethiopia lost an important tool by which Christianity and cultural assimilation could be enhanced among the non-Christian peoples of the kingdom. Moreover, as monasteries became increasingly rich they no longer appealed to the pagan masses, but rather as owners of vast tracts of *gult* land, they were identified with the conquerors, who exploited the labour of the farmers-serfs and were considered part of the conquering political establishment.[43]

Devoid of local allegiances and dependent on the king's goodwill, the leadership of the church and the monastic orders, literate and usually able, were in most respects ideal for service in the central administration. They, and others who owed their position to the king, were appointed governors and officials of different ranks.[44] New districts and provinces were formed and existing ones sometimes were grouped together and put under a royal appointee. This innovation was introduced by Amda Siyon but under Zara Yaeqob such an official held, for a time, much more administrative and military power.[45] On the lower level, a new class of appointed governors now existed at the side of traditional rulers and undermined the authority of the latter. Both systems were now, however, directly supervised by an official of the court. Partly to undermine the economic power of the feudal governors, large 'fiefs' in their territories were granted to the new administrators for their maintenance and for the upkeep of their retainers or armies, which some of them were expected to form. The process which had begun during the reign of Zara Yaeqob's predecessors, of granting estates *(gult)* to churches, monasteries and royal favourites, was accelerated in many cases at the expense of traditional rulers or even of disloyal or corrupt *Chewa* regiments.[46]

One of the most important innovations introduced by Zara Yaeqob in the field of administration was probably the creation of a body of officials which resembled a government and the reorganisation of the court officials under this body. Two *Bitwada-dotch*[47] fulfilled the office of prime minister and minister of war and the office of minister of the interior, responsible for all governors and the administration, respectively. Such high officials, to whom the king delegated authority in different fields, were supposed to control and direct the administration when the monarch was occupied in his frequent wars, and also in time of peace to enable him to devote more attention to major problems such as assimilation and integration of his subjects and reorganisation of the armed forces. This innovation was, it seems, far too revolutionary at this stage, especially as the monarch grew more suspicious of his courtiers. The king found it prudent, therefore, to abolish the offices of the *Bitwadadotch* and reduce the power of the court stewards who, he thought, threatened his position and may have even allied themselves with the provincial nobility against him. Consequently, he reassumed direct supervision of the army and administration through his daughters, who were appointed governors but, in reality, through appointed administrators. In short, he attempted to institute an absolute monarchy which rested upon the narrowest possible base of support and avoided as much as possible delegation of authority.[48]

With the help of the upper hierarchy of the church, the monarch coordinated a massive campaign to proselytise the pagan population of the kingdom. For this purpose priests, and especially monks, were sent to the most remote areas to supervise, and when necessary force, the process of conversion upon the pagans. Numerous people, pagans and even Muslims, adopted Christianity in this period, but their motivation and faith were questionable. After Zara Yaeqob's death and on other occasions, such nominal Christians discarded their new religion as quickly as they had adopted it.

Zara Yaeqob's coerced evangelisation was unsuccessful, in the final analysis, not due to the resistance of the Cushite pagan and Muslim population, but rather because he failed to appreciate the magnitude of the problem – the spiritual and organisational feebleness of the church – upon which he depended and its inability to rise to his expectations.[49]

Notwithstanding the fact that they benefitted substantially from his generosity and reforms and despite the *abun*'s support, the majority of the rank and file of the church, unable and unwilling to change their way of life and frame of mind, resented the new role entrusted them and their exile to remote areas to govern or proselytise 'uncouth' pagans.[50] Pampered in the past, leaders of the order of Tekla Haymanot were aware that the monarch, a supporter of a 'national' church, sympathised with the cause of their rivals. They were, therefore, even more bitter concerning the church conciliation and unity of belief, which the monarch coerced them to accept.[51] Misinterpreting the relations which Zara Yaeqob had begun to develop with European Christian powers, priests and even members of the order of St. Ewostatewos watched with consternation the growing number of Catholic Europeans who reached his court. Ignoring the fact that Zara Yaeqob was only interested in acquiring European technology and support in fighting the Muslim countries, they accused the monarch of deviating from the true faith.[52] Thus, during the occasional rebellions which broke out against the monarch, monks and priests were nearly always in the forefront of the ranks of those who fought the king.

It was to be expected that the traditional nobility and new governors who succeeded in consolidating their position in remote provinces would oppose Zara Yaeqob's reforms, clearly aimed at eroding their base of power. But even *Chewa* regiments, meant to offset the feudal forces in their respective areas, proved untrustworthy.

By the middle of the fifteenth century the royal *(Chewa)* army no longer functioned as a mobile striking force, nor according to the concepts which guided Amda Siyon, who had transformed it into a territorial army. The *Chewa* soldiers took women from among the population of the areas in which they were settled and raised families. Their commanders integrated in the local nobility (through marriage and common interests) and together with the latter resisted the monarch's attempts to change the existing *status quo*. Some regiments, established in provinces which had for long ceased to be frontier areas, opposed royal attempts to dispossess them of *gult*s in the heartland of the kingdom, and settle them in border areas or reform them into a mobile striking force. Others became tired of the continued and bitter campaigns which Zara Yaeqob carried out against his enemies and above all the Muslim principalities.

Aware that the corrupt *Chewa* regiments were incapable of coping with the new problems of the country and rather hampered his reforms because of vested interests and alliances with the provincial feudal administrative system, Zara Yaeqob was determined to reorganise the royal army. He attempted to considerably strengthen and expand the royal bodyguard battalions by channelling to them many new recruits and imported arms. Simultaneously he attempted to keep some *Chewa* regiments in the royal camp as part of a mobile striking force. He also tried, it seems, to introduce into his army new technologies and methods of warfare, borrowed from Mamluk Egypt and Christian Europe. All these innovations naturally did not endear him to the traditional decentralised-oriented *Chewa* framework and his chronicler reported several occasions on which the *Chewa* rebelled against their master, supported the regional nobility against him, or deserted to the enemy, even to the rulers of Adal.[53]

Although Zara Yaeqob succeeded in overcoming the most serious rebellion against him, which broke out in 1453, the Ethiopian monarch by now became bitter and suspicious. Despairing of implementing his reforms, he attempted to centralise completely all authority by dispensing with the help of his stewards and ostensibly ruling directly through his daughters. But instead of putting the kingdom on a firmer infrastructure he became completely isolated and suspected even his closest kin and friends of plotting against him and punished them in the most cruel way. Obviously he could not function properly in such circumstances and as the power of the monarchy began to decline, he was forced, in his last years, to compromise with realities and abandon many of his original goals.

Gifted and strong as Zara Yaeqob was, the revolutionary reforms which he wished to implement necessitated more than the life-span of a single king and a reliable base of support, which the monarchy in mediaeval Ethiopia did not enjoy. Zara Yaeqob's main mistake was, however, that in complete contradiction to the prudent policy of checks and balances of his predecessors, he attempted to challenge all the centrifugal forces in the kingdom and solve its complex problems simultaneously, rather than dealing with them piecemeal. His extremist approach backfired because it created a common cause for traditionally rival factions and united all the power elements whose privileges were threatened as a result of his reforms.[54]

NOTES

1. *Siyum, Makwonen, Kantiba, Nagash* etc.
2. Such as *Negarit,* or cattle drums and trumpets and the many other symbols of royalty.
3. King of Kings.
4. Although most of the scanty material available has been supplied by foreign travellers since the 16th century, it seems that the kingdoms which sprang up in western and southern Ethiopia were the outcome of processes similar to that which led to the emergence of Axum. See below, text.
5. The Chronicles from the period of the Solomonic dynasty are clearly biased.
6. Tamrat, pp. 67-8, 72-5.
7. For instance the population was barred from seeing the king, nor was anyone, even his closest followers and wives, allowed to see the king while eating or drinking. When in public his face was covered by a veil and he was separated by a curtain from his companions while travelling – Alvarez, Vol. II, p. 338; Whiteway, *Castanhoso,* p. 92; Almeida, p. 81; Tellez, F. B., *A View of the Universe or a New Collection of Voyages. The Travels of the Jesuits in Ethiopia,* London, 1710, p. 181; Ludolphus, p. 211. On this subject see: Constantin De Renneville, *Recueil des Voyages de la Compagnie des Indes,* Amsterdam, 1736, Tom. IV, Pt. I, pp. 36-7. The Solomonic myth predates Yekuno Amlak.
8. Lit. the glory of kings.
9. This problem was not unique to Ethiopia and the same pragmatic solution was adopted by the Ottoman and many other Asian dynasties. However, this solution, not as cruel in its methods in Ethiopia as in the Ottoman Empire, was later corrupted.
10. For a different version as to who was the founder – Alvarez, Vol. I, p. 237; Paez, Pero, *Historia de Ethiopia,* Vols. II and III of Beccari, C., *Rerum Aethiopicarum scriptores occidentales inediti a saecule XVI ad XIX,* Roma, 1905-1906, Vol. II, pp. 1⋈-12.
11. Singular *Bitwadad.* Literally, the king's beloved friend. See below, text.
12. Alvarez, Vol. I, pp. 241-7; Whiteway, *Castanhoso,* p. 17; Almeida, *Some Records,* pp. 100-1; Tellez, p. 46; Paez, Vol. II, pp. 111-2, 129-31; Ludolphus, pp. 194-5; Wolde Aregay, Merid, *Southern Ethiopia and the Christian Kingdom 1508-1708.* Ph.D. thesis, University of London, 1971, pp. 61-3.
13. The term feudal is used in this book for convenience sake despite obvious differences from European feudalism.
14. Maintained by revenue accrued from their governorships.
15. This is not strictly true. The use of salt bars from the northern Dankali desert was widespread all over the plateau. Iron bars and cloth were also known to be used as currency and gold dust was also occasionally used for expensive purchases. See above, pp. 8-9. Also: Almeida, *Some Records,* p. 44 – on gold and iron; Tellez, p. 34; *Lobo,* p. 74; Ludolphus, p. 205; Bruce, Vol. IV, p. 815.
16. Correa, C., *Lendas da India* (ed. R. J. de Lima Felner), Lisbon, 1858-64, Vol. II, pp. 33-7. Alvarez, Vol. I, pp. 306-7, note 1 – of 1000 guards dressed in glittering coats of mail, Mecca velvet and silks with gilded plates and studs, and armed with shields, spears, battle axes and swords. These arms were imported from Cairo (beginning of 16th century).
17. Tellez, pp. 62-3.
18. On the name see: Wolde Aregay, p. 82.

19. Soldiers' class and other elements, especially landless Tigreans who became a synonym for mercenaries or military settlers.

20. Literally meaning head.

21. *Chroniques de Zar'a Ya'eqob*, p.58; Ludolphus, p.233; Alvarez, Vol.I, p.116. On the army commanded by the *Tigre Makwonen*, including many *Chewa* – Alvarez, Vol.II, p.428.

22. Paez, Vol.II, pp.172-3; Baratti, G., *The Late Travels of S. Giacomo Baratti*, London, 1670, pp.60-2.

23. Alvarez (Vol.I, pp.129-30) compares the superior armament of the *Chewa* to that of the armies of the nobility.

24. Bahrey, *History of the Galla* in Beckingham, C. F. and Huntingford G. W. B. (trans.) *Some Records of Ethiopia, 1596-1646*, London, 1954, pp.25-6; Tellez, p.56 – on limitation of soldier class.

25. When the governor of Gojjam died in 1574 his private army, which was about to disperse, was organised by the king in *Chewa* regiments and allotted *gult* land – Conti Rossini, C., 'Historia regis Sarsa Dengel (Malak Sagad)', *Corpus Scriptorum Christianorum Orientalium*, Vol.III, 1907, p.54.

26. Bahrey, p.115; Alvarez, Vol.II, p.412; Wolde Aregay, pp.88-91; Tamrat, p.74 – on regiments composed of foreign elements in the north.

27. See period of Serse Dingil, pp.152-4 below.

28. Tamrat, pp.89-92.

29. The taxation of certain districts and provinces included a fixed number of horses. A substantial regiment of Sabrad, in the second half of the 16th century numbered 5000 infantry but only 30 cavalry – Rossini, 'Sarsa Dengel', pp.16-7, 47. Tellez, p.56 – on proportion. Alvarez (Vol.II, p.429) mentions a commander of 15,000, but probably he was *Azmatch*. More likely an average *Chewa* unit consisted of a few hundred up to a few thousand. On *Chewa* commanders (colonels) called for a campaign, who carried their supplies with them – Baratti, pp.60-2.

30. See example of the elite Giyorgis Haylo regiment placed under the command of Harbo about to desert to the rebel Yishaq in 1574 – Rossini, 'Sarsa Dengel', p.54. Of land taken from disloyal *Chewa* and returned to them by Yohannis – Guidi, I., 'Annales Iohannis I, Iyasu I et Bakafa', *Corpus Scriptorum Christianorum Orientalium: Scriptores Aethiopici*, V, Paris, 1903, p.37.

31. See post-Serse Dingil's period, pp.181-3 below.

32. Tamrat, pp.207-15. See also below, pp.143-4.

33. Kammerer, A., *La Mer Rouge, l'Abyssinie et l'Arabie aux XVIe et XVIIe Siècles,*, Cairo, 1947, Vol.I, pp.9-10; Huntingford, G. W. B., *The Land Charters of Northern Ethiopia*, Addis Ababa – Nairobi, 1965, pp.9-10; Beccari, C., *Il Tigre Del Secolo XVII*, Roma, 1909, pp.8-10; Alvarez, Vol.I, pp.116-17.

34. Alvarez, Vol.I, pp.116-7, 124; Vol.II, p.461.

35. There are claims, mainly Jesuit, that the Ethiopian rulers did not wish to incorporate some of these areas within the administrative borders of their empire because they preferred to pillage them and enslave their population. See below, pp.160-2. Wolde Aregay, pp.104-5, concerning the 16th century; Alvarez, Vol.II, p.461 – Libna Dingil refused a request of Nobiis to receive priests and monks, because he claimed he depended on an imported *abun*. However on other occasions mention is made of raids on Nobiis. See also period of Susinyos, pp.200-2 below; also p.167 on another approach to the problem.

36. For instance: *Bahr Nagash, Makwonen, Tsefaha Lam, Negus*. The king had estates in each province – Alvarez, Vol.I, p.248; Kolmodin, J., *Traditions de*

Tsazzega et Hazzega, Upsala, 1915, pp. 51-5; Beccari, *Tigre*, p. 9; Tamrat, pp. 93-6; *Land Charters*, pp. 9-10.

37. Alvarez, Vol. II, p. 429.
38. Wolde Aregay, pp. 66-7.
39. Wiet, 'Les Relations', p. 126; Maqrizi, p. 8 – on Mamluks and Copts used by Negus Ishaq to reorganise his army, administration and fiscal machinery. General sources on administration reforms and classification of different areas: Paez, Vol II, p. 5; Almeida, *Some Records,* pp. 11-2, 72; Tellez, pp. 9-10; *Lobo,* Le Grand, pp. 254-6; Ludolphus, pp. 201, 232-4; Wolde Aregay's (pp. 60-80) division between administrative and military functions and interpretation of Amda Siyon's reforms seems illogical.
40. There is a striking similarity between Zara Yaeqob's fundamental argumentations in the 15th century and those of Susinyos at the beginning of the 17th, even though the latter was completely disillusioned with the national church. See below Chapter IX.
41. Tamrat, pp. 213-14.
42. On the struggle between the church and the monastic orders see Tamrat, Chapter V; on evangelisation, pp. 157-205.
43. About a huge property of land of the church in Amhara see: *Chroniques de Zar'a Ya'eqob,* pp. 122-3, 169-76.
44. Alvarez, Vol. I, pp. 232-3, 257; Vol. II, pp. 463-4; *Chroniques de Zar'a Ya'eqob,* pp. 122-3, 169-70. Angot Ras, a learned priest who was one of the most scholarly people in the country, was made later on *Bahr Nagash* – Alvarez, Vol. I, p. 232.
45. Wolde Aregay, pp. 66-7.
46. *Chroniques de Zar'a Ya'eqob,* pp. 46-7, 169-70. The king owns estates in every province – Alvarez, Vol. I, p. 248; Vol. II, pp. 445-6; Tamrat, pp. 98-102 – on *gult.*
47. Singular *Bitwadad* – the king's beloved friend.
48. Later the office of *Ras,* or the equivalent of commander-in-chief, was established, but the positions of *Bitwadadotch* were reintroduced by Zara Yaeqob's successors. Alvarez, Vol. I, p. 270, note 1; *Land Charters,* p. 10; Almeida, *Some Records,* p. 72; Tellez, p. 54; *Lobo,* Le Grand, pp. 254-5; Paez, Vol. II, p. 48.
49. Even during the crisis of the Jihad of Grañ the church was unable to give up minute ecclesiastical differences – Perruchon, *Sémitique,* 1893, p. 283.
50. On coercion against priests who did not co-operate – *Chroniques de Zar'a Ya'eqob,* p. 82.
51. Council of Debra Mitmaq – Tamrat, pp. 220-31.
52. See rumours concerning his interest in Catholicism – Wansleben, pp. 5-6, on messenger from Pope to Zara Yaeqob and from Zara Yaeqob to Pope. Also Suriano, p. 86. This information does not agree with Tamrat's thesis (pp. 265-7) on the monarch's intentions concerning European kings; also below pp. 215-16.
53. *Chroniques de Zar'a Ya'eqob,* pp. 46-7, 139-40.
54. The many rebellious nobles against Zara Yaeqob attempted to exploit the princes of Amba Geshen, who were cruelly punished by the monarch – Paez, Vol. II, p. 114; *Chroniques de Zar'a Ya'eqob* pp. 46-7.

CHAPTER IV

The Rise of the Muslim Kingdom of Ethiopia in the Sixteenth Century – Power Politics

Political decline and Jihad

Immediately after Zara Yaeqob's death, the nobility abolished or eroded the remnants of his reforms. Moreover, the clash with the feudal administrative-military system led rather to a decline of the power and prestige of the monarchy. Fearing the rise of another strong monarch, who would again attempt to eliminate their privileges, the feudal nobility consolidated its position vis-à-vis that of the king and until the rise of Ahmad Grañ in the sixteenth century contrived to select only relatively weak or young monarchs, who were dominated by their regents. Consequently, the struggle for power among the chief nobles and courtiers was also intensified. All this undoubtedly further undermined the power of the kingdom and helped to prepare the ground for the great victory of the coastal Muslims led by Grañ.

Despite the initial successes of his army in the war against the Adali amirs, Na'od, a timid, inexperienced and weak ruler, was unable to halt the process of decline and Muslim raids on Ethiopia were constantly accelerated.[1] The sultan of Adal, Muhammad ibn Azhar ad-Din (r. 1488-1518), whose capital was Dakar[2], attempted to maintain cordial relations with the Christian kingdom. Nevertheless the real power in Adal from the late 1490s was in the hands of the Amir of Harar, Mahfuz, who took the title of Imam. Since the reign of Eskender, Mahfuz had constantly raided Ethiopia, especially in the month of Lent, when the Christian Ethiopians were weak from their long fast. Such raids made him very popular among the Muslims, because, among other things, they resulted in the exportation to Arabia of tens of thousands of prisoners of war.

69

Many were given to the Sharif of Mecca and other Arabian rulers and others were sold in the slave markets. Towards the end of his reign, at the beginning of the sixteenth century, Na'od succeeded in defeating Mahfuz and the latter kept his peace for a short time.[3]

When Na'od died in 1508 the succession of his younger son Libna Dingil, at the age of 11, was engineered by Illeni with the help of Abuna Marcos, Bitwadad Wasan Sagad and other courtiers. The excuse for overlooking the older brother was that he was unsuitable for the position. Obviously the true reason for this choice was the age of the new king, which guaranteed Illeni and her friends a relatively long period of regency.

The struggle for power within Ethiopia's feudal nobility which had begun immediately after Zara Yaeqob's death not only eroded the power of the monarchy, but resulted in chaos. Law and order declined and the economy of the country suffered. Nobles and courtiers who were out of favour and members of the royal family rebelled in different provinces. Some, who unsuccessfully challenged the clique in power, did not hesitate to desert to the Muslims. Consolidation and expansion of Ethiopian government and cultural influences in the Agaw and Falasha provinces suffered a setback. Indeed, while evangelisation and Christianity, as a whole, rapidly declined, the clergy and monks were occupied in politics, with power struggles or with dogmatic controversies. Thus, by the beginning of the sixteenth century the centrifugal forces in Ethiopia had again triumphed.[4]

The situation in the Red Sea region changed dramatically with the arrival of the Portuguese in the Indian Ocean at the end of the fifteenth century. By the beginning of the sixteenth century this development had already gravely affected the economy and politics of the Red Sea countries. Nevertheless, the Muslim rulers of the region remained, for a time, preoccupied with internal affairs and their traditional rivalries.[5]

In the middle of the fifteenth century Yemen was again in a state of anarchy. The weak Rassulid dynasty, established in the thirteenth century, had long since degenerated and lost the little control which it exercised over the numerous insignificant dynasties, whose base of power were tribes or different towns of the coast and the highlands. This situation was exploited by the Banu Tahir who, supported by other Zaydi tribal elements, succeeded in asserting themselves in the Tihama and made Zabid their centre of government. Soon afterwards, the three Tahirid brothers became the masters of Aden and parts of the central plateau, but Tahirid authority was, in many cases, nominal and was often challenged. San'a, moreover, was captured only in 1505, just a decade prior to the conquest of Yemen by the Mamluks. Thus, despite the role it had played in radiating cultural influences to the Horn and its being the centre of regional and international trade, Yemen remained weak and was unable to intervene more decisively in the affairs of her neighbours or play a significant role in the politics of the region in a most crucial era.

The bitter fratricide among the Mamluks in Egypt, which reached an unprecedented intensity in the last decades of the fifteenth century, greatly harmed Egypt's economy and its transit trade with the Far East. Venice and Genoa, declining anyway due to the expansion of Ottoman power on sea and land, were also affected by the situation in Egypt and its impact on international commerce. Their trade with Egypt was so important, however, that despite the unbearable exactions of the authorities, many Italian merchants were still to be found in Alexandria, desperately trying to retain their monopoly on trade between Egypt and Europe. These watched with exasperation the apathy of the Mamluks regarding the advent of Portuguese power in the Indian Ocean.

Because of the prolonged internal strife in Egypt, Sharif Barakat II of Mecca (r. 1495-1522) succeeded, at the end of the fifteenth century, in consolidating his autonomy in Hijaz. Obviously the Mamluks were also in no position to exploit the anarchy in Yemen or intervene (if they wished to do so) in the affairs of the Horn of Africa. Hence, even after the appearance of the Portuguese in the Indian Ocean, the Mamluks, considered the major Muslim power of the region, whose revenue from trade gravely decreased, were slow to respond to this threat to Muslim power and economy, nor were they fully aware of its magnitude and significance, until about 1506. Ironically, the Venetians were the first to raise the alarm concerning the far-reaching meaning of the developments and to press the Mamluk rulers to take direct action against their Portuguese rivals and curb the growth of their power in the Indian Ocean.[6]

Arriving annually in the Indian Ocean Portuguese fleets since the beginning of the sixteenth century systematically destroyed the Muslim trading complex there and as early as 1503 succeeded in diverting much of the trade of India to Portugal. The disastrous debacle of their fleet when it encountered the Portuguese navy off Diu in 1508 convinced the Mamluks of the urgent need to invest greater efforts and resources in preparations to overcome the Portuguese threat.[7]

That the Portuguese contemplated an anti-Muslim alliance with Ethiopia is an established fact. Pero da Covilhão was sent to the Ethiopian court by king João of Portugal for this specific purpose. Albuquerque, the great Portuguese admiral, despatched messengers to the Ethiopian court in 1504 and in 1507.[8] The Portuguese admiral's plan was to bottle up the Muslim forces in the Red Sea and the Persian Gulf by capturing strategic islands at their entrances. For this purpose, and possibly to co-ordinate an attack on the Muslims in the Red Sea, the Portuguese wished to gain Ethiopian co-operation. Socotra was taken in 1507, but Muslim shipping was harassed in the Gulf of Aden even earlier. When found strategically useless Socotra was abandoned and a half-hearted attempt was made in 1513 to capture Aden, the key to the Red Sea.[9] The Portuguese threat to the heart of the Islamic world seemed, nevertheless, imminent and an alliance between them and the Ethiopians was considered a realistic possibility by the Muslim rulers of the region.

Mahfuz's struggle against the Christian Ethiopians was admired by all the Muslims and in addition to volunteers from Arabia, who flocked to his camp, he enjoyed the support of the rulers of Yemen and Hijaz. When he declared a Jihad and renewed his campaign against Ethiopia following the succession of Libna Dingil (after the arrival of the Portuguese in the Indian Ocean) he was presented with the green flag of Islam by Ulama from Arabia. Many more volunteers and substantial quantities of arms were now shipped from Arabia to the Somali coast[10] and the struggle against the Christian kingdom assumed a new dimension.

Some historians claim that the overwhelming Christian military successes in the conflict with Ifat and Adal since the turn of the fourteenth century, led to increasing religious undertones in the struggle of the Muslim sultanates and peoples of the eastern part of the Horn against Ethiopia. Tamrat[11] even claims that such undertones can be found as early as the time of Yekuno Amlak. Shaykh Muhammad abu 'Abdallah declared a Jihad against Christian Showa in 1299 and the 'Muslim question' was a factor of growing importance in the political-economic struggle between Amda Siyon and the eastern sultanates.

The use of terminology associated with Jihad is prevalent in Muslim sources related to Ethiopia, especially from the fourteenth and fifteenth centuries.[12] But equivalent expressions can be found in Ethiopian sources emanating from the first centuries after the rise of the Solomonic dynasty. What is usually overlooked by historians is the fact that this was a style of writing in the period, and that the literary element to which most contemporary writers belonged were Ulama, or scholars associated with them, and priests or monks, whose concepts were usually oriented to religion and who due to their training employed as a matter of course most naturally, religious terminology in their writings. It is usually difficult to avoid the pitfall of accepting the written word as being the reflection of reality rather than to seek the true factors which motivated conflicts and to assess the true attitude of the people and rulers who participated in them. What may seem an inconsistency between purely politico-economic motivated wars and the deep religious sentiments of the rulers, accentuated by the occasional employment by the sources of terminology associated with religious conflicts, may not be a paradox at all. It is a reflection by the Chroniclers of the reality concerning a heterogeneous, relatively tolerant society, in which the religious sentiments of the rulers were, in most cases, dissociated from politics, and the religious beliefs of the masses were generally superficial.

There was a fundamental difference in the attitude of Ethiopian monarchs to 'their' Muslims, who enjoyed complete freedom and toleration, despite their (partial) exclusion from the ruling classes and who considered themselves 'Ethiopians', and their attitude to the eastern Muslim principalities. The endless wars, economically and politically motivated, caused the Ethiopian rulers extremely grave problems relating to their ability to control and govern their kingdom and to develop its commerce. Their failure to solve the eastern 'Muslim problem' due to climatic, geographical and human constraints coupled with the realisation about the possible implications of the ties between these principalities and their wider Muslim hinterland, caused the Ethiopian monarchs in the fifteenth century to adopt a drastic solution to the problem. Whenever possible Islam was to be uprooted from the area by replacing the population with loyal elements or converting it to Christianity, and by a systematic destruction of the economy of regions which could not be incorporated in the kingdom for reasons mentioned before. But even this 'religious' policy had a politico-economic motivation.

Ethiopia's foreign relations were influenced by the wish to participate in Red Sea politics and trade in a period in which they were becoming increasingly important. The kingdom was also influenced by the special relationship existing between the Coptic church and Ethiopia and the Ethiopians' sentiments, through their heritage, about the Holy Land. Finally, they were also related to the attempts of several Solomonic monarchs to strengthen the monarchy, partly through modernisation and imported technology. All this, notwithstanding the distorted impression created by European sources about the religious factor in the conflicts in the Horn, was the outcome of wishful thinking or a misinterpretation of Ethiopian politics and the motivation of Ethiopian monarchs.

It is significant that the assumed religious undertones in the relations between Ethiopia and its neighbours became even more noticeable from the reign of Ba'eda Maryam, when the Ethiopian monarchy began to decline and after it had abandoned its previous aggressive policy towards its Muslim neighbours. The feebleness of the Ethiopian monarchy and the policy of appeasement which it adopted encouraged the different elements of Adal and the pastoralists, whose power was on the rise at this time, to unite and co-ordinate their attacks on Ethiopia, a step which they had failed, in most cases, to achieve in the past.

The more orthodox Muslim mercantile and agricultural communities of Adal, whose economic foundations and political power were completely undermined by the Ethiopian expansionism and repeated invasion of their territories, joined the new union led by Imam Mahfuz, hoping to regain the self-respect and some of the assets which they had lost in the past. Always envious of the cultivators of the plateau, the poverty-stricken coastal pastoralists, nominally Muslim, if at all, and especially the Somali tribes, whose presence and power in the Horn became more prominent in the region from the second half of the fifteenth century, also joined the cause of Islam. They hoped that the Imam would enable them to get back at the Ethiopians, who systematically undermined their livelihood and looted their cattle. But it seems that their movement towards the plateau was a syndrome of a far wider migration in the area of the Horn.

The pastoralist element

Until recently it was believed that originally the Galla pastoralists, who call themselves Oromo, inhabited the southeastern and eastern part of the Horn of Africa, presently occupied by the Somali and Afar (Dankali) people. It was also believed that the Dankali and the Somali, coming from the north, gradually pushed the Galla southwards and westwards from the beginning of the second millenium A.D. Hence, by the sixteenth century, the Galla had come to inhabit semi-desert areas of the southern borders of the Ethiopian plateau and the northern parts of present-day Kenya,[13] and from there, under the pressure of the expanding Somali tribes, they had begun their migration into Ethiopia. However, scholars now argue[14] that in fact the Galla tribes did not inhabit the southeastern and eastern parts of the Horn before the turn of the fifteenth century. It is most likely that for an extended period they inhabited the area to the south and southeast of the Ethiopian Rift Valley lakes and that the Somali and Dankali migrated with their herds from south to north rather than from north to south. This migration was probably triggered off by population growth and the insufficiency of grazing land and, finally, mounting pressure of Galla tribes, who had begun their two-pronged expansion, it seems, in the fifteenth century.

The Galla expansion southeastwards, along the Webi Shebelli, a minor branch of the great Galla migration in the sixteenth century, began, it seems, before that century, although the vanguard of the Galla reached the delta of the Juba only at the beginning of the seventeenth century. This relatively limited Galla migration, submerged in the following century by a migration of Somali tribes, is responsible for the existence of Galla enclaves, questionable archaeological evidence and traditions about Galla presence in parts of present-day Somalia. Be that as it may, the growth movement of the pastoralist groups created a chain reaction among the peoples of the Horn which was the reason, *inter alia*, for the incessant pressure of coastal-nomads on the eastern escarpments of Ethiopia from the fourteenth century until the beginning of the sixteenth century.

Somali tribes inhabited the hinterland of the Benadir coast and possibly the Ogaden at least as early as the beginning of the second millenium A.D.[16] Gradually the northern Somali, including the

Girri, Bartiri and Marehan,[17] pushed their way from the marginal lands of the Ogaden to the Somali coast and into the Harar-Chercher plateau where they replaced some of the previous inhabitants or inter-mingled with them.[18]

The Dankali, who had arrived it seems in the southeastern part of the Horn even earlier than the Somali, were gradually pushed northwards out of the Chercher-Harar region into the inhospitable deserts of the Ethiopian-Eritrean coast beyond the Awash, although they persistently clung to the slopes of the Harari plateau. Consequently they became the neighbours of the Saho pastoralists, who inhabited the coastal plains north of the bay of Zula and the salt depressions at the foot of the Tigrean plateau.[19]

The intermittent but systematic ravaging of the Harar-Chercher plateau and of Aussa, the punishment inflicted by the Ethiopian armies on the settled population, and the harassment of the pastoralists in the fourteenth and fifteenth centuries, actually facilitated the Somali expansion and entrenchment in the area. This northward expansion, the origin of which may have been population growth, as well as Bantu or Galla pressure, reached its peak by the turn of the fifteenth century. At the beginning of the sixteenth century the Somali tribes, only nominally Muslim, had already replaced the semitised cultivators in the area between the coast and Harar and begun to exert pressure on the Amirate of Harar, its smaller satellites and the southern Afar.[20] In addition to their involvement in the politics of the smaller amirates in the region, they occasionally attacked trade caravans and greatly contributed to the disorder in the region. The border line between the Somali and the Afar territories remained fluid and gave rise to endless raids and counter-raids, but, generally speaking, it could be said that the dividing line between the two peoples stretched from the Bay of Tajura along the northern slopes of the Chercher-Harar range to the Awash and the Doba country in the gullies falling from the highlands on the verges of Angot.

Population movement along the coastal plains of the Horn of Africa and the Harar-Chercher plateau, which gradually built up between the twelfth and sixteenth centuries, undoubtedly affected relations between the coastal people and Ethiopia. As the power of the Muslim principalities in the area diminished, due to the rise of Christian Ethiopia, their ability to withstand the incursion of the pastoralists declined. Thus, by the last decades of the fifteenth century Somali tribes became a predominant factor in the struggle which took place in Adal and a catalyst for the incessant raiding carried out against Ethiopia by Imams who disregarded the authority of the Walasma sultans.[21] The pressure of the Somali tribes on the southern Afar was indirectly responsible, as well, for the intermittent eruptions of the latter from the coastal deserts into the fertile plateau. The rise of the power of Christian Ethiopia in the fourteenth and fifteenth centuries, however, not only curbed such eruptions but also led to severe Ethiopian retributions against the Afar and Somali tribes. However, when the kingdom began to decline towards the end of the fifteenth century, the pastoralists were the first to take advantage of the new circumstances and initiated, or were always ready to join, raids and campaigns against Ethiopia, which would enable them to loot and devastate the rich plateau. The Somali thus became the backbone of the armies of the Adali amirs, including Imam Mahfuz who attacked Fatagar and Showa, whereas the Afar 'sultanate' (or 'sultanates') increased their pressure on the eastern escarpments north of Showa.[22]

The background for Muslim victory – the reign of Libna Dingil

Jihads were conducted against Ethiopia on several occasions in the past, but they are ignored by historians because they had limited objectives and support, went unnoticed and were unsuccessful. Although periods of decline and interregnum in Ethiopia were nearly always successfully exploited in the past by the eastern Muslims and pastoralists to step up their incursions into the plateau, such periods were relatively short and were followed, in most instances, by the rise of powerful kings who quickly defeated the Muslims. In the last decades of the fifteenth century, however, Ethiopia's internal weakness was seriously aggravated by its previously rapid territorial growth, extremely heterogeneous society and the rise to power of the feudal nobility. Not only was the period of decline lengthy, but the possibility of a true revival of the Solomonic power was extremely difficult to achieve.

For some time the Muslims of the Red Sea basin followed the development of Ethiopia's relations with Western Christianity with consternation. By the end of the fifteenth century, however, the speculation and fears concerning Christian ambitions became a reality and a junction between Western Christianity and Ethiopian

Christian interests seemed a possibility which not only threatened Muslim economy, but the very heart of Islam. Ethiopia could no longer be considered a 'tolerated' Christian country, excluded from Jihad. It was not long, therefore, before local *Mujahidun* and pastoralist warriors were joined by volunteers from other Muslim countries, and the rulers of nearby Arab countries actively supported the movement. This development can be attributed also to Mahfuz' success, the substantial loot taken in the raids on Ethiopia and the general fear of a junction between Ethiopia and European Christianity. Nevertheless, Ethiopia was immense in size and rich in resources and manpower. Not realising Ethiopia's internal weakness the Muslim leadership, dependent on a relatively small, poor and disunited pupulation, was still unable to conceive a conquest of Ethiopia or a permanent occupation of territories lost to the Solomonic kings in the previous century.

The religious undertones in the conflict between the Muslim settled and pastoralist population of the eastern part of the Horn and Ethiopia became far more meaningful by the turn of the fifteenth century with the appearance of a Christian European power in the Indian Ocean. It was enhanced by Christian European efforts to develop relations with Ethiopia, reciprocated by the attempts of the Solomonic monarch to receive technical aid from their co-religionists. The new momentum infused into the struggle against Ethiopia and its intensity were also partially the outcome of migrations in the southeastern and eastern parts of the Horn which inevitably was related to the rich plateau. But a major factor in the success of the Jihad of the coastal people against Christian Ethiopia was the internal weakness of the kingdom, the erosion of the power of the government and central authorities. Not less important was the ineffectiveness or failure of integrative forces and steps which should have united the extremely heterogeneous population of Ethiopia.

The reign of Libna Dingil coincided with one of the most eventful and difficult periods in the history of Ethiopia. Just to handle power politics, which seriously affected the region in this period, would have necessitated a very able ruler. But due to Illeni's appeasement policy and the reign of court officials and their allies in the feudal aristocracy, the process of decentralisation in the kingdom reached a peak. Hence only a strong and gifted monarch could halt the disintegration of Ethiopia.

Disgruntled nobles who were out of favour, as well as the rulers of newly conquered border provinces, sought to establish their autonomy or were openly in rebellion. The central authority, in most cases, was incapable of suppressing them because it did not hold real power and because the *Chewa* system became progressively more ineffective and the soldiers were unwilling to fight for their master.[23] Thus the monarchy became even more dependent on feudal armies whose loyalty was questionable, and was unable to stem the rise of Muslim power. Ethiopian Christianity and cultural dynamics also reached a low ebb in this period with Christians intermarrying with Muslims and animists, while pagan customs, universally practised, even penetrated the royal court. As Christianity degenerated, Islam not only held its ground, but continued to expand in the highlands.

As early as 1508 Iman Mahfuz, at the head of Somali pastoralists and Adali amirs, renewed his attacks on the eastern and southeastern provinces of the plateau and the Dankali and Doba made inroads into Angot. Such hit-and-run raids resulted in the disruption of normal life and caravan trade along the eastern escarpments and tens of thousands of Abyssinian prisoners and vast quantities of loot were shipped to the markets of Arabia. While the Ethiopians resorted to defensive tactics, Mahfuz exploited to its fullest potential the advantage of surprise and mobility which enabled him to strike swiftly at a chosen frontier province or provinces. Always elusive and careful not to present to the royal Ethiopian army a 'hard' target, the main body of his forces, made up of Somali and Afar pastoralists, quickly dispersed after every operation to the semi-deserts of the Horn.

Mahfuz's astounding successes should be attributed to a combination of factors. On one hand, the disintegration of Ethiopia's frontier defences, the corruption of the *Chewa* and feudal military-administrative systems, and the lack of determined leadership in the Christian camp. On the other hand, Mahfuz's victory was made possible by the flexibility of his army, his tactics and success in avoiding a headlong confrontation with the royal army (made even slower by the fast of Lent) in areas favourable to the latter. Finally, the extensive aid which he received from Arabia and the many volunteers who joined his camp should also not be ignored.

Greatly exaggerated, Mahfuz's victories produced enormous quantities of loot and many thousands of slaves and led to the spread of his fame in Ethiopia and nearby Muslim countries. His victories over the Christians were especially welcomed by the Muslim people of the Red Sea region, whose morale and economy had suffered a serious blow as a result of the Portuguese activities in the Indian Ocean. In reality Mahfuz and his followers did not constitute a serious threat to Ethiopia and his achievements were limited. Proportionally his power, organised *ad hoc* and composed mainly of volunteers and irregulars, was insufficient to challenge the vast resources of the Ethiopian kingdom, nor did Mahfuz even contemplate a permanent occupation of the Ethiopian plateau or part of it, which would have made him an easy target for the Christian army. His strategy of harassment could be compared to that carried out by the Walasma sultans against Ethiopia, after the decline of their power in the second half of the fourteenth century. Although nearly always successful, his campaigns were just spontaneous eruptions and not part of a strategy aimed at conquering Ethiopia or at least of re-establishing Adali government in its eastern provinces.

The real danger to the kingdom emanated from within and was the outcome of the existence and success of an irresponsible and corrupt feudal military-administrative system which continued to undermine the strength and unity of the country. It was also helped by a church which, rather than curb centrifugal forces in the greatly heterogeneous kingdom, contributed to them. And finally by the uninspiring, irresolute and weak government of Illeni, which because of its character always chose compromises and was partly responsible for the decline of the authority and power of the monarchy.[24]

Illeni's regency ended only about 1516, but all the ills which befell Christian Ethiopia a decade later are generally attributed to the reign of Libna Dingil, whose policy and character, it is claimed, caused Ethiopia's total collapse in the face of Grañ's attack and the terrible calamities which the kingdom suffered as a result of this event. Libna Dingil is usually considered a weak, irresolute, greedy, despotic and cruel monarch and a poor military leader, who had completely alienated Ethiopia's aristocracy and Muslim population. His avidity, lust and immorality, it is further claimed, were directly related to the disregard he showed for the Christian faith – another reason for the astounding collapse of the Christian kingdom.

The undeniable asymmetry between the huge resources, human and others, of Ethiopia and the relatively limited resources of Grañ in the first stages of the 'conquest of Ethiopia' tend to strengthen such claims. So does the evidence from contemporary and later Portuguese, Ethiopian and other sources, the poor performance of the monarch in the crucial battles of 1527 and 1529 and the total collapse of the Ethiopian kingdom after Grañ's victory in 1529.[25] It seems that historians, wishing to explain the astounding and swift victory of the coastal and Harari Muslim forces against the huge and seemingly powerful Christian kingdom, tend to accept the evidence without examining its bias, the context and the circumstances in which it was written; nor do they attribute the proper weight to the realities which existed in Ethiopia when Libna Dingil assumed power. Unfortunately, the Ethiopian royal chronicles of this period are very short and laconic and, in many instances, they even neglect the unfortunate monarch and rather describe the successes of Grañ and the ravages which he brought upon Christian Ethiopia as God's punishment.

The crucial question which should be re-examined is whether Libna Dingil was, in fact, an outstandingly bad and incapable ruler, who came to power in the worst possible time for Ethiopia, or whether he was a victim of circumstances who, in another context, would have emerged as a reformer or even a great king, who contributed to the restoration of the power of the monarchy and the revival of the Christian kingdom.

When the period of regency ended and Libna Dingil assumed power about 1516, the centrifugal forces in Ethiopia were completely triumphant. The courtiers who had ruled the country with the support of factions of the feudal nobility for half a century, were constantly struggling for power. The provincial aristocracy continued to consolidate its autonomy there by eroding the power of the central authorities. The corrupt and inefficient military-administrative apparatus, which the monarch inherited, was also involved in the internal politics of the country. The revenues of the monarch greatly diminished due to the rise of the power of his feudal lords, Illeni's appeasement policy in relation to the tributary Muslim rulers and the disruption of the caravan trade by the raids of the pastoralists and the exactions of the nobles.[26] The church, which lacked dedicated and inspiring leadership, ignored the heterogeneous population of the vast conquered territories and the spiritual substance of Christianity and, in addition to minute dogmatic controversies, also became involved in internal power politics and intrigues.[27] In short, at a low ebb, the huge kingdom was held together by a flimsy administrative framework and a government which disregarded the erosion which threatened the existence of the Christian kingdom.

When he came of age and assumed the government of the country, Libna Dingil, in the tradition of the great kings who preceded him, took upon himself the command of the army. He was determined to terminate Mahfuz's raids, which caused a traumatic fear in the eastern part of Ethiopia. With pre-knowledge of the latter's intended target he managed to ambush him in 1516 in Fatagar, when Mahfuz was encumbered by booty and prisoners.[28] The Muslim army was completely annihilated and Mahfuz and many of his amirs killed. Exploiting his success, the young monarch immediately invaded Adal and devastated it. His victory over Adal, however, was just as meaningless as those of his predecessors because of its limited aims, temporary effect and the composition and character of the Adali population.[29]

Mahfuz's death and the annihilation of most of the commanders of his army sparked off a struggle for power in Adal and between pastoralists and agriculturists. The chaos in Adal gave Ethiopia a few years of grace and enabled the monarch to consolidate his government and deal with troublesome elements in the different parts of Ethiopia.

Once free from the Adali threat Libna Dingil's first and foremost aim was to break the stranglehold of the feudal nobility over the government of the country and to restore the authority of the monarchy. In this he was resolute, uncompromising and ruthless. He relied at first, to some extent, on the support of some important northern nobles to whom he was related through his mother. This, of course, further alienated the Amhara nobility which hated him anyway for stripping it of its privileges and fortunes. Once he had firmly established his power the turn of the Tigrean nobility came and Libna Dingil dealt with it just as ruthlessly. Notwithstanding the power and influence which Illeni retained after she ceased to be regent, and despite her own and Libna Dingil's mother's efforts to intervene on behalf of their protégés, it was evident when Roderigo da Lima reached the court in 1520 that the young monarch was the absolute master of his country. Even though the aristocracy hated the king for his despotism and unwillingness to share power with them and was ready to betray him in suitable circumstances, it recognised the absolute power of the monarch, submitted to his wishes and fearfully obeyed all his orders.[30]

In full control of the government, Libna Dingil consolidated his hold over the provinces of his kingdom and renewed Ethiopian expansion, which virtually ceased after the death of Zara Yaeqob. Thus Ethiopian authority was further extended in the north into the Falasha provinces and, after overcoming the resistance of the Muslim Belaw, towards Sawakin and Sennar.[31] Damot served as a springboard for Libna Dingil's armies, which penetrated further into the southwestern and western plateaux, thereby strengthening Ethiopia's control over the provinces which were the source of the country's trade.[32]

Despite the arrival of the Portuguese in the Indian Ocean and the disruption of the Red Sea trade with the Far East, or rather because of it, commercial activities in the Horn of Africa flourished and many foreign merchants arrived in Ethiopia. The consolidation of the authority of the monarchy and the expansion of Ethiopian government in the plateau also contributed to the kingdom's prosperity in this period. Libna Dingil, who wished to benefit as much as possible from this development and hoped at first to maintain friendly relations with his Muslim neighbours, attempted to foster such relations especially in matters of trade.

In 1516 a Mamluk fleet disembarked troops which occupied the Yemeni coast. This navy, commanded by Mir Hussayn and Reis Sulayman, was provisioned later at Zayla by the Adali government. But rather than confronting the Portuguese, the Mamluk admirals made an abortive attempt to capture Aden and later returned to Jedda.[33] In the meantime an embassy, carrying many presents, was sent by Libna Dingil to Sultan Qansaw al-Ghawri in order to strengthen Ethiopia's relations with Egypt and facilitate the trade with the latter.[34] This gesture within the framework of Libna Dingil's economic and external policy, badly timed because it nearly coincided with the Ottoman conquest of Egypt, may have also reflected the growing apprehension of the Ethiopian monarch in regard to the maritime activities of the Muslims in the Red Sea. It was also related to the monarch's need for resources to combat his feudal nobility and the need for a new *abun*.

Personally involved in commercial activities in a substantial way,

Libna Dingil co-operated with his Muslim neighbours to secure the passage of caravans to, and from, the sea. Muslim merchants daily arrived in his court from far away countries and among other things kept him informed of the situation in the region. His agents, mostly Ethiopian Muslims, exported Ethiopian merchandise, including slaves, to the markets of the Muslim countries and imported to Ethiopia cloth and other foreign luxuries, for the use of the monarch and his officers.[35]

European foreign trade very much depended on Muslims. Some of the king's governors, especially in the eastern provinces, and a not inconsequential number of administrators in the king's court, were also Ethiopian Muslims. Yet Libna Dingil extorted heavy taxes and other payments from the merchant community, predominantly Muslim, and he instituted discriminatory and oppressive measures against his subjects who were Muslims. Refraining from marrying daughters of his Muslim vassals, as was the custom in the past, Libna Dingil exacted, whenever necessary by force, the tribute due from these rulers, which his predecessors had waived, due to marital relations, or Ethiopia's weakness. This seeming dichotomy in the monarch's policy concerning the Muslims in the Horn of Africa emanated from purely economic motivations but, even more, from goals which somewhat resembled the 'nationalist -religious' policy of Zara Yaeqob.[36]

Cognizant of the growing role and importance of religious factors in the politics of the region, Libna Dingil was fearful of the growing influence, prestige and power of the highlands Muslims which they acquired through their control of the country's economy and their wealth. In contradistinction to the inability or indifference of the church to convert the mass of the pagan population and integrate them in the kingdom, Islam was quickly spreading all over the plateau, especially through the activities of the caravan merchants and the Ulama who accompanied them. Libna Dingil was determined to curb the spread of Islam and its influence in the plateau not only on religious grounds but also because of the political implication of this development. Measures were taken to humiliate and segregate the Muslim population, similar to the discriminatory practices against Christians in Muslim countries. Muslims, even administrators and governors for instance, were prohibited from carrying arms and riding horses. Mosques were destroyed and permission was refused to build new ones. Intermarriage of Christians with Muslims was prohibited and a poll tax was levied on all Muslim subjects.[37]

Efforts to encourage the assimilation and integration of the Cushitic population of Gojjam in the Ethiopian 'commonwealth' reached a new peak under Libna Dingil. Gojjam served, moreover, as a springboard for the diffusion of Christianity in Damot and beyond it to the southwest. The area near Lake Tana and Begemder as a whole served to radiate Christian influence into the provinces inhabited by the Falasha. Moreover, when Ethiopian authority was re-established by Libna Dingil in Hadya, the monarch founded monastic centres in the lake region of the Ethiopian Rift Valley.[38] However, proselytising, in some cases achieved by coercion, was not properly supported by the necessary infrastructure and its impact was generally extremely superficial.

In complete contradiction to the claims of later sources, the words of the elderly Abuna Marcos to Alvarez[39] in 1523-1524 concerning Libna Dingil are most illuminating: 'so strong and valiant in the Christian faith and so resolved to destroy the Mourama (Islam)'. This very different evaluation of the monarch's attitude to Christianity and his goals is strengthened by Libna Dingil's proposal to the Portuguese that if they established strongholds on the Ethiopian coast they should jointly attempt to conquer Jerusalem and liberate the Holy Land from the yoke of Islam.[40]

The situation in the Red Sea changed very dramatically after the conquest of Egypt by the Ottomans at the beginning of 1517. Ottoman overlordship was immediately recognised by the authorities of Hijaz and part of the Sudanese coast. Soon afterwards, the Mamluks in Yemen followed suit.[41] For the first time in centuries a major Muslim power, with capabilities far beyond those of the Mamluks, became involved in the struggle for the control of the trade of the Indian Ocean and hegemony in the Red Sea. However, at this early stage, the primary aim of the Ottomans was to protect the holy places of Islam and re-establish Muslim control over the Far East trade, rather than the conquest of additional territories in the region. Yet, indirectly, the change in the balance of power in the Red Sea basin was bound to affect Ethiopia and the Muslims of the Horn of Africa. Not only did the Ethiopians fear the Ottoman power, but many more volunteers for the holy war were arriving in Zayla and firearms of different types became available to the amirs of Adal.[42]

Illeni's delegate Mathew finally returned to India in 1517 with Roderigo da Lima's embassy. He and his companions were sent to the Red Sea in the fleet commanded by Lopo Suarez. This fleet, which penetrated the Red Sea as far as Jedda and burnt Zayla on its return, failed to disembark the ambassadors because the Ethiopian coast was considered unsafe. Only in 1520 was the da Lima embassy put ashore at Massawa by a small Portuguese flotilla.[43]

When the Portuguese embassy reached Libna Dingil's court it found to its dismay that the situation there had changed since Illeni's regency and that the vain monarch had dissociated himself from Illeni's original intention to form an alliance with Portugal. As it transpired later on, Libna Dingil was, nevertheless, interested to develop a relationship with Portugal in view of his fear of the Ottoman intentions, demonstrated by the massacre of Ethiopian pilgrims by Turks in 1518 and 1525. In fact, the Ethiopian monarch encouraged the Portuguese to establish a presence on the Ethiopian coast at Sawakin, Massawa and above all in Zayla.[44] Moreover, the period of grace from Adali attacks was nearing an end and in 1525, even before Roderigo da Lima departed from Ethiopia with the false impression that everything was well and that the king was in full control of the situation, Imam Ahmad Grañ became the *de facto* ruler of Adal.

By the early 1520s Libna Dingil's camp was nearly always to be found in the southwestern provinces of his kingdom which were previously independent sultanates and whose population was still partly Muslim. It is possible that the king's presence in the area was necessitated by mounting Galla pressure from the south, but even more so by the intermittent raids of enterprising amirs and the Somali tribes. The latter, already a major factor in the politics of Adal in Mahfuz's time, became predominant in the sultanate with the rise to power in 1515/16 of Garad Abun, the Wazir of the puppet Walasma sultan. Somali raids into Ethiopia, however, brought retribution and Libna Dingil's army devastated Adal. Hence, already in 1519 the Adali sultan found it prudent to move the seat of the sultanate from Dakar to Harar, further eastwards.[45] But the meaningless raids of the Ethiopians only served to intensify the hatred of the population of Adal and the coast against Christian Ethiopia. When Garad Abun was killed in 1525 in a clash with a Somali tribe, Ahmad ibn Ibrahim (Grañ) inherited his place after a short struggle for power.

The Muslim conquest (futuh) of Ethiopia

Probably of Somali origin, Ahmad ibn Ibrahim, popularly called Grañ – the left handed – served as a soldier in Garad Abun's army and married Imam Mahfuz's daughter. After Abun's death he suppressed the restless Somalis and succeeded in gaining the recognition and loyalty of all the amirs of the sultanate and the support of the pastoralist tribes. Disregarding the puppet Walasma sultan, he took to himself the title of Imam and in 1525/6 led an abortive raid into Fatagar. However, this raid could be considered a preliminary probe of the enemy's defences. In 1527 Imam Ahmad launched a two-pronged attack against Dawaro and Ifat in which he proved himself a daring general and an outstanding tactician. This battle, moreover, demonstrated the devastating impact of the firearms which he used against the Ethiopian army.

Grañ used the coming two years to prepare the conquest of Ethiopia. In addition to his trained soldiers and original supporters, many more pastoralist tribes joined his camp. Mercenaries were recruited from Arabia, arms were acquired and the dissatisfaction of the Ethiopian nobility and the Muslim population was fully utilised to subvert the power of Libna Dingil.[46]

The 'conquest of Ethiopia' *(Futuh al-Habasha)* began in 1529 when Grañ's forces met the royal Ethiopian army commanded by Libna Dingil at Shembra Koure. Notwithstanding the vast numerical superiority of Libna Dingil's army the Muslims were completely victorious and the Ethiopian forces literally disintegrated under their attack. Many nobles and their private armies, as well as *Chewa* regiments, flew from the battlefield rather than fight, but many others betrayed their master, deserted to Grañ and joined his forces.

Libna Dingil's 'character' and incompetence notwithstanding, it would be inaccurate to attribute the success of Grañ just to his ability and charismatic leadership and to the internal weakness of Ethiopia. The rapidly changing situation in the Red Sea region had much to do with the dramatic achievements of the Muslims of the eastern part of the Horn.

Harar and its smaller satellites, which together made up the amorphous sultanate of Adal, were facing in this period increasing Somali pressure and even interference in their internal affairs. It was beneficial, if not essential, for the rulers of Adal to channel the energy of the pastoralists toward the efforts against Ethiopia. Moreover, the threat which the appearance of the Portuguese in the Indian Ocean posed to Islam and to the Muslim economy sparked off a political and possibly a spiritual revival among the Muslims of the Red Sea basin. Invariably, this threat drew the attention of the Muslim world to the Horn and to the Christian-Muslim conflict in that region.

Portuguese attempts to contact the Ethiopian ruler from the Indian Ocean and the presence of many Europeans in his court were probably reported to the Muslim authorities by the many merchants who visited the royal camp. Albuquerque's activities in the Gulf of Aden in 1507 caused great consternation to the Muslim population of the region. But the abortive expedition of Lopo Suarez to the Red Sea in 1517 and the arrival of Roderigo da Lima's embassy in Ethiopia in 1520 had actually frightened the Muslims and caused them to consider Ethiopia a realistic threat and not just a potential danger to the Muslim sphere of the Red Sea and the holy towns of Islam. The occasional visits paid by Portuguese flotillas to Massawa in order to maintain contact with da Lima only served to increase the suspicion of the Turkish-Muslim authorities in the Red Sea concerning Libna Dingil's and the Portuguese intentions.

The Ottomans, whose position as a super-power at the time was unquestionable, replaced the ineffective Mamluks in the Red Sea in 1517. After establishing their authority in the Hijaz, the Ottomans captured part of Yemen in 1525, making Zabid their headquarters. By this time, the conflict in the Horn was generally considered a Jihad, worthy of the support of all believers. Indeed, even before the conquest of the Yemeni coast by the Ottomans, the flow of weapons and material support in general, and of *Mujahidun* and mercenaries from Arabia, was substantially accelerated. After their arrival, however, firearms and military aid, as well as Ottoman soldiers, were sent by the Pasha of Zabid to Grañ.[47]

The vast numerical superiority of the Ethiopians in the battle of 1527 and at Shembra Koure in 1529 is unquestionable. However, the power of the Muslims should not be measured quantitatively but considered qualitatively. In addition to the advantage of mobility and inspiring leadership, the Adali army and cavalry were by now far better armed than the Ethiopians. According to contemporary reports, the psychological effect of the firearms, especially the artillery, used by Grañ against the Ethiopians was devastating because the latter were completely terrified by the very noise of such weapons, which they had never experienced before.[48]

By the time Grañ became the recognised leader of the Harari and the coastal agricultural and pastoralist population, the conflict with Ethiopia had long since assumed a clear religious dimension. Imam Ahmad's war against Ethiopia was not just a Jihad, but intended to be a *Futuh*, a permanent conquest of the Christian kingdom and its transformation to a Muslim sultanate. The tense atmosphere in the region following the arrival of the Portuguese, and the religious character of the conflict with Ethiopia, assured Grañ of the support of most of the population of the Harar-Chercher plateau and a good part of the highland Muslims who, until this period, were loyal to the Ethiopian monarch and in some instances even supported his struggle against the Muslim trading sultanates and the coastal pastoralists.[49]

Imam Ahmad exploited his victory at Shembra Koure and pressed on during 1529 with the conquest of the plateau. Tired, encumbered by enormous quantities of loot and somewhat overwhelmed by their success and the final aims of their leader, many of Grañ's original supporters pleaded with him to return to Adal as long as the road was open to them. By this time Grañ's army was swollen by Ethiopian forces who deserted to him and Muslims who had joined his flag,[50] and the Imam, aware of the situation in Ethiopia, was determined to continue his *futuh* until the whole of the country was in his hands.

Composed largely of new converts and highland Muslims around a core of Somali and other coastal Muslims, several forces commanded by Grañ's lieutenants continued the conquest of most of southern and central Ethiopia. In 1531 Imam Ahmad marched northwards to Tigre and from there turned to the Agaw-Falasha territories. Here he was helped by Christian and Muslim traitors and by the Falasha, who rose against the Christian monarch who had oppressed them in the past. Later on Grañ conquered Gojjam and sacked Amhara, probably Ethiopia's richest province, where enormous art and spiritual treasures had been deposited over the centuries in numerous churches and monasteries.[51]

By 1533, having captured the provinces around Lake Tana, Grañ was more than ever determined to rule Ethiopia, considering himself the founder of the new Muslim dynasty of that country.

So confident was he in his success that he, his amirs and their immediate followers sent to Adal for their familes, whom they wished to settle in Ethiopia.[52]

Grañ's chronicler did not continue his account of events beyond the year 1534 A.D. Moreover, the Muslim forces systematically sacked the churches and the monasteries and slaughtered the clergy and the monks, who were the literary elements in the country. Our sources concerning the period between 1534 and the arrival of the Portuguese in 1541 are, therefore, extremely meagre.

We know that by 1540 all the territories of the Christian kingdom were captured by Grañ. In the north, the Muslim conquest was facilitated by a general rebellion of the oppressed Falasha and elsewhere Grañ was helped by traitors from among the traditional nobility and by local Muslims. Whatever resistance remained to Grañ's *futuh*, it was not serious, and Libna Dingil and the handful of his loyal supporters were constantly hunted by Grañ's forces and their local allies and were forced to flee from one place to another.

When law and order were restored by Grañ, many of his original supporters from among the pastoralists chose to return to the lowlands. The Ottoman support in armament and manpower was no longer an asset but a liability. Not only was it costly, but also dangerous in view of Ottoman aspirations in the Red Sea region. Consequently, the Ottoman soldiers were paid off and sent back to Zabid with their artillery together with Arab mercenaries, who had joined Grañ at the beginning of his Jihad. This cautious policy was fully justified by the Ottoman high-handed behaviour in Yemen, the conquest of Aden and the atrocities committed there and in other places in the Red Sea, after their abortive expedition to India in 1538/9.[53] Gradually life returned to normal in the highlands and the population became accustomed to their new ruler. It looked as if a new dynasty, founded by Grañ, would replace the house of Yekuno Amlak and rule a Muslim Ethiopia.

In a sense Grañ took up the expansionist policy of the Solomonic kings. His armies penetrated and conquered new areas in the south, west and especially in the north. Here, his authority was extended in the direction of Sawakin, Kassala and Sennar and many of the local chiefs came to his camp to have their position confirmed.[54] Considering the vast territories which Grañ controlled, the coastal elements who remained with him, and upon whose loyalty he could absolutely depend, became thinly spread and the Imam became increasingly dependent on local elements for the administration of the country.

Once he had conquered Dembiya, Grañ established the centre of his government near Lake Tana. The Imam, however, began to organise his administrative system in the plateau even earlier. This administration relied, to a great extent, on traditional administrators and feudatories, who deserted to the Muslim camp and who, if Christians, converted in most cases to Islam.[55] However, together with this civil administration Grañ maintained a military superstructure composed of his original supporters. The Ethiopian governors were subordinated to Grañ's lieutenants, who were Somali, Afar and Harari amirs. Such military commanders, with their troops, composed of coastal pastoralists, Ethiopian Muslim and converted Christian troops, garrisoned fortified *amba*s in each district, supervised the Ethiopian administrators, helped with the collection of taxation, preserved the Imam's authority and constituted a kind of foreign military aristocracy.[56] Not unlike the previous Ethiopian system, fiefs were granted to units of this new military aristocracy, whose commanders were chosen from amongst the Imam's closest friends.[57]

The founding of a Muslim-Ethiopian sultanate by Grañ initiated a rapid social, political and cultural upheaval in Ethiopia. The Ethiopian nobility, partly responsible for the conquest of their country by the people of the lowlands, gradually found out to its dismay that it had gained little, if not lost, by exchanging one master for another. Considered in the past the elite of the kingdom, the Christian Tigrean and Amhara semitised and other feudals now became subordinated to Muslim amirs and pastoralists, who enforced the Imam's authority. Ethiopia being a conquered country, all the land belonged by Muslim law to the Muslim community and the taxation from it went to the central treasury. Whoever remained loyal to his Christian faith was also supposed to pay *Jizya* (poll tax) to the Muslim government. The peasants were virtually serfs, but it seems that under Grañ they were taxed more heavily in order to support the traditional feudatory-administrative class and, in addition, the new Muslim military aristocracy. The ecclesiastics, considered by the Muslims the pillar of the Christian kingdom, were systematically hunted and exterminated and, having little to lose, were in the forefront of whatever resistance existed to the Muslim government. The soldiers, if they joined Grañ, probably retained most of their privileges. However, the Muslim Ethiopian community, over and above its past economic achievements, was now elevated in the social stratification of the country from an inferior to a superior position and many Ethiopian Muslims served in Grañ's administration and army, some in the highest positions.

The Christian semitised culture, which lost its hegemony, further declined in the plateau during Grañ's reign. On the other hand, Islam and the 'culture' of the conquerors made great strides. This process, however, did not have a sufficient time-span to consolidate itself and Islam and its cultural influences remained superficial in the non-Christian Cushitic provinces. In the north and parts of Showa, where Christianity and the semitised heritage were more deeply rooted, the influence of the conquerors was even more superficial and gradually produced a cultural ethnic tension between the coastal pastoralists and their Muslim allies and the plateau nobility and agriculturalists. Nevertheless, to all intents and purposes Grañ succeeded in transforming Ethiopia into a Muslim sultanate and, had it not been for the Portuguese intervention in 1541, the Imam might have consolidated his achievements and Ethiopia have changed its character during the course of the sixteenth century.

NOTES

1. Perruchon, J., 'Histoire d'Eskender, d'Amda Seyon II et de Na'od, Rois d'Ethiopie', *Journal Asiatique*, 1894, Vol. III, pp. 43-4.
2. 'Documenti Arabi', p. 52. The sultan was assassinated in 1518, but just before that his capital was moved to Harar.
3. Alvarez, Vol. II, pp. 409, 411; Winter Johns, J., *The Travels of Ludovico Di Varthema, 1503-1508*, London, 1863, pp. 63-4 – of slaves in Aden's and Yemen's armies; p. 86 – the many thousands of slaves exported via Zayla in 1503-1504.
4. Of a *Bitwadad*'s son in Mahfuz's camp and similar desertion – Alvarez, Vol. II, p. 413. Of a member of the royal family who became a Muslim and was Zayla's governor in 1517 – Kammerer, A., *La Mer Rouge, l'Abyssinie et l'Arabie Depuis l'Antiquité*, Cairo, 1935, Vol. II, p. 273.
5. Sharif Barakat II temporarily overthrew the power of the Mamluks in Hijaz in 1505, while the Tahirids were fighting the Imam of San'a (*Varthema*, p. 61).
6. Heyd, Vol. II, pp. 512-25; Boxer, C. R., *The Portuguese Seaborne Empire*, London, 1969, p. 47; Lane, F. C., 'The Mediterranean Spice Trade', *American Historical Review*, Vol. 1839-1840, pp. 464-8. In 1503 *Varthema* (pp. 37-8, 50,

61) reported from Mecca on an extensive pilgrimage season with brisk trade, notwithstanding the fact that the Portuguese captured seven ships from India, thus preventing the Indian merchants from participating in the annual fair.

7. Kammerer (1947), Vol. I, pp. 16, 67; Dames, L.. 'The Portuguese and the Turks in the Indian Ocean', *Journal of the Royal Asiatic Society*, London, 1921, pp. 8-9. Mogadishu was bombarded by Albuquerque in 1507 and Socotra was taken in the same year. See also below, pp. 109-12.

8. Alvarez, Vol. I, pp. 276-9.

9. Boxer, *Portuguese*, p. 47; Ozbaran, Salih, *The Ottoman Turks and the Portuguese in the Persian Gulf*. Ph.D. thesis, London, 1969, pp. 21-2; Dames, 'The Portuguese'.

10. Alvarez, Vol. II, p. 408; Serjeant, p. 18. The Mamluks of Egypt now also supported Mahfuz – Wiet, 'Les Relations', p. 131. In the early 1520s Alvarez (Vol. II, p. 408), a member of da Lima's embassy, reported that the 'king of Adal' was considered a saint by the Muslim kings due to his wars against the Christians; 'they also say that he receives supplies from the king of Arabia and the xeque of Mecca and other Moorish kings and lords with many horses and weapons. In return he sends to Mecca annually large offerings of Abyssinian slaves which he takes in his wars and also sends slaves as presents to the king of Arabia and to other rulers.' On Messianic-Mahdist expectation in South Arabia, related to the struggle in the Horn following arrival of the Portuguese – Cerulli, E., *La Lingua e la Storia di Harar*, Vol. I of *Studi Etiopici*, Roma, 1936, p. 29.

11. Tamrat, p. 126.

12. Such as Al-Umari, Qalqashandi, Maqrizi and others, using, in addition to *Jihad*, terms associated with it such as *Shahid, Istashhada, Mujahid, Kafir-Kufara, Ghazi* etc.

13. Cerulli, E., *Somalia, Scritti Vari Editi ed Inediti*, Roma, 1957; Lewis, I. M., 'The Somalis Conquest of the Horn of Africa', *Journal of African History*, I, 1960, pp. 213-30; Lewis, I. M., 'The Galla in Northern Somaliland', *Rassegna di Studi Etiopici*, XV, 1959, pp. 21-38; Huntingford, G. W. B., *The Galla of Ethiopia*, London, 1953, p. 19.

14. Mainly Lewis, H. S., 'The Origins of the Galla and Somali', *Journal of African History*, VII, 1966. Also: Asma-Giyorgis Gabra Mäsih, *Ya Galla Tarik* (an unpublished manuscript, a copy of which is to be found at the Institute of Ethiopian Studies, Addis Ababa), p. 87; Guillain, C., *Documents sur l'histoire, la géographie et le commerce de l'Afrique Orientale*, Paris, 1856, Vol. III, pp. 169-70; Salt, H., *A Voyage to Abyssinia in the Years 1809 and 1810*, London, 1814, p. 176; Lobo, Le Grand, pp. 19-22.

15. See below, text.

16. Cerulli, E., 'La Città de Merca e tre sue inscrizioni Arabe', *Oriento Moderno*, 1943; Lewis, H., 'The Galla'; Guillain, Vol. III, pp. 169-70. Somali tribes are first mentioned in the 12th century.

17. Part of Habar Magadi.

18. On a Muslim from Jelebe (Jeledi?), forced by the Somali to escape from his homeland and granted a *gult* in Bali when he became the commander of the Ethiopian forces there – *Futuh*, text, pp. 242-3. On disorder in Adal due to Somalis – *Futuh*, text, pp. 14-15.

19. Of early pressures by pastoralists on the Muslims of the Showan plateau and Amhara – Cerulli, 'Il sultanato', pp. 11-12; Huntingford, *The Glorious Victories of Amda Seyon*, pp. 30-2.

20. See: Curles, A. Y., 'The Ruined Cities of Somaliland', *Antiquity*, Vol. X, 1936, p. 100; Vol. XI, 1937, pp. 316-27; *Futuh* (translation), p. 16 (Somali amirs); *Varthema*, p. 88, note.

21. Cerulli, 'Documenti Arabi' – Sultan al Zahir ad-Din murdered by Somalis 1518 – p. 52; Whiteway, xxxiii; *Futuh*, p. 16.
22. Alvarez, Vol. I, pp. 180, 190-3, – on intermittent eruptions of pastoralists, Dankalis and Somalis into plateau. For an indication of the role of the pastoralists in the incursions into Ethiopia and its conquest by Gran see the lament of the Abyssinians in Rome – Ludolphus, pp. 221-2.
23. Alvarez, Vol. II, p. 412.
24. Illeni's policy was also responsible for the abstention from communicating with Portugal for ten years after Pero de Covilhao's arrival. Sources for this period are extremely meagre and the chronicles understandably poor. Churches and monasteries, which served for many centuries as depositories for Ethiopia's spiritual-cultural treasures, were the first targets of the invading Muslims. Alvarez's excellent account, based on his impressions of Ethiopia only a few years after Libna Dingil came to power, and Shihab ad-Din's account of Ethiopia, undoubtedly also reflect the situation in the first part of Libna Dingil's reign.
25. Kammerer, A., *Routier de Dom Joam de Castro. L'exploration de la Mer Rouge par les Portugais en 1541*, Paris, 1936, p. 76; *Futuh*, p. 221; Ludolphus pp. 221-2; Almeida, p. 69. Merid Wolde Aregay (pp. 133-6) also assumes, without proof, that Libna Dingil was manipulated by one faction of the nobility.
26. Alvarez, Vol. I, p. 187.
27. Such controversies did not subside even during Gran's conquest – Perruchon, *Sémitique*, 1893, p. 283.
28. Alvarez, Vol. II, p. 413.
29. Alvarez, Vol. II, pp. 408-11.
30. Alvarez, Vol. II, pp. 433-4; also: Vol. I, p. 173. Admiral de Castro (*Routier*, p. 76) attributes the collapse of Ethiopia to the persecution of the aristocracy by the monarch and its having plotted with Gran even before 1527-1529. Recalled from banishment after Gran's victories, Bitwadad Wassan Sagad remonstrated with the monarch for alienating the nobility and told him that God was helping Gran because of Libna Dingil's tyranny – *Futuh*, p. 221. On Illeni's death in 1525 the court officials and nobles told Alvarez (Vol. II, pp. 433-4) 'that since she had died all of them had died, great and small, and while she lived, all lived and were defended and protected; and she was the father and mother of all, and if the king took this road, his kingdoms would become deserts.'
31. The Hamaj, called Nobiis by Alvarez, were the inhabitants of the previously Christian kingdom of Alwa, who had reverted to paganism and asked for the monarch's help to be reconverted to Christianity. This happened shortly after the Muslim Funj dynasty came to power in Sennar. The 'Nobiis' remained loyal to the king even after he was completely defeated – Alvarez, Vol. I, pp. 124, 129; Vol. II, p. 461; *Futuh*, text, pp. 339-41, 346-7.
32. On annexation by attrition see below, p. 168.
33. See below, p. 112.
34. Alvarez, Vol. I, pp. 304-10; Kammerer (1947), Vol. I, pp. 16, 67; Kahle, P., (ed.) *Die Chronik des Ibn Ijas*, Leipzig, 1932, pp. 9-11; Wiet, 'Les Relations', pp. 136-9. On commercial co-operation of Libna Dingil with his Muslim neighbours – Andrea Corsali to Lorenzo de Medici, letter of 18 Jan. 1517 in Ramusio, Vol. I, p. 186; p. 290B, Barbosa (probably from 1520) – on many prisoners of war exported via Massawa; Dames, 'The Portuguese', pp. 10-12.
35. Alvarez, Vol. I, p. 187 – On merchants from Hijaz, North Africa, Greece, India, the Persian Gulf and Egypt in Ethiopia. Also: Alvarez, Vol. I, pp. 193,

251; Vol. II, p. 405; Ramusio, Vol. I, p. 186. On Muslim merchants arriving from India and other countries nearly daily in Libna Dingil's court – Alvarez, Vol. II, p. 405.

36. Alvarez, Vol. I, pp. 186-7, 251. See above, pp. 32-3.
37. Alvarez, Vol. I, p. 174; Vol. II, pp. 427-8; *Futuh*, text, pp. 275-6.
38. Alvarez, Vol. I, p. 193; Vol. II, pp. 427-8. The Ethiopian church must have been very short of priests or was not very enthusiastic to co-operate with the ruler, because Libna Dingil was unable to provide Christian clergy to the Hamaj population of the border with Sennar when requested to do so. *Futuh*, text, pp. 16, 275-6; Ramusio, Vol. I, p. 186. See also his attempt to get a new *abun* in 1515-16.
39. Alvarez, Vol. II, p. 368.
40. Alvarez, Vol. I, p. 287.
41. *De facto* Ottoman government was established in Yemen only in 1525. Kammerer (1947), Vol. I, p. 69. Also Stripling, G. W. F., *The Ottoman Turks and the Arabs, 1511-1574*, Urbana, 1942, Vol. I, pp. 188-9.
42. See below, pp. 109-14. On the crucial role of firearms in Gran's campaigns in 1527 and 1529 – *Routier*, pp. 62-71, 285-7; Ludolphus pp. 222-3; Budge, E. A. W., *A History of Ethiopia, Nubia and Abyssinia*, London, 1928, Vol. I, p. 332; Alvarez, Vol. II, p. 414 note 1, according to de Barros. See also below, pp. 88-9, 116-17.
43. Kammerer (1935), Vol. II, p. 272.
44. Alvarez, Vol. I, pp. 273, 287, 305-6; Vol. II, p. 451; Correa, *Lendas da India*, Vol. II, p. 180. Libna Dingil was even ready to pay the expenses which would be incurred by such a presence. See also below, pp. 114-16.
45. Cerulli, 'Documenti Arabi', p. 52. Also: Perruchon, *Sémitique*, 1893, p. 280.
46. On many defectors, Christians and Muslims, in Gran's camp – Ludolphus, p. 221. On Muslim defectors – Cerulli, *La Lingua*, Vol. I, pp. 33-4. On support from many Muslim rulers – Cerulli, *La Lingua*, Vol. I, p. 36. On Messianic-Mahdist expectations aroused by Gran *'Imam Akhr az-zaman'* – Cerulli, *La Lingua*, Vol. I, pp. 29-30.
47. Libna Dingil feared direct Ottoman military intervention to support Ethiopia's Muslim enemies. Alvarez, Vol. I, pp. 287, 305-6. Not only the Turkish Pasha of Yemen but also the Tahirid ruler of Aden and also Muslim rulers, including in India, had sent help to Gran – Cerulli, *La Lingua*, Vol. I, p. 34. See below, pp. 138-40.
48. For a naive description by Ethiopian contemporaries see: Ludolphus, pp. 221-2. Also: Kammerer, *Routier*, pp. 62-71, on impact of firearms; Whiteway, pp. xxx, 32; Morié, Vol. II, p. 239; Budge, Vol. I, p. 332; Gallina, F., 'I Portughezi a Massaua nei secoli XVI, XVII', *Bollettino di Società Geografica Italiana*, Mars. 1890, p. 226; Alvarez, Vol. II, p. 414, note 1. On quality of arms and armoured cavalry in Gran's army – *Futuh*, pp. 254-5. On presence of Arabs and other foreign Muslim elements in Gran's army – *Futuh*, pp. 233-4.
49. See Cerulli (*La Lingua*, Vol. I, p. 35) on differentiation by Hararis between Gran and his nephew Nur ibn Mujahid, considered the true saviour of Harar proper.
50. For the crucial part of pastoralists in conquests, see the lament of the Abyssinians in Rome – Ludolphus, pp. 221-2; *Futuh*, pp. 248-9, 362-3.
51. *Futuh*, pp. 256-7. On the Falasha rebellion or war according to Jewish sources, Eshcoly, *Hareuveni*, pp. 47-9 and letters from year 5285 (Jewish Calendar) in Scholem, G., *Kiryat Seffer* (Hebrew) shana zain (7th year), Jerusalem, pp. 415-16, 443-4.
52. *Futuh*, pp. 300-1; Whiteway, *Castanhoso*, pp. 43-4.

53. See below. See also: Kerr, R., *Collection of Voyages,* Edinburgh, 1812, Vol. 6, pp. 264-6, on Venetian officer in this expedition; Dames, 'The Portuguese'; Ramusio, Vol. I, pp. 274-6.
54. *Futuh,* pp. 301, 304-5, 321, 343-5, 346-7; Trimingham, p. 87.
55. See Libna Dingil's letter to Bermudez in 1540 – Correa, Vol. IV, pp. 138-9.
56. Whiteway, *Castanhoso,* pp. 24, 30-1, 58-9. See similarity to relations between Arab conquerors who constituted a military aristocracy in *amsar* (fortified camps) and *mawali* (new converts) in the 7th century Muslim empire.
57. *Futuh,* pp. 300-1, 332-3, 338-9, 343-7.

CHAPTER V

The Revival of the Solomonic Monarchy and the Decline of Muslim Power in the Horn

The Portuguese expedition to Ethiopia and the rise of Gelawdewos

Libna Dingil may have been irresponsible, tyrannical and have lacked military ability. But his tenacity, persistence, determination and pride should be admired. Despite repeated defeats, the disloyalty of the *Chewa* and the highland Muslims and the fact that he was betrayed by most of the Christian nobility, the monarch, constantly pursued by his enemies, some of whom were previously his subordinates, continued the war against Grañ and refused offers of honourable submission.[1]

In 1535, in the hour of his greatest distress, Libna Dingil despatched Joao Bermudez, the surgeon of da Lima's embassy (who had chosen to stay with him) to the Portuguese king to request aid, promising to accept Catholicism if such aid would be forthcoming. Bermudez reached the Portuguese court after many difficulties and the Portuguese authorities, still believing that all was well in Ethiopia – as was reported by da Lima – were shaken by his account of Grañ's Jihad. Bermudez arrived in India in 1539 carrying royal orders to send aid to the Ethiopian king. The Viceroy was expecting at this time an Ottoman naval attack and needed all the forces that he could muster. He was entrusted with the protection and control of the vast Portuguese empire in the Indian Ocean, which necessitated manpower and material resources far beyond what Portugal could supply. At this stage, therefore, he was unwilling to commit any forces to the Red Sea arena. Portuguese interest in the latter area, which had proved of minor commercial importance, was limited to gathering information about the activities of the Ottomans and especially about the fleet which, it as rumoured, they were preparing. The Viceroy nevertheless despatched two small boats to Massawa in 1540 to gather information about the situation in Ethiopia and to deliver letters to the Ethiopian king from himself and from Bermudez.[2]

Once in Massawa the Portuguese captains became fully aware of the desperate situation of Libna Dingil and the virtual conquest of Ethiopia by the Muslims. Before their departure they received letters from Libna Dingil addressed to the Portuguese authorities and to Bermudez in which he described the state of the country and his own plight, and urgently requested Portuguese military aid. Shortly after the departure of the Portuguese boats Libna Dingil died, or was murdered, and his son Gelawdewos succeeded him.[3]

News of the letter which Libna Dingil received from the Portuguese quickly became general knowledge in Ethiopia. Informed of this letter, Grañ acted quickly and marched against Gelawdewos in an attempt to eliminate the last threat to his government, before the arrival of the Portuguese. For the same reason, Mujahid, Grañ's wazir, attacked Amba Geshen, which had successfully withstood previous onslaughts, conquered it and executed all the princes of the royal family who were found there.[4]

In 1541 a large naval expedition commanded by the Portuguese Viceroy in India, Estavao da Gama, entered the Red Sea. The expedition, it seems, had nothing to do with Ethiopia but had as an objective the destruction of the fleet which, it was rumoured, the Ottomans were preparing in the northern parts of the Red Sea. Nevertheless, da Gama intended to exploit the opportunity to disembark at Massawa Bermudez and a number of soldiers and artisans which he had recruited. While part of the Portuguese Armada was anchored off Massawa, the Portuguese were informed of the full extent of the calamity which had befallen Ethiopia and were entreated by the king's mother and some important Ethiopian lords to save Christianity in the area. Nevertheless, it was only after the Viceroy returned to Massawa with the major part of the fleet that it was decided to land a relatively large force to help the Ethiopian king. Hence about 400 soldiers and 130 servants and slaves, amply equipped with firearms and artillery and commanded by the Viceroy's younger brother, Christovao, were landed near Arkiko.[5] This spontaneous adventurous decision, probably meant to be a temporary intervention to save the Christian kingdom,[6] had a momentous influence on the immediate history of Ethiopia, but was also to have a substantial impact on Ethiopian Christianity and culture.

Grañ was determined to capture the king before the arrival of the Portuguese or, at least, to prevent a link-up between them and the Ethiopian monarch once they should arrive. Consequently, Gelawdewos (r. 1540-1559), who succeeded his father in 1540, was pursued from the environs of the northern coast into the interior, as far as Showa. When informed of the Portuguese landing, Grañ quickly marched towards Tigre in order to intercept them before they could reach Gelawdewos' camp. Thus the Portuguese, who marched southward from the Eritrean plateau, found their way blocked by Grañ's army when they reached Wojarat. Notwithstanding the overwhelming numerical superiority of the Muslim army, da Gama, by sheer audacity and bravery, making the best use of his fire power, managed to defeat Grañ in two engagements. The Portuguese were, however, prevented from advancing to meet the king by the advent of the rainy season.

During the coming months Grañ, who fortified himself on the verges of the plateau overlooking the Dankali plains, applied for, and received, reinforcements and artillery from the Ottoman Pasha of Zabid who, due to the Portuguese expedition, became increasingly more interested in Ethiopia. When the two armies clashed again in the beginning of 1542 the Portuguese were totally defeated. Many were killed and Christovao da Gama was captured and executed.[7] In spite of this catastrophe, there is little doubt that the quixotic campaigns of the latter helped save Christian Ethiopia and the Solomonic dynasty. Hypothetically it is possible, of course, that Grañ's Muslim empire would have collapsed or disintegrated at some time in the future as a result of internal developments in Ethiopia even without Portuguese intervention.

Resenting the exactions of the Turks and fearing Ottoman domination, Grañ again dismissed the Turkish reinforcements, and returned to his headquarters near Lake Tana. In the meantime Gelawdewos, a far more gifted and tactful person and a far better general than his father, was able to recruit a few thousand soldiers. Considering the strength of Grañ's army, it was probably fortunate for Christian Ethiopia that he had been unable to join da Gama before the fatal battle in Wojarat. When Gelawdewos finally reached the northern provinces, he was joined by the remnants of the Portuguese. During 1542 he won a number of victories over

Grañ's local commanders but avoided a confrontation with the Imam's main army. These victories, although far from being decisive, together with the support of the Portuguese fusiliers and his own inspiring leadership, enhanced the prestige of the young king and attracted new volunteers to his camp.

Grañ completely underestimated Gelawdewos and the potential of the remnants of the Portuguese force. He still thought of the Ethiopians in terms which suited the reign of Libna Dingil rather than the new circumstances, for which he himself was partly responsible. Therefore he did very little to prepare for the decisive battle with the Ethiopian king. When the two armies finally met in 1543 at Weyna Dega (Dembiya), Grañ's army was still larger than that of Gelawdewos, his cavalry was superior to that of the Ethiopians and the number of his fusiliers greater than that which Gelawdewos had on his side. Yet, the Muslims were this time faced by a determined and desperate army, led by a gifted and beloved monarch. Nevertheless, it seems that the shooting and killing of Grañ by the Portuguese soldiers actually determined the battle and Ethiopia's future. Once the Imam fell, his army quickly disintegrated, his Muslim sultanate collapsed and Christian Ethiopia was revived.[8]

Accepted as a matter of course, the above proves how dependent on Grañ's personality was the shaky Ethiopian sultanate. Yet the Muslim conquest left deep scars on Ethiopia, which could not be easily healed. The cultural and artistic heritage of the country suffered an irreparable blow as a result of the ravages of Grañ's followers. The framework of the Ethiopian church, always weak in the past, was literally eradicated by the Muslims and its inadequate spiritual infrastructure was further eroded. The tension and distrust between the monarchy and feudal nobility, temporarily covered up, in reality deepened under the surface. Processes of assimilation and integration of the heterogeneous population, which achieved limited success, experienced a substantial set-back. Islam became further entrenched in the plateau and even influenced, it seems, the Ethiopian Christian semitised culture. Last but not least, with the collapse of Ethiopian defences and the period of interregnum in the south, the Galla (Oromo) tribes succeeded in making deep inroads into the highlands and, thereafter, became increasingly a major factor in the development of the region, leading gradually to the eclipse of local Muslim and Solomonic power.

The reconsolidation of Christian Ethiopia and the decline of Adal

After the death of Grañ at Weyna Dega the Ethiopian nobility flocked to Gelawdewos' camp and swore allegiance to the emperor. Nearly all were forgiven for past disloyalty and the imperial armies quickly took possession of the whole of the northern and central plateaux. Many Adali soldiers perished in the battle with the Christians, while some, accompanied by Ethiopian converts, escaped to the lowlands and still others joined forces with feudal rulers and found refuge in peripheral provinces. The large indigenous Muslim community of the plateau, however, submitted to Gelawdewos and was not harmed. It was not only that he was tolerant toward his Muslim subjects and aimed at national conciliation, but he also appreciated their crucial contribution to the economy of his country. Later on, when conditions permitted, Ethiopia's relations with some Muslim rulers in Arabia, the Red Sea islands and in the Horn were also improved[9] and trade with them encouraged.

The reconquest of southern and especially southeastern Ethiopia (with its many Muslim inhabitants) proved to be far more difficult and lengthy than that of the north and Showa. Here, Grañ's lieutenant, Wazir Abbas, in command of a strong army, succeeded in carving out for himself an empire to the east and around the Rift Valley lakes composed of Dawaro, Bali and Fatagar. Some Sidama rulers, mainly Muslim, in areas west of the Rift Valley, were also unwilling to give up their newly regained independence and continued the struggle against the Ethiopian monarch. Moreover the Galla, who had succeeded in penetrating the southeast immediately following the collapse of the Ethiopian empire, again took advantage of the period of confusion caused by Grañ's death and stepped up their migration into the southeastern plateau and into Adal. It took Gelawdewos several years before he was able to establish his authority in the south.[10] In a way, however, by breaking the power of the local potentates, he unwittingly opened the area to the Galla in the future.[11] Moreover, some of Grañ's Amirs and many of his supporters in the southeast continued the bitter struggle against Ethiopia and the Galla continued to erupt into the plateau from the direction of the Webi Shebelli.

Once the conquest of the south was completed, Gelawdewos marched with the bulk of his army westwards to Damot. This ancient kingdom and the provinces adjacent to it, especially to the southwest, contributed an important part of Ethiopia's revenues and trade. As the country's economy was in a shambles, it was imperative to re-establish the monarch's authority in this region. Also, it seems that strong Muslim forces found refuge and settled in these areas. But while Gelawdewos was trying to consolidate his government in the west and even raided the peoples of peripheral areas of the empire, it became evident that his governors in the southeastern provinces were unable to cope with local Muslims' resistance, Adali attacks and Galla raids. Consequently, from about 1549 until his death in 1559, with certain outstanding exceptions when forced to march to the western provinces, Gelawdewos devoted most of his time to campaigns against Adal and the Galla, and the royal army was nearly always to be found in Waj.[12]

Gelawdewos was not only an outstanding monarch but in many ways his vision and policy concerning some basic problems of the empire resembled that of his great forefathers. Christian northerners were settled as garrisons *(Chewa)* in the midst of the Sidama population of the south and on the borders of Adal. The new *Chewa* regiments were not only meant to defend the empire against invasion but also to facilitate integration by the diffusion of Christianity and the northern culture among the indigenous population. This process was further enhanced by the nearly uninterrupted presence of the royal camp in the southeastern provinces during the last decade of Gelawdewos' reign, which temporarily helped curb Galla expansion as well. His policy regarding Adal also resembled that of his predecessors and was aimed at eroding the power of the sultanate and its pastoral allies by attrition through continuous harassment and the disruption of their economy. Hence Ethiopian armies repeatedly ravaged Adal's sedentary and nomadic population beyond Aussa and as far as Zayla.[13]

By the mid-1550s Ethiopia was again united within its old borders. With the exception of the areas adjacent to the Falasha provinces of the north, security and peace reigned throughout the empire.[14] Yet Gelawdewos was aware that most of the factors which had contributed to the collapse of the empire in the time of his father were still in existence, if not aggravated by the upheavals caused by Grañ's conquest, the period of continuous wars which followed it and by the Galla's penetration of parts of the southeastern plateau. Ethiopia was no less heterogeneous and the regime had a very narrow base of support. The framework of the national church, if it could be considered an integrative force, was nearly destroyed by the Muslims. The traditional aristocracy was still selfish and jealous of the authority of the crown, and the military-administrative system of government by its very nature contributed rather to the centrifugal forces which always unsettled the shaky unity established by strong rulers.[15]

Gelawdewos, who emerged from the battle of Weyna Dega with tremendous power and prestige could, if he had wished, have attempted to break the power of the treacherous ruling class. He prudently refrained from doing so because the empire, hardly recuperated from the traumatic period of Grañ, still faced enormous challenges. His first consideration was to rebuild the unity of the Christian-semitised nucleus of Ethiopia and he therefore avoided revolutionary changes in its traditional structure and institutions. Nevertheless he sought to establish greater centralisation by gradually tightening the monarch's control over administration and the nobility with the help of loyal followers.[16]

The gifted, scholarly and deeply orthodox monarch considered the rehabilitation of the Ethiopian church, a pillar of the Solomonic kingdom which had suffered systematic destruction during the Muslim Jihad, one of his first priorities. Not unlike his great forefathers who attempted to reform the country's administration and government, Gelawdewos believed that the church should become a major integrative force and a tool for bridging the cultural and ethnic diversity of Ethiopia's population. But aware of the state of the church after Grañ's period, its intellectual shortcomings and the cultural inferiority of most of the ecclesiastics, he became personally involved in the spiritual revival and the reorganisation of its framework. Hence Gelawdewos attempted to strengthen the philosophical foundations of the dogmas of the Ethiopian church, clarify its basic beliefs and find common denominators where different interpretations existed.

Shortly after his final victory over Grañ's generals in the south, the King of Kings imported two new *abuns* from Egypt.[17] These were urgently needed not for spiritual purposes but in order to replace the many thousands of priests and other clergymen massacred during the Muslim invasion (not to mention the numerous monks who also perished). These were essential to the efforts to revive Christianity in the country and improve the relationship of the church with the nobility and population, many of whom had betrayed it. Nevertheless, the propagation of Catholicism by the Portuguese and the aggressiveness of some of them, who challenged the dogmas of the national church and semitic-Cushitic customs and traditions incorporated into it, produced tensions and challenges which the church and the emperor could not ignore. But the importation of the *abun*s had an important political, as well as a spiritual, significance.

The presence of the Portuguese in Ethiopia gradually became a grave embarrassment to the monarch. Some, under the leadership of Joao Bermudez,[18] insisted even before Grañ's death that Gelawdewos submit to Rome, as Libna Dingil had promised to do when he applied to Portugal for help. Moreover, by openly propagating Catholicism and engaging in controversies with the monarch, monks and Ethiopian priests, the Portuguese spread increasing unrest. Further, by challenging customs such as observing the Jewish Sabbath, they contributed to the revival of traditional ecclesiastical disputes which further confused the shaken population, whom Gelawdewos wished to unite.

Even before the battle of Weyna Dega the emperor had informed the Portuguese soldiers that although ready to reward them handsomely for their services he had no intention of abandoning the faith of his ancestors. Showing great patience and toleration as long as he could, Gelawdewos was finally forced to exile Bermudez and the more vociferous among his supporters who defied the monarch and refused to stop their activities. Many of the Portuguese soldiers, however, opposed Bermudez' extremism and co-operated with the emperor.[19]

Unaware of the state of affairs in Ethiopia and misinformed by the Viceroy in India, Rome and Lisbon still believed that Gelawdewos and his subjects were willing to convert to Catholicism.[20] The task of instructing them in the Roman faith was entrusted to the young and vigorous Jesuit Order. Consequently, an embassy, including a Jesuit Father, was sent from India to Ethiopia to prepare the ground for this undertaking. The ambassadors coming by way of Massawa found the emperor in the southeast.

Informed of the purpose of the embassy Gelawdewos was clearly displeased with the idea and reiterated his determination to remain loyal to the Ethiopian national church. To make his position even clearer and at the same time strengthen the spiritual framework of the national church Gelawdewos, while in Damot in 1555, compiled and publicised a treatise encompassing the main points of his belief according to the dogmas of the national church, which came to be known as the 'Confession of Gelawdewos'.[21]

The arrival of the delegation from Goa brought to the surface the discontent latent among many ecclesiastics and part of the nobility caused by the monarch's reforms and government. In addition to its theological aspects it became evident that the matter of the emperor's relations with the Portuguese was emerging as a grave political issue. The anti-Catholic and anti-Portuguese feelings were running high and many nobles, it was reported, warned the emperor against the conversion of Ethiopia to Catholicism. It was rumoured, moreover, that the ambassadors were spies and the Portuguese were exploiting matters of faith to cover up their true intentions of colonising Ethiopia and gaining control of its trade. Fearing for their freedom, if not their life, and in view of Gelawdewos' unqualified refusal to convert to Catholicism, the ambassadors departed in 1556 aboard a Portuguese warship which had arrived in Massawa.[22]

That the emperor did not attempt to capture any part of the Ethiopian coast, notwithstanding the revival of the Red Sea trade, could be explained by his preoccupation elsewhere and the intensive maritime activities of the Ottomans since the late 1540s.[23] But Gelawdewos, who admired European culture, technology and military skill, was reluctant to request Portuguese aid despite the difficulties he faced after reconquering the plateau. His bitter experience with Bermudez and his companions, and his apprehension concerning the reaction of the ecclesiastics, may have been a major reason for this conduct. But it is also likely that suspicions of Portuguese aspirations in the region, strengthened by reports of Ethiopian and foreign Muslim merchants of events in India, was a factor which influenced his foreign policy as well.[24]

Several members of the Jesuit Order led by Nunez Barreto, appointed Bishop of Ethiopia, left for India in 1555. Barreto remained, however, in Goa to await developments and the Jesuits who reached Massawa in 1557 were under the arrogant and bigoted Andreas Oviedo. They were received by Gelawdewos in his camp with courtesy but the monarch immediately informed them of his determination to remain loyal to the Ethiopian church. In fact, in letters and proclamations publicised before and after the Jesuits' arrival, the emperor rejected the Catholic dogmas and emphasized his devotion to the national church. He also encouraged, if not initiated, the writing and translation of anti-Catholic polemical works and actively and most successfully participated in debates with the Jesuits which took place in his court. Disillusioned and frustrated, Oviedo attacked the monarch and mocked the Ethiopian church and traditions and customs of the country. With tension and anti-Catholic feelings rapidly mounting, and no longer welcomed by Gelawdewos, Oviedo decided in 1559 to retire to Tigre where he and his companions were given refuge by Bahr Nagash Ishaq.[25]

Notwithstanding Gelawdewos' determined and proud defence of the Ethiopian church, the Portuguese mission of 1555 and the arrival of the Jesuits soon afterwards brought to the surface the opposition to the monarch's government and policy. Many warlords or nobles who had prudently reconciled themselves to Gelawdewos' administration now found the opportunity to criticise their master over his relations with the Portuguese, the toleration shown to the Jesuits and other matters. The emperor's efforts to bring about the spiritual revival of the national church and to suppress theological differences in its ranks and among the monastic orders had already caused resentment in the past. However, the criticism voiced by the Jesuits over different customs of Ethiopian Christianity gave new impetus to the bitter controversy over the question of the Sabbath among the ecclesiastics, and in addition to increasing tension in the country the emperor was censured for allying himself with the 'Franks' *(Ferenjoch)*.[26]

The departure of Oviedo from the royal camp did not terminate the controversies nor did it relieve the tension in the country. Cognizant of the disastrous impact that the religious strife and unrest were having on the cohesiveness and politics of the country, at a time when Ethiopia was threatened by powerful enemies, Gelawdewos decreed the discontinuation of theological polemics and suppressed any attempt to disobey his orders.[27]

When summarising the situation following Gelawdewos' death in the battle against the Adalites in 1559 his chronicler[28] makes a point of stressing the fact that 'controversies stopped, there was a general consensus and all were united.' Other sources, disregarding circumstances, the character of the king and the universal love for him, claim that the frustrated and disillusioned Gelawdewos chose to become a martyr and purposely marched to his death against Nur ibn Mujahid's superior army. Be that as it may, the early death of the able, scholarly, just and compassionate king proved a calamity for Ethiopia.[29]

NOTES

1. Perruchon, *Sémitique,* 1893, p. 283 – of proud answer of Libna Dingil to Grañ's offer of submission in the year 1537/8.
2. Correa, Vol. IV, pp. 107-10. On Portuguese policy concerning the Red Sea see below, p. 119.
3. Kammerer (1947), Vol. I, pp. 32-3, 96-7; Ludolphus, pp. 22-3; Tellez, pp. 119, 130; Correa, Vol. IV, pp. 107-10, 138; Guidi, I, 'Di due frammenti relativi alla storia di Abissinia', *Rendiconti della Reale Accademia dei Lincei,* series 5, Vol. II, 1893, p. 585; Bruce, Vol. III, p. 19; Vol. IV, pp. 321-2.
4. Whiteway, p. xxxviii.
5. Kammerer (1947), Vol. II, pp. 32-3, 97-8; Conzelman, W. E., *Chronique de Galâwdêwos,* Paris, 1895, pp. 8-9; Correa, Vol. IV, pp. 138, 341, 361, 372; Whiteway, *Bermudez,* pp. 137-8, 140-4; Whiteway, *Castanhoso,* pp. xxxviii, 3-4, 9, 11, 19, 22, 31, 44-5, 49-53, 107-8; Basset, R., 'Etudes sur l'histoire d'Ethiopie', *Journal Asiatique,* 7th series, Vol. XVII and XVIII, 1881, pp. 104-5.
6. Christovao da Gama was already appointed governor of 'East India'.
7. Whiteway, *Castanhoso,* pp. 43-4, 55-6, 140; Correa, Vol. IV, p. 361; Kammerer (1947), Vol. I, pp. 35-7, 146-8; Basset, 'Etudes', pp. 103-5; Bruce, Vol. III, pp. 203-8; Perruchon, *Sémitique,* 1893, pp. 282-4.
8. Guidi, 'Due Frammenti', p. 584; Whiteway, *Castanhoso,* pp. 76-83; Perruchon, *Sémitique,* 1894, pp. 263-6; Basset, 'Etudes', pp. 105-6.
9. Beccari, C., *Rerum Aetiopicarum scriptores occidentales inediti a saeculo XVI ad XIX,* Roma, 1903-1917, pp. 97, 155. On Muslim military elements in Damot and Dembiya, see below, text. On relations with rulers of 'Tarais', the 'islands', 'Saba' and 'Arabia' – Conzelman, pp. 170-1. Ichege Embagon, a Yemenite merchant who converted to Christianity, a scholarly and enlightened head of the monastic orders, was most helpful to Gelawdewos and in addition was the author of polemical and other theological compilations – Trimingham, p. 90, note 1; Conzelman, p. 153.
10. Conzelman, pp. 139-41; Basset, 'Etudes', p. 106; Beccari, Vol. II, pp. 245-51; Vol. X, pp. 41-6.
11. Conzelman, pp. 141, 149; Whiteway, *Bermudez,* pp. 229-31; Beccari, Vol. X, pp. 45-8; Paez, Vol. II, pp. 405-420. On renewed struggle in the southeast – Conzelman, pp. 154-7.
12. A key province near the Rift Valley lakes, Conzelman, pp. 140-2, 144-6, 149, 151-4, 157; Whiteway, pp. 202, 230-1; Cerulli, E. *La Lingua e la Storia dei Sidama,* Vol. II of *Studi Etiopici,* Roma, 1938, p. 30. Gelawdewos, nevertheless, conducted a campaign against the southwest in 1552 – Conzelman, pp. 151-3.

According to Serse Dingil's chronicler (Rossini, 'Sarsa Dengel', p. 44) he was defeated in Enarea. In Damot in June 1555 he wrote the so-called 'Confession of Gelawdewos'. Joao Bermudez' account of events is not only biased, but completely untrustworthy and inaccurate. See: Whiteway, *Bermudez.*

13. Conzelman, pp. 140, 145-6, 149, 154-5, 174; Conti Rossini, C., 'La Guerra Turco-Abissina del 1578', *Oriente Moderno,* 1921-1922, p. 687. See also below, p. 142.
14. Conti Rossini, C.: 'L'autobiografia de Pawlos monaco Abissino del secolo XVI', *Rendiconti della Reale Accademia dei Lincei,* Vol. XXVII, 1918, p. 291; Conzelman, pp. 170, 174-5; Wolde Aregay, p. 165, according to the Jesuit Gonçalo Rodrigez, in Ethiopia in 1555-6.
15. See below, pp. 142-3
16. Whiteway, pp. 84-5; Almeida, *Some Records,* p. 74; Perruchon, *Sémitique,* 1894, p. 264; Conzelman, pp. 147-8; Rossini, 'Pawlos', p. 285; *Land Charters,* p. 103.
17. Beccari, Vol. I, p. 7; Vol. X, p. 28; Rossini, 'Pawlos', p. 199 – on a second *abun,* who arrived in 1552-3; Guidi, I., 'Le liste dei metropoliti d'Abbisinia', *Bessarione,* Vol. VI, 1899, p. 10, note 7; Tellez, p. 284.
18. Himself a layman with superficial theological knowledge. On Bermudez' incompetence in theological matters – Beccari, Vol. X, pp. 28-9; Vol. V, pp. 365-6; Paez, Vol. II, p. 345.
19. They were given land and presents of gold. Beccari, Vol. II, pp. 247, 345, 413-16; Vol. III, p. 19; Vol. V, pp. 321-2, 365-6; Vol. X, pp. 28-9; Whiteway, *Castanhoso,* p. lxxiv; Perruchon, *Sémitique,* 1894, pp. 266-7; Basset, 'Etudes', pp. 106-7.
20. Whiteway, *Castanhoso,* pp. 112-14.
21. The full English text is in Budge, Vol. II, pp. 353-6.
22. Paez, Vol. III, pp. 28-30; Beccari, Vol. V, p. 358; Vol. X, pp. 46-7 – Bermudez left Ethiopia with the ambassadors; Basset, 'Etudes', p. 107. On fears of Portuguese imperialism and reaction to the embassy – Tellez, pp. 135-7; Ludolphus, pp. 320-1.
23. See below, text.
24. See below, pp. 146-7.
25. Whiteway, *Castanhoso,* pp. 112, 115, 117; Tellez, pp. 134, 137; Beccari, Vol. III, pp. 28-30; Vol. V, pp. 383-5; Vol. X, pp. 68-78; Bruce, Vol. III, pp. 216-18, 223.
26. Perruchon, *Sémitique,* 1894, p. 267; Conzelman, p. 158 – the chronicler considers the controversies with the Jesuits one of the main problems which the emperor faced. Also *Ibid,* p. 169; Wansleben, p. 12. On Gelawdewos' ability in theological debates – Tellez, pp. 139-40.
27. Conzelman, p. 174; Tellez, p. 140; Wansleben, p. 12. To ensure that the controversies would stop the monarch retained the heads of the different factions in his camp.
28. Conzelman, p. 174.
29. On the suicidal martyrdom of Gelawdewos – Guidi, 'Due Frammenti', p. 585. The chronicler is undoubtedly sympathetic to the Catholics. Also: Wolde Aregay, p. 172. On the many ecclesiastics who died in the battle – Basset, 'Etudes', pp. 107-109; Tellez, p. 140; Conzelman, p. 169. For a discussion of Gelawdewos' period leading to the succession of Minas, his brother: below pp. 142-3.

CHAPTER VI

Trade and Power Politics in the Red Sea and the Indian Ocean in the Sixteenth Century

Following the accord of Tordesiles of 1494, which co-ordinated the imperialist activities of Spain and Portugal, the Cape route to India, explored in the second part of the fifteenth century, was left to the latter. By diverting the Far East trade to Lisbon the Portuguese hoped to break the power of the Muslims and to punish the Italian towns, whose prosperity they envied and whom they accused of betraying Christianity. The ambitions of the rulers of Portugal, however, far exceeded the meagre resources of their country and its relatively small population (about two millions). These factors were to prove a major drawback to the astounding expansion of the Portuguese empire in the sixteenth century.

Vasco da Gama's first successful voyage to India in 1497-9, with only three boats, could be considered just a reconnaissance expedition. Arriving in western India just after the disintegration of the kingdom of Delhi, the Portuguese found the situation there conducive to their intervention in the affairs of the region. Muslim Gujjerat, the only kingdom of consequence with a maritime and military power, was extensively involved in the trade of the Red Sea and the Persian Gulf. However, Gujjerat and its smaller sisters, accustomed to deal with individuals or groups of foreign merchants, were incapable of confronting a major sea power such as Portugal, which annually despatched to the area substantial Armadas with tremendous fire power. Consequently, Gujjerat and the weak Tahirid rulers of Yemen, who began to suffer from Christian maritime warfare since 1500, sought help from Mamluk Egypt and promised its ruler their full co-operation.[1]

Significantly, the substantial fleet, led by Vasco da Gama to India in 1500-1501, carried on board priests and missionaries and

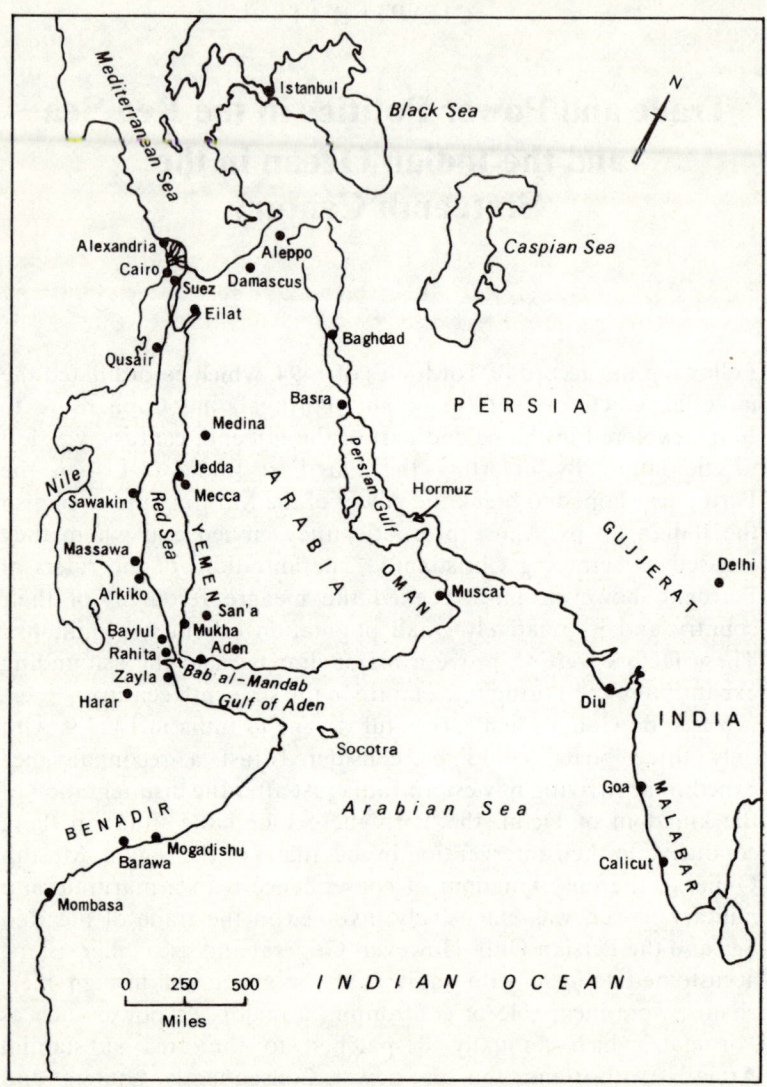

WESTERN PART OF INDIAN OCEAN LITTORAL

had been instructed by the king to destroy Muslim shipping in the Indian Ocean. Sailors of this fleet had already exchanged blows with Muslim merchants in Calicut and the captain of the flotilla, whom Vasco da Gama left behind with orders to cruise in the Arabian Sea, attacked and burnt ten Egyptian ships.

The ease with which the Portuguese established their maritime hegemony in the Indian Ocean was the result of vastly superior naval technology, seamanship and fire power, compared to anything which existed in the region. Hence, already by 1502/3 the Portuguese were able to undermine the whole network of Muslim shipping and trade in the Indian Ocean, and maintained constant patrols near the entrance to the Red Sea. By 1504 Egypt already experienced a shortage of spices and a year or two later, after the Portuguese established a systematic blockade on the entrance to the Red Sea, Far Eastern products disappeared altogether from the markets.[2] Only then, following the pleas of the Venetian and the Muslim rulers, did the Mamluks decide to act. A naval expedition, organised in Suez (1507) and commanded by Mir Hussayn al-Kurdi, sailed into the Indian Ocean in 1508 in an attempt to destroy Portuguese power there. But its debacle, off Diu, only aggravated the situation. Ironically, Mir Hussayn, returning to Jedda with the remnants of his fleet by way of Aden, confiscated the small Tahirid navy, thus completely exposing the shipping of the Gulf of Aden and the Red Sea to the mercy of the Portuguese.

Probably the greatest naval strategist of his period, Albuquerque, the admiral of the Portuguese navy in the Indian Ocean, began his activities against the East African coast and in the Gulf of Aden and attempted to contact the Ethiopian court in 1505. Realising the limitations of his resources, his grand strategy for establishing Portuguese hegemony in the Indian Ocean was based on the idea of gaining control of all the maritime straits leading to it and of obtaining local allies to supplement his meagre forces. In this context Socotra was captured in 1507 and soon afterwards the Portuguese began the campaign which led to the conquest of Hormuz and nearby strategic locations. These activities undoubtedly influenced the Mamluks' decision to launch the abortive expedition of Mir Hussayn (1507/8).

Albuquerque, appointed Viceroy of India in 1509, proceeded with his plan to gain control of a network of strategically and economically important bases, which was a departure from the concept of a 'seaborne empire'. Within the context of this policy, Goa was captured in 1510 and became the centre of the Portuguese government in India and efforts to extend Portuguese hegemony into the Persian Gulf were stepped up. Moreover, exploiting favourable circumstances Albuquerque negotiated an agreement with Shah Isma'il, the founder of the Safawid dynasty of Persia, by which the latter undertook to attack the Mamluk flank and was promised Portuguese aid. Preoccupied with unrest in Egypt, rebellions in Syria and clashes with the Ottomans, the Mamluks were unable to direct all their resources against the Portuguese. Qansaw al-Ghawri, nevertheless, temporarily made up his differences with the Ottoman ruler Bayezid in 1510 and the latter even agreed to supply him with artillery, wood and other materials needed to construct a new fleet, which could challenge Portuguese sea power.[3]

An abortive Portuguese attempt to capture Aden in 1513 prompted the Mamluks to speed up the construction of the new navy in the northern part of the Red Sea. Once it completed its preparations in 1516 this navy, commanded by Mir Hussayn and Reis Sulayman, disembarked Mamluk troops on the Yemeni coast near Zabid and then continued to Zayla, where it was provisioned by the Adali governor. The ruler of Aden, however, did not welcome the Mamluks and repulsed all their attacks. Having failed to capture the town, the Mamluks returned to Jedda.

The reappearance of the Mamluk navy in the bay of Aden triggered off in 1516/17 a Portuguese expedition to the Red Sea. Commanded by Lopo Suarez, it unsuccessfully attempted to attack Jedda and on its return trip burnt Zayla, probably because it helped provision the Mamluk navy. Yet this expedition was motivated by defensive rather than offensive objectives because it was meant to preempt and destroy the Mamluk fleet in its home base before it could erupt again into the Ocean.

By this time, having reached the sources of the spice trade in the East, the Portuguese no longer considered the Red Sea on their list of economic priorities. Moreover, with his forces thinly spread over a vast area, the Portuguese Viceroy in India realised that any large Muslim naval expedition arriving in the Indian Ocean could constitute a major threat to his 'empire'. Therefore, the Portuguese continued to keep an eye on the Red Sea. But, due to the enormous demands on the Lusitanian navy, the blockade of Bab al-Mandab was somewhat relaxed and some Far East ships, carrying spices and other merchandise, occasionally succeeded in the second decade of the sixteenth century in breaking through the blockade and reaching the Red Sea ports. But the arrival of such boats was an exception and until the 1540s the spice trade in Egypt remained limited and the price of spices extremely high.

Mamluk-Ottoman relations were strained throughout the fifteenth century and on several occasions between 1482 and 1491, during the reign of Bayezid II (r. 1481-1512), the Mamluks even succeeded in defeating the Turks. At the beginning of the sixteenth century, however, the Mamluks were threatened by the growing power of the Portuguese in the Indian Ocean and the virtual siege of the Red Sea which they failed to break, whereas the Ottomans were being challenged by the rising power of the Safawids in Persia. Consequently, relations between Egypt and the Turks rapidly improved. Just at this time (1511/12) Bayezid was replaced by his son Salim 'the Great'.

The conflict between the Ottomans and the Shi'i Safawids, augmented by religious differences, was aggravated by the rise of Sultan Salim to power. Ottoman expansionism under Salim was reoriented and directed towards the Arabic-speaking territories and India, whose wealth was legendary. The Safawid Empire, ruled by the ambitious Isma'il Shah, was not only a thorn in the side of the Ottomans; it also stood in their way of advance to India. After he was defeated by Salim in 1514, Isma'il Shah attempted to create an anti-Ottoman alliance between himself, the Mamluks, the Portuguese and the king of Georgia. However, while he was in Samarkand, Salim defeated his army in Mesopotamia and conquered Kurdistan.

Realising that he was to be the next victim of Salim's ambitions, Qansaw al-Ghawri quickly mobilised the largest army that he could muster and marched in 1516 into Syria. In the battle which ensued, the Mamluk army was completely routed near Aleppo and Qansaw was killed. Salim immediately marched into Egypt and in January 1517 defeated its new ruler, Tuman Bey. Once Salim became the master of Egypt, Sharif Barakat of Mecca and the Mamluk commanders in Jedda, on the Sudanese coast and in Yemen declared their loyalty to the Ottoman sultan.

The fall of Constantinople in 1453, the Ottoman advance towards the heart of Europe, the rise of Ottoman sea power in the

Mediterranean and the decline of the Venetian and Genoese maritime empires[4] since the second half of the sixteenth century had already convinced Europe that the Turks, rather than the decaying Mamluk sultanate, were the leading Muslim power. With the arrival of the Ottomans in the Red Sea in 1517, the threat to the Portuguese from this direction became even more imminent. Moreover, in 1519 an Ottoman-Mamluk navy, under the command of Hussayn al-Rumi, Jedda's governor, even sailed to Yemen to establish direct Ottoman authority there and make preparations for an expedition against the Portuguese. News of Salim's death, however, caused this fleet to return to Jedda before it accomplished its goals. Notwithstanding, Ottoman activities in the Red Sea greatly alarmed the Portuguese.

The Portuguese captured the 'kingdom' of Hormuz and its smaller satellites between 1507 and 1509 and further entrenched their position in the region during the governorship of Albuquerque. Yet, with their seaborne empire stretching as far as China, they were exploiting their meagre resources to their limit. Naturally, they were forced to decide on priorities and the Red Sea was not very high on their list. On the other hand, when the Ottomans took command of the Mamluk navy and gradually established their hegemony in the Red Sea, the Portuguese became increasingly apprehensive lest they might undertake a major maritime effort from this direction against their centres of government in India. An alliance with Ethiopia seemed now even more desirable; they intensified their naval operations in the Red Sea in order to gather information about Turkish movements in the region and renewed their attempts to capture Aden.

The death of Salim 'the Great' in 1519 sparked off rebellions in many provinces of the empire. The Knights of St. John, whose centre was to be moved from Rhodes to Malta in 1522, intensified their struggle against the Ottomans. In 1520 the French made an abortive attempt to conquer the main ports of the Levant. Consequently the new Sultan, Sulayman 'the Magnificent', was fully occupied in the first years of his reign with domestic and other matters and unable to pay attention to the southern peripheries of his empire and the Indian Ocean. His authority in the Hijaz and Yemen was ignored and rebellions broke out in Syria and Egypt in which many Mamluks participated. In fact, the rebels in Egypt even succeeded temporarily in overthrowing the representatives of the central government and did not hesitate in 1523 to apply to Christian Europe and to the Pope for help.

The Portuguese, who failed to take Aden in 1513 and in 1516/17, were quick to exploit the weakness of the Ottomans and the anarchy in Egypt and Yemen. Since 1520, when their warships disembarked da Lima's embassy in Massawa, they regularly despatched small flotillas into the Red Sea to gather information about Ottoman-Muslim activities there, to attack shipping in the area and to maintain contact with their embassy in Ethiopia. With Ottoman-Mamluk authority degenerating in Yemen, and the seas controlled by the Christians, the ruler of Aden was forced in 1524 to recognise Portuguese overlordship and undertook to co-operate with Portugal in its efforts to prevent merchants from sailing into the Red Sea and the Ottoman fleet from erupting into the Indian Ocean. In the coming years this agreement was renewed under duress on several occasions and, although in reality worthless, it enabled the Portuguese to use Aden for intelligence purposes and reflected the temporary decline of Muslim power in the region.[5] But the tide was rapidly changing.

Once firmly established on the throne and in control of the situation in the heartland provinces of the empire, Sulayman despatched to Egypt in 1524 his Grand Vezier and friend, Ibrahim Pasha, who quickly re-established Ottoman authority in this important province. Ibrahim Pasha, a most talented administrator, used the opportunity to reorganise the administration of Egypt and to consolidate Ottoman authority in Hijaz and along the Sudanese coast.[6] Ottoman authority, represented by the Viceroy of Egypt in charge of the Red Sea region as a whole, was later extended to Massawa and the delta of the Baraka, and a Turkish presence in Massawa is also reported in this period.[7]

Hijaz enjoyed a period of relative tranquillity and prosperity during the long reign of Sharif Muhammad Abu Numay II (r. 1526-1584). Ottoman authority was maintained by the Pasha of Jedda, a subordinate of the viceroy of Egypt, and by the armies which annually arrived with the Haj caravans. The revival of the Red Sea trade since the 1530s, coupled with the generous donations of the sultan for the construction of religious institutions and shrines and for other charitable purposes, benefitted the population and even the Beduin tribes remained relatively tranquil. Conse-quently Ulama from all over the Muslim world flocked to the holy towns and together with their local counterparts were responsible for a spiritual-religious revival, which also affected nearby countries.

Yemen was far less fortunate. It was governed by Ottoman officers, who were sent thither by the governor of Egypt or bought their appointment from the Porte. Motivated in most cases by greed, they exacted whatever taxes they could from the population. But the relatively small forces which they deployed were insufficient to overcome the militancy of the tribal population and the followers of heterodox imams, strongly opposed to the strict Sunni Hanifi *Madhab* to which the Ottomans adhered.

The reign of Sultan Sulayman 'the Magnificent' (1519-1566) was one of the most impressive periods in the history of the Ottoman dynasty. Although the main thrust of Ottoman expansionism during Sulayman's reign was once again directed towards Europe through the Balkans (and the Maghrib·), attention was also devoted to the situation in the Indian Ocean and the main avenues leading to it, the Red Sea and the Persian Gulf. The Turks realised by then that the prosperity of Egypt and Syria, and of the empire as a whole, depended to a great extent on the revival of the international trade with the Far East by the traditional routes to the Middle East.[8] Moreover, the many Turks and Ottomans employed in India were a source of information about the wealth of this subcontinent and some of their chiefs repeatedly invited their kinsmen to conquer it. Yet, despite Ottoman attempts during Sulayman's reign to launch expeditions against them, the Portuguese, on the whole, managed to maintain their hegemony in the Ocean because the resources earmarked by Sulayman for this purpose were insufficient. Nevertheless, the Ottomans succeeded in consolidating their control over the Red Sea and gradually began to undermine Portuguese predominance in the Persian Gulf.

Sulayman Reis, whom the Ottomans inherited from the Mamluks, was confirmed in 1525 in his position as admiral of the Red Sea navy. On this occasion he submitted a most impressive report on the trade of the Indian Ocean and its importance to the empire, as well as an evaluation of Portuguese military and naval strength in the East. Yemen was considered especially important to the Ottomans due to its strategic position in relation to the 'gates' of the Red Sea and the Indian Ocean and future attempts to revive the trade between Egypt and the Far East. Shortly after submitting his report, Sulayman Reis sailed with his fleet to the Kamran islands and from thence, in 1526, to the Yemeni coast, where the Mamluks were quick to pledge, once again, their loyalty to the Ottoman sultan. This time, however, Turkish forces were disembarked on the coast in order to establish, once and for all, the authority of the 'Sublime Porte' in the region. The Ottoman governor and his officers aroused, however, the immediate antipathy of the population and the traditional rulers because of their misgovernment and because they mishandled the complex situation in Yemen.[9] Nevertheless, the Ottoman presence in Yemen undoubtedly contributed to the Muslim success in the Horn of Africa, although this area remained peripheral to Ottoman aspirations.

A major Ottoman effort to break Portuguese maritime hegemony and to dislodge them from their strongholds in the Indian Ocean was already under way in 1528/9. The Red Sea fleet was constantly strengthened by new warships built in Suez or transported thither, in parts, from the Mediterranean. Much was done to improve the fire power of the warships and many Greeks and Italians were recruited to serve in them.

Additional incentive for the first Ottoman naval expedition against the Portuguese in India was the urgent requests for help received from the heirs to the Mogul empire and from many Turkish administrators who were employed by the rulers of western India. Indeed, many thousands of Turks, some of them Ottomans, served in the armies (especially in the artillery) and the administration of Indian states and some reached the highest positions. The latter had already invited their brethren to the rich subcontinent during the reign of Bayezid, but now they repeatedly pleaded with Sultan Sulayman to intervene in local rivalries and help them in their struggle against the Portuguese.[10]

Commanded by Mustafa Bayram and Seffer Bey, the Ottoman fleet, comprising 36 vessels and 20,000 men, of whom 7,000 were Janissaries, sailed in 1530/31 from the Red Sea to India. Although they succeeded in breaking the Portuguese siege on Diu and encouraged the Mogul empire's resistance to Christian pressure, the Ottomans failed to achieve their major goals of dislodging the Lusitanians from the region or of breaking their naval hegemony in the Ocean. Yet, for the first time since their appearance in the Indian Ocean, the Portuguese were confronted by vessels of war nearly equal to their own, with artillery which, in some instances, was superior to that of the Portuguese.[11] Evidently, with their resources stretched to the limit, the Portuguese became even more apprehensive of Ottoman aspirations in the region.

In the Persian Gulf opposition to Portuguese expansion until about the middle of the sixteenth century emanated from tribal leaders and from some Safawi rulers. As a result of the importance of maritime power in the Gulf and the relative power vacuum there, Portuguese influence was gradually extended as far north as Bahrayn, al-Hasa and Basra. Putting economic considerations before religious ones, the Christian authorities permitted Muslim merchants to trade in Hormuz and the Gulf as long as they undertoook not to trade with the Red Sea. Thus the Portuguese centre at Hormuz flourished and became the most important trade centre and entrepôt for the whole region.[12]

Baghdad, and most of Iraq, were conquered by Sulayman in 1534/5. Thereafter the Turks strove to extend their influence to the head of the Persian Gulf. But, although they gained a partial success in 1545, they did not establish a firm foothold in the region until the 1550s.[13] In the meantime their achievement enabled them to gain control of the silk route from Tabriz and the secondary spice route via the Gulf and Basra. But this only whetted their appetite for the economic rewards of the Far East trade and they continued to strive to undermine the Portuguese infrastructure in the Indian Ocean.

Under increasing Portuguese pressure in the mid-1530s, the kingdom of Gujjerat repeatedly implored the Ottomans to come to its help. At this time the Turks were still reorganising their naval forces in the Red Sea and consolidating their gains in Mesopotamia. But it is evident that Sultan Sulayman was contemplating the conquest of India. The war with Venice afforded the governor of Egypt, Khadim Sulayman Pasha (al-Rumi), an opportunity to put his hands on all the Venetian vessels in Egypt's ports. Even more important, their crews were pressed into service in the Ottoman Red Sea navy. Thus in 1537 this fleet set sail from the northern part of the Red Sea, committing acts of atrocity in Jedda and in Aden, which they captured by treason in 1538. From Aden Sulayman Pasha sailed to Diu with a huge fleet and a substantial army on board, but after a short stay in Indian waters and despite the strength of his fleet, the cowardly admiral ordered his captains to return to the Red Sea without giving battle to the Portuguese. In 1539 Sulayman Pasha appeared before the coast of Yemen and consolidated Turkish authority there, though not without additional atrocities, and returned to Egypt.[14]

Even if Turkish efforts to dislodge the Portuguese from India and the Indian Ocean could be considered a failure, they resulted in establishing Ottoman hegemony in the Red Sea and in the conquest of Aden, whose strategic and, to some extent, economic importance was unrivalled in the region. Moreover, with their forces dispersed from Mombassa to Nagasaki, the Portuguese no longer aspired to establish themselves in the Red Sea basin or at least to control its entrance, and rather awaited with apprehension a Turkish attack from this direction. On the other hand, Sultan Sulayman, deeply committed to the drive towards the heart of Europe and the attempt to establish Ottoman hegemony in the Mediterranean[15], was unable to allocate sufficient forces and resources seriously to challenge the Portuguese in the Indian Ocean. Unaware of the state of affairs in Constantinople, the Portuguese occasionally despatched vessels into the Red Sea to gather information about Ottoman activities. Their suspicions were further strengthened by the small fleets despatched by the Turks, unaware of the state of affairs in Goa, into the Indian Ocean to harass the Portuguese and to gather information about their movements.

Expecting a new attack from the direction of the Red Sea after the unsuccessful Ottoman expedition of 1537/9, the Portuguese authorities in India, mobilising all their resources,[16] organised an Armada and despatched it to the Red Sea in order to destroy the Muslim fleet in its home ports. It was commanded by India's Viceroy, Estavao da Gama (Vasco da Gama's son), who, *inter alia*, intended to disembark Bermudez and his followers in Massawa. This navy entered the Red Sea in 1541, but achieved very little, with the exception of the historic decision to land in Massawa 400 soldiers, commanded by Christovao da Gama, the Viceroy's brother, to help the Ethiopian king.

All the above notwithstanding, a *de facto status quo* was emerging by which the Portuguese were left in control of the Indian Ocean and the Ottomans of the Red Sea. Moreover, the struggle between the two powers was no longer ideologically oriented, but rather a conflict over the mastery of the Far East trade with the

Mediterranean and Europe. In fact the Portuguese blockade of the Red Sea was relaxed; trade by this ancient route rapidly revived and its volume quickly surpassed former dimensions and, after the middle of the century, even doubled and tripled.[17] In the Persian Gulf and even in Hormuz, Ottoman and other Muslim and non-Muslim merchants traded freely with the Portuguese and the way was open for limited co-operation between the two powers. Indeed, in 1542, the Portuguese king even offered to supply spices to the Ottomans in Basra against wheat, if the latter would limit their presence in Aden and concede the Portuguese blockade of the Red Sea.[18] The Turks, however, still infuriated by da Gama's expedition and with their eyes on India, did not reply to the Portuguese offers and continued to consolidate their infrastructure at the head of the Persian Gulf.

Ottoman authority was established in Basra in 1546 and by 1550 it was expanded to the head of the Gulf. A year later the Turks were in possession of the province of al-Hasa and by 1555, despite incessant wars with Beduins in Iraq and in eastern Arabia and Safawi pressure, the Ottoman flag was implanted as far as Qatar. However, their government in the Gulf remained precarious and they were unable to develop maritime activity in the region. Yet their activity prevented the extension of Portuguese domination and influence to Iraq and its consolidation in the upper parts of the Persian Gulf. However, the Ottomans realised that as long as the Portuguese held Hormuz and several supporting bases nearby, they could not hope to use this route to challenge the Portuguese power in India.[19] The main effort of Sulayman in the direction of the Indian Ocean was focused, therefore, on the Red Sea, whose gates he controlled.

Following da Gama's expedition and the Christian victory in Ethiopia, the Ottomans renewed their endeavours to prepare a naval expedition against the Portuguese. To facilitate this expedition they moved the headquarters of their fleet in 1546 from Suez to Mukha, using Aden as a staging base. Squadrons belonging to this fleet constantly patrolled the coast of southern Arabia, attacking Portuguese shipping in the northwestern part of the Indian Ocean and even attempted, unsuccessfully, to attack the Portuguese in Mombasa.[20] As elsewhere, their government in Yemen proved extremely despotic and chaotic. Rebellions were very frequent and in 1547 the population of Aden temporarily succeeded in regaining their autonomy. Expecting Turkish retribution, they invited the Portuguese to occupy their town in 1549/50, but the latter arrived only after Aden was recaptured by Pirie Reis, the new Ottoman admiral of the Red Sea fleet.[21]

In command of 30 warships and 16,000 soldiers, Pirie Reis was ordered to break the Portuguese stranglehold over the Gulf by conquering their strategic infrastructure focused around the Straits of Hormuz. The Turkish admiral sailed to Hormuz in 1551/2 and gained, at first, limited successes, but when he encountered the main Portuguese navy he was totally defeated. The major part of what was left of the Ottoman fleet escaped to Basra, but Pirie Reis returned to Suez in 1553 and was summarily executed for cowardly behaviour.[22] In the coming years Ottoman efforts in the region were aimed at saving the remnants of their fleet trapped in the Persian Gulf. The heyday of Ottoman sea power was over and the Porte abandoned its plans to conquer India.

Pirie Reis' replacement as *Kapudan* (admiral) of the Red Sea fleet, Murad,[23] failed to force his way through the Portuguese defences in the Straits of Hormuz and shamefully returned to the Red Sea. In its desperation, the Ottoman Porte appointed in 1554 Sidi Ali Reis, a famous admiral, navigator and scholar, as *Misr Kapudan* (Admiral of Egypt) and ordered him to save the fleet trapped in the Persian Gulf. Sidi Ali Reis reached Basra by land and took command of the fleet. All along his way to Hormuz, and beyond Hormuz, he was constantly engaged by the Portuguese in naval battles. Probably as a diversionary action, to help Sidi Ali Reis, Seffer Reis, who commanded the Ottoman navy in the Red Sea, erupted into the Indian Ocean in 1554. But despite such tactics and Sidi Ali's personal bravery and superb seamanship, his fleet was completely destroyed and his flagship was carried by the winds to the coast of India. Sidi Ali Reis returned to Istanbul by land only in 1557[24] and was accorded a hero's welcome. Thereafter the Ottomans did not attempt any more to challenge Portuguese naval hegemony in the Indian Ocean.

The Ottomans, and the Venetians who helped them, were used to the conditions existing in the Mediterranean and tried to transplant naval techniques and tactics, common in that sea, to the new environments. Even a gifted admiral and seaman such as Sidi Ali Reis was at a disadvantage when fighting the Portuguese in the Persian Gulf and the Indian Ocean because, in addition to better seamanship, the latter, established in the region for fifty years, had adapted their navy to the special climatic and other conditions existing in the area. Moreover, the Portuguese had organised in the Indian Ocean, the Red Sea and the Persian Gulf an intelligence network and a defence infrastructure which, exploiting local auxiliary forces, greatly contributed to the efficiency of their navy. In the Persian Gulf, moreover, they enjoyed by this time the co-operation of the Persian rulers and some Arab chiefs.

On the whole, Ottoman efforts to reach India and break Portuguese sea power distracted their attention from the Horn of Africa. By the beginning of the second half of the century the situation in the Red Sea was radically different from what it had been in the first decades of the century. Both powers were preoccupied elsewhere and the *status quo* which began to emerge around 1540 was further cemented in the 1550s and early 1560s, partly due to exhaustion of the combatants.[25] In such circumstances the Turkish authorities in the Red Sea became increasingly interested in Ethiopia and its trade.

Some merchandise from the Far East was already reaching the Red Sea in the 1520s despite the Portuguese blockade.[26] By the 1540s the Portuguese blockade of Bab al-Mandab was no longer effective and the quantities of spices and other products of the Far East arriving in Egypt were constantly on the increase. Moreover, Venetian merchants were permitted to settle in Cairo already in 1532 and, bypassing Jewish and other brokers, traded directly in the Indian Ocean. It was not long before the quantity of spices carried to Europe by way of Egypt surpassed that which reached Lisbon. By 1560, it was evident that the Portuguese monopoly on the trade of the Far East was completely broken, and merchants who had previously come to Portugal for spices returned to the Italian towns and especially to Venice.[27]

The interest of the Muslim commercial communities in the trade of the Red Sea in the first decades of the sixteenth century was sustained, to some extent, by the booty and tens of thousands of slaves taken in the Jihad against Ethiopia. An additional incentive was the increasing demand for 'Mukha' coffee in the markets of the Muslim countries. The coffee plant grows wild in certain parts of Ethiopia and it probably derived its name from the Ethiopian province of Kaffa. By the fifteenth century coffee had been introduced to Yemen and was cultivated especially on the western slopes of the Yemeni plateau, climatically ideal for this purpose. The use of coffee as a beverage began to spread and in the sixteenth century coffee houses opened in many centres of the Ottoman empire, including Mecca and Istanbul.[28]

Insofar as the ports of Yemen were considered the centre of the coffee trade, many merchants arriving in the Red Sea until the sixteenth century to trade in luxury commodities and *Habsha* slaves also acquired coffee for their own use and for commercial purposes. Inevitably when the Far East trade ceased to reach the Red Sea (and the Middle East as a whole), coffee as a trading commodity grew in importance. Indeed, even when the trade in spices fully revived by the 1540s, coffee, increasingly in demand in the different parts of the Muslim world, remained an important trade item, in volume and in value, and many merchants arrived in Mukha and even in the Horn of Africa for the purpose of acquiring high quality coffee.

Part of the coffee exported from Yemen came from the southwestern parts of the Ethiopian plateau and from the area of Harar. The coffee was transported to the coast by relays of caravans which penetrated the interior as far in the southwest as the Omo river basin and Kaffa in search of more luxurious commodities. Considering the quasi-monopoly of the Muslims over caravan trade and the contribution of caravan merchants to the diffusion of Islam in the past, this development could have had an important impact on Ethiopia in general and the expansion of Islam in the area in particular had it not been for the Galla migration in the plateau.[29] Such a development, however, became evident especially in the eighteenth and nineteenth centuries. Coffee cultivation and trade became essential, however, for the economy of the Harar-Chercher plateau.

All in all, trade in the Red Sea was rapidly increasing in the second part of the sixteenth century and the revenue from it was substantial. Inevitably it became evident that whoever controlled the outlets of this trade was ensured of a substantial source of revenue. Hence, as Turkish maritime activities declined, the interest of the Ottoman authorities and officials in the Ethiopian region began to increase. Moreover, the historic apprehension of a possible European-Ethiopian alliance which could threaten the heart of the Muslim world did not completely subside.

It was realised by both Portuguese and Turks that Abyssinia was important for the possession of the spice route. Situated near the Red Sea and on the Indian Ocean, its possession was, if not absolutely necessary *per se* to the Turks for the control of the Red Sea, at least desirable to keep the Portuguese from becoming permanently established there and so threatening the Ottoman possessions as they had those of the Mamluks. Besides Abyssinia's products were valuable.[30]

In the second part of the sixteenth century it seems that the last consideration, rather than the former, was the most important motive in shaping Ottoman policy regarding Ethiopia, if such a policy was ever formed. It is far more likely that the initiative for further conquest in such remote parts was left by the Porte to entrepreneuring Pashas, motivated by greed whetted by the legendary wealth of the plateau.[31]

Small Portuguese flotillas arrived in Massawa in 1555 and 1556 in order to examine the situation in Ethiopia and sound Gelawdewos' reaction to the possible arrival of Catholic missionaries and priests in his country. This, and the landing of the Jesuit Fathers near Massawa in 1557, caused great apprehension among the Muslims of the region. Immediately after Oviedo and his comrades had advanced into the plateau, Uzdamir Pasha[32] in Sawakin marched by land to Arkiko and from there into Hamasin, while the Ottoman fleet attempted to destroy the ships which brought the Jesuits.

After serving as *Kashif* (district governor) in the Ottoman administration of Egypt, Uzdamir was appointed in 1549/50 *beylerbeg* of Yemen. When he lost this governorship six years later, he acquired from the Porte an appointment to command 'the conquest of Abyssinia' with the title *beylerbeg* of *Habesh.* In Jedda he organised in 1555/6 an army of 3,000 mercenaries whom he gradually transported to Sawakin, a handful of whom he may have stationed in 1557 in Massawa.[33] The latter, or Turkish merchants, informed him of the arrival of the Portuguese ships and the landing of the Jesuits. Thus the arrival of the Jesuits in Ethiopia, in addition to the embarrassment it caused Gelawdewos, triggered off the first Turkish invasion of the plateau. But Ottoman plans for the conquest of Ethiopia, or more likely its Eritrean provinces, were already in an advanced stage at this time.

Once on the plateau, the Ottoman soldiers quickly captured the capital of Bahr-Midir, Dabarewa, which became the centre of Uzdamir's activities. Encouraged by the initial successes of the Turks, some local Muslims as well as rulers of peripheral Muslim principalities, hoping for a new Muslim 'conquest of Ethiopia', immediately allied themselves with the Turks. Considering the size of his army, it seems however that Uzdamir's objectives were relatively limited. Though he raided Tigre, whose governor and army were in the south with the King of Kings, he did not seriously try to extend his conquests beyond Bahr-Midir.[34]

The news of the Turkish invasion reached Gelawdewos while he was camped on the southeastern borders of the kingdom, following a Galla eruption from Bali into the provinces east of the Rift Valley lakes.[35] Thus Azmatch Ishaq, the *Bahr Nagash*,[36] a leading Tigrean noble and one of the officials closest to the monarch, was sent northwards to deal with the situation. Exploiting his knowledge of the area and the numerical superiority of his army, Ishaq completely defeated the Turks and their local allies and Uzdamir escaped to Sawakin with only a handful of survivors.

Uzdamir's 'invasion' of Ethiopia should be examined in its true proportion and context. It was a limited military expedition of a greedy Pasha, attempting to carve for himself a rich governorship. Indeed it was not even co-ordinated in any way with the ruler of Adal-Harar. At the time of this incident, with an increasing volume of the Far East trade reaching the empire by way of the Persian Gulf and the Red Sea, and short of military-naval resources, the Ottomans were more amenable to the idea of giving up their ambitious plans concerning the Indian Ocean and concentrated on consolidating their position in the Red Sea.[37]

After Uzdamir's main army had been wiped out the small garrison in Massawa, and for that matter the whole Ethiopian coast, were at the mercy of Ishaq. However, the latter chose to leave the Turks and the Sultan of Dahlak in possession of Ethiopia's most important maritime outlet, probably because of the tradition-al Ethiopian antipathy regarding their coast. Bahr Nagash Ishaq, moreover, was motivated by the fact that the Turks were willing to sell him firearms and that the Muslims furnished an insatiable market for all the slaves which he could supply.[38] Thus, the Ottomans were left with a foothold on the coast, which served as a listening post and a springboard for their intermittent attempts in the second half of the sixteenth century to expand the 'Pashalik of Habesh'. Though unsuccessful, these campaigns contributed to the erosion of the power of the Ethiopian kingdom and helped facilitate the great Galla migration in the plateau in the following decades.

Correspondence between the frustrated Jesuits, who left Gelaw- dewos' court and settled in Tigre,[39] and the Portuguese authorities in Goa, gave rise to rumours in the late 1550s concerning the possible arrival of another Portuguese expedition in Ethiopia. The Ottomans became even more apprehensive because of what seemed an intensification of Portuguese naval activities in the Red Sea.[40] Consequently, the appearance of several Portuguese war- ships off the Ethiopian coast in 1560 brought Uzdamir Pasha, once again, from Sawakin to Massawa.

Uzdamir had been closely watching developments in Ethiopia following Gelawdewos' death in 1559 and the struggle for power following the succession of his weak brother Minas. Bahr Nagash Ishaq, who had rebelled against the new king, joined forces with Uzdamir in 1562 and their combined army invaded Bahr-Midir and defeated the Ethiopian army commanded by Minas. Soon afterwards, when he heard of Minas' death, Ishaq drove his new ally back to the coast. Uzdamir succeeded, nevertheless, in persuading the Viceroy of Egypt, who feared a Portuguese-Ethiopian alliance, to send him reinforcements[41] and again marched into Bahr-Midir in 1563. However, before the Ottoman army achieved anything, Uzdamir died and most of his army was sent to Yemen to quell the rebellion there.

By the late 1550s the resistance to the Ottoman rule in Yemen was led by a new dynasty of Zaydi imams, whose base of power was in the area of San'a. Within a few years the insurrection spread all over the plateau as well to the Tihama coast. By 1564 the position of the Turks became so desperate that the governor of Egypt was forced to instruct the Pasha of *Habesh* to sail with all his forces to the Tihama.[41] Still, the situation continued to deteriorate and Ottoman authority in Yemen was nearly eradicated.

Shortly after coming to power Selim II ordered his Viceroy in Egypt to re-establish Ottoman government in Yemen in view of its economic and strategic importance. Thus Sinan Pasha, a most able officer and administrator, was despatched in 1569 to Yemen. Aden, having experienced Ottoman atrocities in the past, promptly requested Portuguese aid. Sinan, therefore, marched directly to this strategic town and conquered it just before the arrival of the Portuguese fleet (1569/70). By 1572 Ottoman authority in the whole of Yemen was so secure that its governor was able to send reinforcements to the *beylerbeg* of *Habesh*, who was preparing a new campaign against Ethiopia.[43]

Aware of the growing instability in Ethiopia and dissatisfied with just the customs revenues of its northern ports, Radwan Pasha, it seems, wished to gain control of the whole trade network of Ethiopia, or at least, of its northern provinces. With the large reinforcements procured from Yemen in 1572 he succeeded in re-establishing an Ottoman presence in Bahr-Midir. In the coming years he was intermittently repulsed to the coast by Bahr Nagash Ishaq, but in 1575 the Ottomans were back in Dabarewa, Bahr-Midir's capital. Allying themselves with the ruler of Harar and the embittered and disillusioned Ishaq, the Turks made between 1576 and 1579 their most serious bid to conquer Ethiopia. However, this campaign ended disastrously and both Ishaq and Radwan perished on the battlefield.[44]

While Serse Dingil became increasingly preoccupied with the Galla migration and trade continued to develop nevertheless, the new Ottoman Pasha of *Habesh* (Kedawred?) abortively attempted in 1589 and again in 1592 to re-establish a foothold on the plateau. Both campaigns were, however, on a far smaller scale than the invasion of 1578/9 and ironically they did not affect the generally cordial relationship between the Turks and the Ethiopian monarch.[45]

By the turn of the sixteenth century Ottoman power had so declined that entrepreneuring Pashas could no longer attempt the conquest of the plateau, despite the complete chaos there. In the following century the Ottoman authorities in the Red Sea were even forced to relinquish control of the Ethiopian coast to the Na'ib of Arkiko, who commanded the local garrison. For a time, although decreasing, Ethiopian trade continued to flow through Massawa and Sawakin.

The death of Sulayman in 1566 marked the end of the era of rapid Ottoman expansionism. The decline of Ottoman power, which had begun in the last decade of Sulayman's reign, became far more evident after the succession of Selim II. The sultan by this time ceased to be an able military leader and became a spoiled oriental despot, who grew up and spent most of his time after coming to power in the harems of the court. Members of the royal family were no longer appointed governors of provinces, the practice of fratricide was annulled and the king's brothers and close relatives were imprisoned in luxurious surroundings, and were in many cases exploited in court conspiracies. The *devshirme* system became increasingly corrupt and the power of the Janissaries grew at the expense of the central authority. Finally the vast quantities of American silver and gold reaching Europe accelerated the inflation in the empire which greatly affected its economy.

Peripheral areas of the empire, such as the Red Sea basin, were the first to be influenced by the erosion of its power and economy. Ottoman government in Egypt began to degenerate and the Turks were no longer able to challenge the Portuguese predominance in the Indian Ocean.[46] Invariably, the Ottoman authorities in the Red Sea became more sensitive to rumours about the expected arrival of Portuguese expeditionary forces in Ethiopia and apprehensive concerning the intermittent appearance of their flotillas in the region.[47]

Thinly spread over a vast empire, the Portuguese in this period had no intention of getting involved in a war with the Turks. In fact, suffering from a chronic shortage of manpower, most of their sailors in the Indian Ocean fleet were by this time of Asian origin.[48] Moreover, King Joao III died in 1557 and his young heir Sebastiao became involved in an unfortunate expedition to North Africa. It was not long (1580) before the government of Portugal was to pass into the hands of Philip II, King of Spain. Indeed, considering their situation, the Portuguese attempted on several occasions to negotiate a peace settlement with the Ottomans.[49] Yet, although they lost interest in Ethiopia and the Red Sea, they continued to send small flotillas to the region, which maintained contact with the Jesuit Fathers in Tigre, but whose main duty was to warn Goa of any preparation for an Ottoman naval attack.[50]

The Portuguese expeditions into the Red Sea not only kept alive Ottoman suspicions about Goa's intentions, but also brought retribution in the form of naval expeditions, despatched by Yemen's governor in the 1570s and early 1580s, to attack Hormuz and East Africa.[51] All this notwithstanding, desperately short of resources and sailors and especially while the Red Sea trade continued to flourish, the Ottomans did not wish to continue the confrontation with the Portuguese.[52] Thus, a *de facto* truce between the two powers emerged in the last decades of the sixteenth century.[53]

Just as Ottoman power rapidly declined from the end of the century, the growing prosperity and political upheaval in Europe, following the Reformation and the wealth derived from America and the Far East, had a dramatic effect on the situation in the Indian Ocean and the Red Sea. Once in control of the Portuguese empire, Philip II of Spain instructed his Viceroy in India to renew, more vigorously, the activities against the Muslims and render help to Jesuit attempts to reach Ethiopia.[54] But whereas the Portuguese were incapable of and unwilling to mount an attack on the Ottomans, the new Jesuit efforts to reach Ethiopia were to have a lasting impact on the history of that country, especially in the first half of the seventeenth century.[55] Spain's control of Portugal, moreover, accelerated the intervention of vigorous new imperialist countries in the Indian Ocean, which undermined Portuguese hegemony in that region.

At war with Spain in 1584, the British began to attack Portuguese shipping in the Atlantic and the Indian Ocean. Moreover, Europe's growing prosperity caused a constant expansion of the market for Far East spices and other luxury products. Having defeated the Spanish Armada in 1588 and envious of the rich Portuguese trade with Asia, the British established the East India Company, which in 1591 despatched to India three ships laden with British merchandise. Dutch merchants, who had acquired spices in Lisbon for the markets of northern Europe and who had been prevented from sailing to Portugal since 1585, thereafter extended their struggle with Spain to the waters of the Indian Ocean.[56] These developments led to a complete change in the balance of power in the Indian Ocean from the turn of the sixteenth century. The declining Ottoman empire, however, could not compete with the Europeans and benefit from this turn of events. Indeed, European trading companies, supported by their respective governments and by freelance pirates from many nations who began to infest the waters of the Indian Ocean and especially the Arabian Sea, produced at the beginning of the seventeenth century a short-lived crisis in the Red Sea trade.

Ironically, just before Catholicism was about to triumph in Ethiopia and when Ottoman power was already declining, the vigorous European nations who reached the Indian Ocean motivated by purely commercial considerations, were not interested in the Red Sea and the country of the 'Presbiter John'. Portuguese India, under Spain, although prompted by the Jesuits and Rome to intervene, was unable and unwilling to do so. Christian Ethiopia, however, was no longer threatened by the Muslims, nor did power politics directly influence its history until the nineteenth century. Indeed, the Galla migration, facilitated to some extent by the wars with the Muslims, and the resurgence of the traditional centrifugal forces, greatly contributed to the enfeeblement of the Solomonic dynasty and prevented its more able monarchs from participating in Red Sea politics. Yet the stagnation of trade and other relations with Europe following the 'Jesuit period',[57] at a most crucial time in its cultural and technological development, was to have a most disadvantageous effect on the spiritual development and progress of Ethiopia.

NOTES

1. See *Varthema*, pp. 64-5. A major source is A.I. Sylvester de Sacy's collection in *La Foudre de l'Yémen*, Paris, 1897-98 (especially p. 522 onwards), with Johanssen, *Historia Yemenae*, Bonn, 1828. On Portuguese activities see: Boxer, *Portuguese;* Major, R. H., *India in the 16th Century;* Dames, 'The Portuguese'; Sousa, F. Y., *The Portuguese Asia* (trans. Stevens, J.), London, 1696.

2. Unconfirmed sources reported a small Portuguese fleet in 1505 in the vicinity of Jedda, the port of Mecca.

3. The shipments of war materials from the Ottomans to the Mamluks were captured by the navy of the Knights of the Order of St. John, at this time still in the Island of Rhodes. See also above pp. 71-2.

4. Haji Khalifeh, *The History of the Maritime Wars of the Turks* (trans. Mitchell, J.), London, 1831; Ayalon, D., 'Hamamlukim vehaotsma hayamit', *Divrei Haakademia Hayisraelit Lemada'im* (Hebrew), Vol. I, No. 8, Jerusalem, tav sheen kaf daled (1964).

5. On Portuguese representatives in Aden reporting on the movements of the Ottoman fleet – Serjeant, pp. 56-7. Also: Kammerer (1935), Vol. II, pp. 283-8.

6. Stripling, Vol. I, pp. 88-9. For a general source on the Ottomans in Egypt see: Stanford Shaw, J., *The Financial Administrative Organisation and Development of Ottoman Egypt, 1517-1798*, Princeton, 1958.

7. Ramusio, Vol. I, p. 290B; 'I Portoghezi a Massaua'.

8. Crichton, A., *History of Arabia and its People*, London, 1852, Vol. II, p. 112.

9. Stripling, Vol. I, pp. 88-9; Ozharan, pp. 47-8.

10. Dames, 'The Portuguese', pp. 3-4; *The Maritime Wars*, pp. 65-6.

11. Dames, 'The Portuguese', pp. 14-5; Serjeant, p. 18.

12. Ozbaran, pp. 22-30.

13. Basra had, however, already been captured in 1547. Ozbaran, p. 28; Lewis, B., 'The Ottoman archives as a source for the history of the Arab lands', *Journal of the Royal Asiatic Society*, 1951, pp. 149-51.

14. *The Maritime Wars*, pp. 65-6; Ramusio, Vol. I, p. 274; Sousa, Vol. I, pp. 433-48; Kerr, *Collection of Voyages*, Vol. VI, pp. 260-5; Ozbaran, pp. 47-8; Serjeant, pp. 19, 79-94; Bombaci, Alessio, 'Notizie Sull' Abyssinia in Ponti Turche', *Rassegna di Studi Ethiopici*, anno III, No. 1, p. 80; Vambéry, A. (ed.) *The Travels and Adventures of Sidi Ali Reis*, London, 1899, Introduction, pp. vi, vii, xiii.

15. *The Maritime Wars*; Ayalon, 'Hamamlukim'.

16. A network of spies in the Red Sea kept the Portuguese informed about the movements of the Ottoman navy and the construction of additional warships in Suez, but these spies grossly exaggerated Turkish militancy. Lane, pp. 584-6.

17. Boxer, *Portuguese*, p. 59; Lane, p. 584.

18. Danvers, F. C., *The Portuguese in India*, London, 1894, Vol. I, pp. 450-1.

19. Ozbaran, pp. 32-43. This was a period of intensive activities in eastern Europe and maritime activities in the Mediterranean. The famous admiral Barbarossa died in 1546.

20. Stripling, pp. 97-9; Boxer, *Portuguese*, p. 43; *The Maritime Wars*, pp. 7, 70-71; Ozbaran p. 43.

21. Serjeant, pp. 107-8.

22. *The Maritime Wars*, pp. 72, 85-6; Ozbaran, pp. 44-6, 49-56; Kammerer (1947), Vol. I, pp. 90-3. Nevertheless a number of Portuguese captives taken in the Persian Gulf were brought to Egypt and were later ransomed by king Gelawdewos of Ethiopia in 1554 – Whiteway, *Castanhoso*, p. lxxiii.

23 Previously the governor of the *Sanjak* (district) of Katif, the northern part of the Arabian coast off the Persian Gulf – Ozbaran, p. 54.

24. Ozbaran, pp. 59-63; *The Maritime Wars*, pp. 63, 73-4; Danvers, Vol. I, pp. 511-13; Orhonlu, C., 'Seydi Ali Reis', *Journal of the Regional Cultural Institute of Iran, Pakistan and Turkey*, Teheran, 1967, pp. 44-57; Vambéry, *Sidi Ali Reis*. Of a Turkish governor in Surat at the time of Sidi Ali's expedition – Dames, 'The Portuguese', p. 23.

25. Danvers, Vol. I, pp. 511-20; Ozbaran, pp. 77-87; Lane, p. 584.

26. See Alvarez, Vol. II, p. 415 on merchants from India frequently arriving in the Ethiopian court.

27. Stripling, p. 95; Lane, pp. 584-7.

28. When a *fatwa* prohibiting the use of coffee was proclaimed in Istanbul in 1584, riots broke out in the capital and in other towns of the empire and thereafter the objection of the orthodox to the drinking of coffee was overlooked.

29. See below, text.

30. Stripling, p. 96.

31. According to the Ottoman traveller Evliya Celebi (*Narrative of Travels in Europe, Asia and Africa in the 17th Century*, trans. Joseph von Hammer, London, 1834, Vol. I, p. 89), during the reign of Sulayman (died 1566) the *khas* (tribute) of the *beylerbeg* (provincial governor) of *Habesh* was one million and eighty thousand aspers, nearly equivalent to the *khas* of the *beylerbeg* of Rumili and a little more than that of the governor of Damascus.

32. Uzdamir (called also Zamur), considered the founder of the Pashalik of *Habesh*, was an ex-Mamluk of Circassian origin, and related to the Mamluk sultan of Egypt Qansaw al-Ghawri.

33. Bombaci, 'Notizie', p. 80; Evliya, Vol. I, part I, p. 85; Ruppell, E., *Reise in Abyssinien*, Frankfurt-am-Main, 1838, 1840, Vol. I, pp. 185-200; Beccari, Vol. X, p. 51. The local ruler of Sawakin was killed by the Portuguese in 1556 – Wolde Aregay, p. 168, note 2, according to Correa.

34. Conzelman, pp. 158-9, 164; Kammerer (1947), Vol. I, pp. 166-7; Rossini, 'Turco' (1921-2), p. 685.

35. See below, text.
36. Literally meaning 'ruler of the sea', the title of the governor of the 'Eritrean' provinces of Ethiopia. According to Wolde Aregay (p. 180) Ishaq held at this time the office of *Bitwadad*.
37. Danvers, Vol. I, p. 511; Tellez, p. 150; Ozbaran, pp. 84-5, 87; Stripling, p. 96; Lane, pp. 584-6.
38. Rossini, 'Turco' (1921-22), p. 688; Conzelman, pp. 166-7; Beccari, Vol. X, p. 104 – on tax agreement between Ishaq, Isma'il, the Sultan of Dahlak and the governor of Massawa.
39. See below, p. 137-8.
40. Beccari, Vol. X, p. 105; Ozbaran, p. 85; Danvers, Vol. I, p. 511; Lane, pp. 584-6. On firearms and Turkish artillery used by Nur ibn Mujahid against Gelawdewos in 1559 – Kammerer (1947), Vol. I, p. 170; Conzelman, pp. 175-6; Budge, Vol. II, p. 350.
41. Beccari, Vol. X, p. 157, the Jesuit F. Freire from Cairo, 30.11.1562. See below, pp. 146-7.
42. Kammerer (1947), Vol. I, p. 175, On several Muslim ships captured by the Portuguese off Jedda in 1564 – Lane, p. 586.
43. Kammerer (1947), Vol. I, p. 176. A major source for the history of Yemen in this period is: Britton, S., *The Rise of the Imams of Sanaa*, Oxford, 1925. Sinan Pasha was appointed in 1571 the governor of Egypt and his brother Berhan replaced him in Yemen. He should not be confused with another governor called Sinan, who ruled Yemen in the 1580s.
44. See below pp. 155-6. Rossini, 'Turco' (1929), pp. 51-6; Rossini, 'Sarsa Dengel', pp 70-93; 'Annales Iohannis', p 35; Tellez, pp. 148-9.
45. Cherubini, an Italian merchant who traded in Ethiopia at the end of the 16th century, writes in a letter from Dembiya on 24 December 1579 (Almagia, R., *Contributi alla storia della conoscenza dell' Etiopia*, Padua, 1941, p. 48) of the good relations between the Ottomans and the Muslims of Tigre and, when not at war, with the king of Ethiopia. On trade relations between Ottoman authorities in Massawa and Arkiko and Portuguese in Diu – Tellez, pp. 161-2, 173.
46. The last factor may have enhanced Turkish interest in Ethiopia and its trade.
47. On rumours about the landing of Portuguese forces at Baylul in 1575 see: Kammerer (1947), Vol. I, p. 176. Also below pp. 155-6.
48. Report of Archbishop of Goa in 1569 concerning 3,000 servicemen rather than 15,000 listed on payroll – Boxer, *Portuguese*, p. 53. On Ottoman exhaustion as a sea power – Stripling, p. 101.
49. On negotiations for a peace and trade agreement – Ozbaran, p. 85.
50. Stripling, p. 96; Kammerer (1947), Vol. I, p. 175; Boxer, *Portuguese*, pp. 52-4; *The Voyage of John Huyghen Van Linschoten*, Hakluyt Society, London, 1885, Vol. I, pp. 37-9.
51. Ozbaran, p. 95; Tellez, pp. 153-8; Sousa, Vol. III, pp. 6, 28-9, 62; Linschoten, Vol. I, p. 38; Serjeant, p. 111.
52. This, *inter alia*, prevented the planned Ottoman expedition to Bahrayn. Ozbaran, p. 91; Stripling, pp. 100-1; Boxer, *Portuguese*, p. 96.
53. Lane, pp. 585-6; *Linschoten*, Vol. I, pp. 43, 50. Tellez, pp. 161-2, 173.
54. Tellez, p. 17; Lane, p. 587.
55. See Chapters IX, X below.
56. Danvers, Vol. II, pp. 67, 105-8; Ryley, J. H., *Ralph Fitch, England's Pioneer to India*, London, 1899, pp. 242-3.
57. See below, Chapter X.

CHAPTER VII

The Rise of Galla Power in the Horn

The Galla and the disintegration of Adal

In the 1550s Gelawdewos was constantly preoccupied in fighting the Galla in the southeastern peripheries of his kingdom and the Muslims of the Harar-Chercher plateau.[1] The monarch's tactics concerning the Galla were relatively successful in the short run, and their eruptions were, on the whole, curbed by new *Chewa* garrisons supported by the royal army. His strategy concerning Adal, however, completely misfired.

Although it enjoyed a period of prosperity and stability while Grañ ruled Ethiopia, Adal lost its political primacy among the Horn's Muslims. The collapse of Grañ's Ethiopian sultanate transformed Adal, once again, into the focus of Muslim activities in the region. Yet the Walasma sultans of Adal lacked the charisma and leadership to rally to their flag all the Muslims of the Harari plateau and the lowlands, nor were they even capable of asserting their authority over their amirs and the Somali and other pastoralist tribes of their sultanate. Adal underwent, therefore, a period of instability and civil war which resembled the years prior to the rise of Grañ. The situation was further complicated by the presence in the sultanate of tens of thousands of refugees from the plateau, many of whom were converted Ethiopians. The latter, who became increasingly involved in Harar's politics, introduced new customs and an indifference to the laws of Islam, not compatible with the relative orthodoxy of the Hararis.

In spite of the internal strife in the sultanate, the Adalites managed to launch several attacks on the eastern and southeastern provinces of Ethiopia. But these attacks, accompanied by uprisings of local Muslims, were ineffective and resembled the raids of the Muslim amirs on Ethiopia a century earlier.[2] The Ethiopians suppressed the rebellions in the southeastern provinces and settled many *Chewa* there. But determined to break Adal's power through attrition, they retaliated by massive raids into the sultanate, constantly ravaged its territories and at one stage even temporarily occupied Harar.[3] Such a strategy, unaccompanied by colonisation, had proved ineffective in the past and it rather rekindled in Adal an atmosphere similar to that which preceded the great conquest of Grañ. Already in 1551/2 differences and rivalries were forgotten and the settled population and nomads united under the command of Grañ's nephew, Nur ibn Mujahid.

Following the example of his uncle, Nur left the Walasma sultan on his throne and took to himself the title of Imam. Within a matter of a few years he had succeeded in reorganising the administration and the army of the sultanate and in 1559 he led his forces into Dawaro. Disregarding an Ethiopian army commanded by Gelawdewos' kinsman, Hamalmal, which invaded Adal, Nur continued his advance in the direction of Fatagar. With the northern regiments watching the Turks and the Borana Galla pinning down the *Chewa* in the area of the Rift Valley lakes, Gelawdewos' army, which confronted Nur, was not only physically weak because of the fast of Lent, but also inferior in numbers and armaments to that of the Muslims. Hence, though the monarch fought heroically he was totally defeated and was killed on the battleground. But rather than continuing his advance into Ethiopia Nur, after garrisoning the southeastern provinces of the plateau, chose to return to Harar, which was threatened by the Galla migration.[4]

The written history of the Horn of Africa from the middle of the sixteenth century does not do justice to the Galla people. It is largely concerned with developments in the kingdom of Ethiopia and, to a lesser degree, with the principalities of the coast. These communities, being literate, produced chronicles and religious monographs, or were visited by foreigners who left behind written material concerning their hosts. The Galla people, on the other hand, illiterate until modern times and hostile to foreign visitors, have been relatively neglected, although the story of their great migration, the evolution of their society and culture, the growth of their political power and their transformation into the predominant element in the Horn is a major theme throughout the period. But through lack of source material concerning the Galla the history of the area is unbalanced and incomplete.

The Oromo,[5] better known as Galla[6], were Cushitic pastoralists with a common language, culture and socio-political organisation.[7] Although, as their traditions indicate, the Galla may have had originally a central political and spiritual leadership in the person of the legendary *Abba Muda*,[8] when first reported in Ethiopia and Adal they were already divided into different groups which operated independently, each having its own elected leader. Basically, the major division among the Galla was between Baraytuma and Borana.[9] But these groups were in their turn composed of a number of 'tribes' and clans stemming from legendary ancestors.

Internally each Galla 'tribe' was organised in five classes called *gada*. The *gada* system was not, however, an age-grade system because a son could join the first of the parallel *gada* classes only after his father had completed the cycle of five classes of the *gada*. Once he was initiated into the first class of the *gada* promotion from one class to the other took place automatically and collectively, irrespective of age, every eight years.[10] Each class had specific functions within the scope of activities of the tribe. But above all the internal organisation of the tribe was geared for warfare. Militarily the most important was the third class, which served as the spearhead of the tribe. But the second class of the *gada*, in training to take over the duties of the third, and the fourth class were also used extensively in battle whenever necessity arose. The fifth class of the *gada*,[11] called in many sources *luba*, could be considered the ruling *gada* as it served in a way as a council of elders and greatly influenced decisions taken by the tribe or clan. Tribesmen who completed the full cycle of the *gada* (five classes) were retired from participation in the activities of the tribe and were usually left with the young children and women in the rear camp to tend the cattle and defend it, if attacked.

Galla society, like most pastoral societies, was egalitarian in the extreme. Each *gada* elected its own leader (*Abba Gada*) and other office holders. One of the most important of these was the war leader of the third class, usually called *Abba Dula*, who was in fact the military commander of the whole tribe in time of war. Another important office holder was the *Abba Buko*[12], in a way the spiritual and to a certain extent the political leader of the tribe. Office holders, unless exceptionally strong and gifted, were considered and treated as *primus inter pares*. Each member of the tribe could voice his opinion and influence decisions taken in the councils of his *gada* or the tribe. Thus the elected officers of the tribe, as well as the *luba*, executed the collective wishes of their tribe rather than of themselves when making decisions.[13]

According to Galla ritual, members of the second class of the *gada* could not be initiated into the next class unless they killed a warrior (or a dangerous animal) and fought an enemy which had not been previously attacked.[14] Such a system gave rise to endemic raids and the constant extension of the radius of Galla penetration. It also explains the correlation between the rhythm of Galla pressure and the rise to power of a new *luba* every eight years.[15] By the middle of the sixteenth century, moreover, the population growth and substantial increase of Galla cattle, accompanied by a few years of drought,[16] undoubtedly influenced the pattern of Galla migration.

Led by their *Abba Dula*, the warriors of each tribe or clan, numbering a few thousand, would swiftly penetrate enemy territory, sometimes across hundreds of miles.[17] Living off the land, they destroyed everything in their path and annihilated anyone whom they met. Obviously the relatively rigid Ethiopian defence system, based on *Chewa*, supported by the cumbersome royal army, could not prevent the penetration of the highly mobile Galla raiding parties. Even the pastoralist forces of Adal and its excellent cavalry, surprised by the attackers, their mobility and viciousness, were unable to stop them. But once they overcame their initial shock, the armies of Ifat and Ethiopia respectively could, in most cases, master the Galla raiding columns. Thus, through necessity or custom, after overrunning and looting a certain region, the Galla invaders quickly retreated to the southeastern peripheries of the plateau.

The problem of the original homeland of the Galla has already been discussed elsewhere.[18] At the turn of the sixteenth century, however, it seems that the Savannah and the semi-desert which they inhabited to the south of Bali could no longer support their growing numbers and their herds and the Galla began to move into the southeastern peripheries of the Ethiopian plateau.[19] The struggle between Grañ and Christian Ethiopia undoubtedly facilitated the Galla migration into the highlands. But this expansion was later curbed by Grañ's armies and by Gelawdewos, once the latter had firmly established his government in the south. The continuous struggle between Ethiopia and Adal after Grañ's death and the chaos within Adal, however, afforded the Baraytuma group, whose attempts to penetrate Ethiopian defences were repeatedly frustrated, an opportunity to advance into Bali and the Chercher-Harar plateau.[20]

Nur ibn Mujahid's campaign against Ethiopia and the destruction brought upon Adal by an Ethiopian army in 1559 further eroded its ability to withstand the Baraytuma's raids. Thus, exploiting the absence of Nur and the bulk of the Muslim army, the Galla overran most of Harar's territories and threatened the town proper. It was in this period, during the cycle of *luba* 'Mesle' (1556-1564), that the pattern of the Baraytuma's expansion changed dramatically and became a full-scale migration, which affected both Adal and the peripheries of Ethiopia.

> The fifth luba was called Mesle ... He devastated all the lands and ruled them; and he entered with his animals, whereas previously the Galla made war coming from the Wabi and had returned there. Our King Ansaf Sagad (Gelawdewos) had fought him, starting from Asa Zanab.[21]

Nur 'the Just and the Pious' is even more glorified by Harari traditions than Grañ 'the Conquerer' because he saved Harar from the Galla and dedicated himself to its protection. Nur's armies continued to hold most of Waj and Fatagar even after 1560, when they were reported to have been defeated by Hamalmal,[22] but rather than carrying on the traditional war against Ethiopia, from 1559 to the time of his death in 1567, Nur gave his undivided attention to the growing pressure of the Galla. Although Nur was unable to dislodge the Galla from the parts of the Chercher-Harar plateau which they had overrun and settled, his tireless campaigning[23] and the wall which, according to tradition, he had built around the town, temporarily curbed the advance of the Baraytuma and saved Harar. Moreover, the relative stability in Harar during Nur's reign enabled the townspeople to participate in the revived trade of the Red Sea, and Harar enjoyed a period of great prosperity and development.[24] Yet although he succeeded in postponing the disintegration of Adal, Nur, by his victory over

Gelawdewos and the breaching of the *Chewa* defence system, unwittingly paved the way for the triumph of Galla power in the Horn of Africa.

After Nur's death Adal reverted again to a state of chaos. Several factions in Harar and the amirs of its different provinces fought each other for power. An Ethiopian convert, supported by the refugee element in Harar, gained control of the government and deposed the last sultan of the Walasma dynasty. The disorder within Adal, however, afforded the Ethiopians an opportunity to re-establish their authority in part of the territories of the south-eastern provinces, which the Adalis still held. Concurrently, the Baraytuma Galla, especially the Ittu, Humbana and Karayu tribes, renewed their advance in the Chercher-Harar plateau, along the eastern escarpments and even into the Dankali desert. Reconciling themselves to the new balance of power and the settlement of the Galla in the region and in order to facilitate their commercial activities, the more realistic elements in Harar attempted at this stage to regulate their relations and trade with the Galla by treaty. This treaty, despite some opposition from the 'traditionalists', may have paved the way for the early islamisation of the Galla in the area of Harar.[25]

Notwithstanding the enfeebled state of their sultanate and its harassment by the Galla, the rulers of Harar tried in 1575 to re-establish their control over the southeastern provinces of the plateau. Sultan Muhammad IV,[26] who co-ordinated his plans with the Ottoman Pasha of *Habesh*, probably wished to exploit the war of succession in Ethiopia. Be that as it may, in 1576 the Adali army was camped in Bali, poised for the attack on Ethiopia, and it punished the Muslim rulers of Hadya for having submitted to the Ethiopian ruler. Aware of the dangerous alliance between the Muslims and the threat to his authority in the southern provinces, Serse Dingil (r. 1563-1597) quickly marched to the south and, taking advantage of the rivalry between the different components of the strong Muslim forces and their commanders, succeeded in defeating them. Sultan Muhammad and some of the most important Adali chiefs were taken prisoner and later executed.[27] This was the last attempt of the Harari and coastal Muslims to attack Christian Ethiopia.

The futile Adali attempts to invade Ethiopia left the Chercher-Harar plateau completely unprotected. Consequently the Baraytuma swept the area and destroyed many hamlets and villages as far as the hinterland of Zayla. The town of Harar itself was besieged for a time and had it not been for the timely arrival of reinforcements from the coast it might also have fallen to the Galla.[28]

In spite of the constant danger to Harar emanating from the Galla, the struggle for power in the sultanate was renewed immediately after the death of Muhammad IV. This time the traditionalist element in the town gained the upper hand and Muhammad ibn Ibrahim Gassa, a descendant of the family of Grañ, became the ruler of Harar and took the title of Imam.[29] But, to the disgust of the indigenous Hararis who supported him, in 1577 the new Imam transferred the seat of his government to the oasis of Aussa, where the Awash river is about to disappear in the sands of the Dankali desert.

Aussa, the site of several villages inhabited by cultivators of different origins, was an important commercial centre for the caravan trade between the coast and central Ethiopia. The salt deposits nearby were also a factor of some importance for its commerce. But the transfer of the seat of Adal to Aussa proved a fatal mistake. It was too far removed from the heart of the imamate to allow effective control of its other centres. Moreover, even the deserts surrounding Aussa were an inadequate barrier against Ethiopian Somali, Dankali and Galla raids. It was not long before Sultan Muhammad's rivals began to plot against him in the other centres of the sultanate and Aussa itself became the battleground for amirs who aspired to rule Adal. In the last decade of the sixteenth century Adal disintegrated and in Aussa one ruler exercising minimal authority followed another and the bulk of its fertile lands was abandoned because of Dankali and Galla raids.[30] In its enfeebled state at the beginning of the seventeenth century the imamate attracted Muslim adventurers from Tigre and its rulers recognised the overlordship of the Ethiopian emperor, or at least maintained friendly relations and exchanged presents with him.[31] The Imams, moreover, wished for Ethiopian co-operation in the struggle against the Galla.[32]

Effective control of the other parts of Adal during the hectic period following the transfer of its seat to Aussa was nearly always in the hands of the amirs or tribal chiefs who ignored the Imam's authority. The governors of Harar became semi-independent, and whenever free from Galla pressure they participated in plots against whoever ruled Aussa. Harar, however, gradually declined because its economy was adversely affected by the occupation of most of its lands by the Galla. The latter, moreover, together with the Somali tribes who lived between Harar and the coast, constantly disturbed the trade in the area, even if they began to participate in it.

Towards the end of the century some Galla tribes between the Webi and the Juba began to move in a southeastern direction. This migration brought the Galla by the beginning of the seventeenth century as far as the southern Benadir coast and beyond Malindi. In the process, some Hawiya tribes and their kinsmen, the Ajuran, who had been living along the Benadir coast and possibly in Mejertaniya at least as early as the thirteenth century, were forced to move northwards, southwards and possibly even into the interior. Although the number of Galla involved in this migration was relatively small[33] it is not unlikely that the displacement of some Somali tribes along the Galla route of advance may have created ripples in the Ogaden and northern Somalia which further contributed to the decline of law and order in Adal. Hence, by the beginning of the seventeenth century, with European pirates appearing in the Gulf of Aden, trade on the Somali coast had greatly declined.[34]

The fortunes of Zayla were always closely connected to those of Harar. It was, therefore, badly affected by Harar's decline and the deterioration of law and order in the whole region. Although it continued to recognise the nominal overlordship of Aussa as late as the 1620s, Zayla frequently served, because of its geographical location, as a springboard for contestants for the Imamship of Adal (Aussa). Moreover, the weak amirs of Zayla, who repeatedly drained the town of its defenders and resources, made it an easy prey to the Somali tribes who lived in the hinterland. Hence, in spite of the prosperity of the Red Sea in the last decades of the sixteenth century, Zayla continued to decline. In the 1620s it was captured by the Ottomans but shortly afterwards it fell into the hands of the Yemeni governor of Mukha.

An independent Dankali (Afar) 'sultanate' was in existence even after the rise of Grañ to power.[35] In the south it touched on Adal near the Bay of Tajura and, bypassing Aussa, it touched on Ethiopia near Amhara (Dobba). Its northern border lay beyond the salt depressions at the foot of the Tigre escarpment and the Bay of

Amphila on the coast. At the turn of the sixteenth century, the seat of the Dankali sultan was the village of Rahita, not far from Assab. The authority of the Dankali sultan over different Afar tribes was at best only nominal. The Afar, like most pastoralists, were an extremely egalitarian society. In their case any form of centralised government was even more improbable because the difficult desert which they inhabited caused them to be scattered over vast areas where the functional unit was the family group or, at most, the clan.[36]

The Dankali (Ethiopian) coast has a number of minor ports such as Tajura, Rahita, Baylul, Assab, Edd and Anphila. However, because of the prohibitive conditions of the Dankali desert and the fierceness and lawlessness of its population, these ports, the site of small and impoverished hamlets, were only rarely visited by caravans from the plateau or by trading boats from Arabia.[37] Naturally, the control of the rich valley of Aussa was always a bone of contention between the unruly Dankalis and the masters of Adal. Consequently Afar tribes intermittently raided the valley of Aussa or deeper into the Harar-Chercher plateau. However, in the last quarter of the sixteenth century the Dankalis in their turn came under pressure from the expanding Baraytuma Galla, who raided their territory as far as the coast.

The greatest asset of the Dankali sultanate was the salt plains of Arho to the east of the Tigrean escarpments. These salt mines supplied Ethiopia with most of the raw salt and with all the salt blocks (amoleh) used as currency all over the plateau.[38] The revenue accruing to the Afar from this source was one of the reasons for their co-operation with the rulers of Tigre. After the death of Nur and the gradual disintegration of Adal, or possibly even earlier, the Dankali sultan prudently recognised the nominal overlordship of the kings of Ethiopia. The constant raids of the Baraytuma into Dankalia, which were occasionally directed towards Arho, made such co-operation even more desirable. Nonetheless, the authority of the Ethiopian king carried little weight in the Afar desert, especially in view of the fact that the Dankali sultan could hardly exert any authority over the tribes of the interior.[39]

By the beginning of the seventeenth century Adal, as a political entity, loosely unifying the different Muslim elements of the Chercher-Harar plateau and the coast, had ceased to exist. It had disintegrated into insignificant political units fighting each other despite growing Galla pressure. Cultivation lost ground to pastoral nomadism and Adal's mercantile centres, unable to take advantage of the revival of the Red Sea trade, were in a state of stagnation. No longer did Muslim power, the Ottomans notwithstanding, threaten 'Christian Ethiopia' and in some cases the weak Muslim principalities even nominally recognised the overlordship of the Solomonic monarch. On the other hand, Christian Ethiopia, preoccupied with its internal struggle for power and the Galla migration, abandoned its aggressive policy concerning the Muslim territories and maintained friendly relations with their petty rulers. With the Galla settling between the combatants, the centuries-old struggle between Christian Ethiopia and the Muslim nomads, cultivators and merchant communities disappeared from the history of the Horn of Africa until the nineteenth century.

The Solomonic dynasty and the rise of Galla power

The premature death of Gelawdewos in 1559 constituted a major tragedy for Christian Ethiopia. The deep scars left by Grañ's conquest were still unhealed and the reorganisation of the military-administrative system and the process of socio-political reintegration of the kingdom were far from complete. Moreover, the revival of the national church, sponsored by the enlightened monarch, was far from successful and the Jesuit presence in Ethiopia only helped to rekindle old controversies.

In the Sidama provinces of southern and southwestern Ethiopia ethnic-cultural fusion, supported by northern military colonisation and evangelisation reintroduced by Gelawdewos, was again interrupted before it had time to take root. Even worse, in the partially Muslim eastern and southeastern provinces and districts even the *Chewa* defence system, systematically reconstructed by the monarch, began to disintegrate following Nur's victory and the activities of Muslim armies in Waj and Fatagar. In the north, the Eritrean region was threatened by the Ottomans and in the Falasha provinces coerced assimilation, always strongly resisted, was the cause of serious disturbances and rebellions.

Gelawdewos, who realised the vulnerability of the Ethiopian state and society after the traumatic experience which it had undergone, pardoned the nobles who had betrayed their country and attempted to incorporate this powerful element, always a detriment to Ethiopian unity and royal authority, in his efforts to rehabilitate the framework of the Solomonic state. Nevertheless, nearly always occupied in the war against Adal and, to some extent, with the Galla, he entrusted the administration and protection of most of the country to nobles devoted to him, especially those who had proved their loyalty during Ethiopia's darkest hours, and many of whom were of northern origin. Excluded from the government of the country other nobles, mainly of Amhara-Showan origin and members of the royal family, including the Queen Mother, Sabla Wengel, became jealous and frustrated. But, fearful of the strong monarch, they reconciled themselves to the situation and bided their time.

The death of a king nearly always caused an erosion of the authority of the monarchy and sparked off a power struggle among the court stewards and factions of the feudal-military administration. Queen Mother Sabla Wengel, in Gojjam with the royal court, attempted to avert such a development by having her third son Minas crowned without delay. A captive of the Muslims for nearly ten years and known for his severity and bad temper, Minas was not popular and was even considered a weakling.[40] Anyway, the most likely candidate to succeed Gelawdewos, who did not have male offspring, Minas was also chosen because his mother, his relatives and their allies among the nobility, hoped to rule the country, or become influential in his administration. Indeed, Sabla Wengel and her supporters were determined to whittle down, as soon as possible, the influence of Gelawdewos' favourites, who were absent from the court when Minas was enthroned.[41] Partially instrumental in Minas' succession, Hamalmal, the powerful cousin of the king, was appointed governor of a vast area, including the southeastern provinces.[42] Other members of the royal family and supporters of the Queen Mother replaced Gelawdewos' governors, with the exception of the ones in the northern provinces.

The nobility of 'greater Tigre', with their different languages, their special cultural-historic heritage, many supporters of the order of St. Ewostatewos and Muslims, more often than not remained aloof from the house of Yekuno Amlak.[43] Gelawdewos, however, had appointed many Tigrean nobles to key positions in the administration. Among the most influential was Bahr Nagash Ishaq, staunchly loyal during Grañ's period, who was awarded, as a sign of esteem and trust, the guardianship of the children of

Yaeqob, the monarch's deceased brother. Constantly busy else-where, the monarch undoubtedly expected that this powerful vassal would maintain royal authority in the turbulent north.[44] When Gelawdewos was killed Ishaq was away in Bahr-Midir carefully watching the activities of the Turks and their allies in the peripheries of the kingdom. Inevitably he was not consulted concerning Gelawdewos' succession and was presented with a *fait accompli* when Minas was crowned King of Kings. Still the supporters of the new emperor did not dare challenge this powerful noble, and Ishaq and his father were left governors of Bahr-Midir and Tigre respectively.

Empress Sabla Wengel and the royal court escaped to Gojjam after the Muslim victory. By now the process of Amharisation and assimilation of this rich province had advanced to the point that it was considered part of the core of the kingdom. It was not long, however, before it became clear that Nur ibn Mujahid had no intention of following in Grañ's footsteps and that he was returning to Harar. Hence, Hamalmal, who had previously fought the Adalites, was despatched to deal with the garrisons left by Nur in Fatagar and Waj. Containing the slow advance of the Galla along the verges of the eastern escarpments[45] did not seem important at the time. Ethiopian complacency could be explained at first by the fact that the main thrust of the Galla migration into the highlands had not yet begun.[46] The Galla, moreover, did not have a united leadership nor were they motivated by an ideology (religion), and pastoralist attempts to settle in the plateau, which led to their integration with the local population, were a common phenomenon. After centuries of struggle with the Muslim principa-lities of the east, culminating in the traumatic experience of Grañ's Jihad, such factors became the determining criteria in forming the policy and priorities of the Christian rulers. This misconception concerning their migration and the disregard shown to their power, enabled the Galla during Minas' reign and following his death to penetrate peripheral provinces of the plateau and establish there bases for further expansion.[47]

Notwithstanding tensions between Tigreans, Amhara and Showans these peoples, the core of the Solomonic kingdom, proud of their historic-cultural heritage, were strongly 'ethnic conscious'.[48] This found an expression in a 'chosen people' complex, already evident in the myths concerning the origin of the kingdom.

Although themselves a product of a synthesis between Semitic influences and the local Cushitic culture, the 'semitised Ethiopians'[48a] ironically looked down at other sedentary Cushites of the plateau, even at their Agaw brethren, who continued to contribute to the expansion of their society. As for the southern Cushites, mainly the Sidama, they did not achieve true social equality even when converted to Christianity and integrated in the kingdom.[49]

Considered uncivilised and inferior, even compared to the plateau's Muslims, the coastal pastoralists, when they succeeded in settling along the eastern escarpments, were kept at arm's length by Ethiopian society.[50] Inevitably, the pagan Galla hordes, with their strange customs and social organisation, when they began their great migration to the plateau, seemed even more inferior in the eyes of the semitised Christian elites than the Somalis and Dankalis. Moreover, whereas contacts with the latter were confined to the population of the eastern provinces, many of whom were themselves of the same origin, the Galla soon overran the plateau's heartlands and came directly in contact with the semitised Ethiopians.

Hamalmal failed to re-establish Ethiopian hegemony in the southeastern provinces and, more or less, ignored their slow northward advance along the slopes of the plateau. The *Chewa* of Showa and Ifat were still sufficiently strong, however, to deter a Baraytuma attempt to penetrate the Ethiopian heartland.

An abortive campaign led by Minas against the Falasha only proved his incompetency as a military leader and strengthened the camp of his opponents.[51] The expedition, however, afforded Minas the opportunity to strengthen his authority in the northern provinces, which traditionally enjoyed a measure of autonomy. Detained in the royal camp, Bahr Nagash Ishaq and his father were dismissed from their offices as governors of Bahr-Midir and Tigre respectively and these provinces were given to members of rival Tigrean noble families related to the monarch through marriage.[52]

Changes in the status of different nobles and courtiers were most common in the Ethiopian socio-political structure and dynamics. Normally, the faction out of favour reconciled itself to the new situation and patiently awaited a change in the situation to regain the monarch's favour and occasionally would even contribute to a change in the internal balance of power. Sabla Wengel's party's determination to prevent the pillars of Gelawdewos' government from re-establishing their influence at the court and the character of the monarch notwithstanding, it is difficult to comprehend the bitterness of the struggle which ensued unless the contribution of the Jesuits and the Showan-Amhara origin of the majority of the Empress' supporters is taken into account.

The number of Jesuits and Portuguese soldiers who settled in Ethiopia may have been inconsequential. But their firearms, contacts with Goa and the doctrinaire aggressiveness of the Jesuits which already had a considerable impact on Ethiopian spiritual dynamics during Gelawdewos' reign, were beginning to affect Ethiopian internal politics. The provocative and haughty behaviour of the bigoted Oviedo drove the short-tempered Minas, who at first attempted to befriend the foreigners, notwithstanding his dislike of their dogmas,[53] to persecute the Catholics. Indeed, determined to convert Ethiopia to Catholicism by coercion, Oviedo exacerbated the situation by inciting Ishaq, other nobles and his Portuguese companions, to rebel against their master and, ignorant of the situation in the Indian Ocean, persistently invited the Portuguese authorities to intervene in Ethiopia.[54]

Ethiopian suspicions about Portuguese aspirations concerning their country were influenced by their easier cultural identification with the Muslims of the region than western Christians (especially when represented by the Jesuits), and were to become a factor of increasing importance in the politics of the Horn of Africa from the sixteenth century. Inasmuch as the Jesuits became involved in Ethiopia's internal affairs and attempted to win Goa's support for their plans, they contributed to the general apprehension concerning Portuguese intervention and colonialism. In addition to their bigoted and narrow-minded concept of 'Christian Ethiopia', its church and cultural heritage, they misinterpreted the religious toleration of the Ethiopians and their superficial affiliation to Christianity. Thus, and in order to justify their impolitic behaviour, they provided a distorted picture of the situation and of the motivation of the different factions in Ethiopia.[55]

At the beginning of 1561 Ishaq, who had slipped away from the royal camp, other Tigrean lords and troops shabbily treated by Minas, disaffected Dembiyan nobles and most of the Portuguese rebelled against the monarch and declared his nephew King of Kings.[56] The rebels in Dembiya were quickly defeated and, fearing a junction between Ishaq and the widely expected Portuguese army, Minas chased the *Bahr Nagash* from Tigre to the coast. When the Portuguese expedition did not materialise, the frustrated Ishaq allied himself with Uzdamir Pasha and agreed to cede to him part of the northern plateau. In 1562 Ishaq and Uzdamir invaded Bahr-Midir and crowned another nephew of Minas.[57] The unfortunate Minas, forced to escape to Showa when his army disintegrated under Turkish artillery fire, died at the beginning of 1563 in Amhara, at the beginning of his advance northwards at the head of the new army.[58]

The absence of many provincial governors and powerful nobles, including Hamalmal, from the royal camp when Minas died, was exploited by the ambitious Sabla Wengel. Supported by Minas' wife, the court stewards and the Showan officers with the royal army, she again disregarded accepted succession procedures involving consultations with the nobility, and enthroned Minas' son, Serse Dingil (r. 1563-1597). A boy of fourteen, the new king, it is evident, was chosen because his grandmother and the court stewards hoped to retain their power and the Showan nobles may have wished to re-establish Showa's primacy and gain influence in the administration. Similar coups were not unknown in the past, but the kingdom was now in a state of extreme crisis, nor did the courtiers have the support of any element among the nobility. Indeed, even Sabla Wengel's previous allies in the royal family, including the powerful Hamalmal, resented her highhanded behaviour and refused to recognise Serse Dingil's succession.

For a short time Hamalmal and his followers allied themselves with Ishaq. Invariably, by the beginning of 1564, the common front between Amhara and Tigrean nobles disintegrated because the former feared that the latter, especially Ishaq, might re-establish their predominance in the court. Denuding the eastern provinces of their *Chewa* regiments, thus facilitating the Baraytuma's renewed advance, the irresolute and irresponsible Hamalmal crowned a 'king' of his own and marched from Angot to western Ethiopia and back to Showa, in a futile attempt to regain his predominant position.[59]

Following his victory over Minas, Uzdamir urgently requested reinforcements from the Pasha of Egypt in order to exploit his success. In view of the circumstances his request was quickly granted.[60] An all-out Ottoman attack, supported by local Muslims, could have constituted a serious threat to Ethiopia, convulsed by civil war. In addition to the northern Muslim principalities, the sultanate of Adal and the armies left by Nur ibn Mujahid in the southeastern provinces, large Muslim forces, which survived Gelawdewos' victory, were active in Damot and Dembiya and Islam was revived through the increased activities of caravan merchants, especially in the Sidama south, where the Sultan of Hadya was strengthening his autonomy and military power.[61] Their bitter experience in 1557, however, taught the northern Muslims caution and Nur, preoccupied with the Galla, could not, if he was approached, join the Ottomans. Most important, when he heard of Minas' death Ishaq chased his ally Uzdamir back to the coast. Moreover, just when the Turkish reinforcements arrived at the end of 1563 Uzdamir died and, after limited successes in the war against the *Bahr Nagash,* the new Pasha was ordered with his troops to Yemen.[62] Be that as it may, frustrated by his inability to play an active role in the struggle for power in Ethiopia due to his preoccupation with the Ottomans, Ishaq even abandoned his 'king'.

In the coming years the power of the feudal lords constantly increased because it was unchecked by any central authority. The lords, able to retain all the revenues of the areas under their control, continued to build their military power. In the Ethiopian feudal system control of land and trade was a synonym for power and nobles and warlords used their armies to expand their territories. While this process was going on many *Chewa* regiments found it prudent to support the cause of local potentates. Others abandoned their strongholds and became nothing more than highway robbers. As the country deteriorated into a state of anarchy, the centrifugal forces became completely triumphant. Nevertheless, the Solomonic monarchy was still considered a pillar of the semitised Christian kingdom and the nobles, as well as generals, could not yet dispense with it. As the chronicler wisely commented:[63] 'les gens d'Ethiopie aiment d'avoir un roi.'

Rejected by the nobility, deserted by the army and with no sources of revenue, Serse Dingil's cause seemed at first hopeless. Yet, by the second part of 1564, the tide was beginning to turn. By 1566 the church leaders, lesser nobility and some army command-ers began to flock back to his camp. In the following year, assured of recognition of their governorships and semi-autonomous status, even the powerful nobles who had opposed Serse Dingil's accession, including Ishaq and Harbo, Dembiya's governor, paid allegiance to the king.[64]

Accelerated in the first year of Serse Dingil's reign, the disintegration of royal authority enabled the regio-centric feudal class to usurp the power and resources of the monarchy. Serse Dingil's long reign of more than fifty years did not lead to a meaningful consolidation of the authority of the King of Kings and the Galla migration even prevented the superficial unification of the country by him. In an attempt to follow Gelawdewos' policy, the monarch strove, whenever he could, to win the recognition and support of the feudal nobility by appeasement and, when necessary, by coercion. But lacking his grandfather's ability and *savoir faire* he failed to win the respect and, to some extent, the co-operation of the aristocracy and despite personal bravery and able generalship he did not succeed in inspiring devotion and discipline among his soldiers. He neglected, moreover, the opportunity to harness the national church to his efforts to maintain the framework and unity of the kingdom. In the final analysis his reign, marked by major policy blunders, resulted, in the long run, in the collapse of the Solomonic dynasty and undermined 'semitised Ethiopia'.

In a socio-political system such as that of Ethiopia, the monarch and his mentors were not unaware of the correlation between sources of revenue and the predominancy of the central government. Having established his authority, although nominal, in the central and northern provinces, Serse Dingil launched several expeditions into the western and southwestern provinces. These fertile and populous parts of the plateau, including Damot and the cluster of Sidama kingdoms around Enarea, were not only an important asset *per se*, but also the main source of Ethiopia's luxury products and the focus of its caravan trade. They were also the home of flourishing communities of Muslim merchants and military elements, the remnants of Grañ's armies, whose power and importance was growing in the area.[65]

Once he had overcome rebels in the west and received the tribute of Enarea and its sister-states, the monarch marched in 1568 to the south against the Muslim ruler of Hadya, who following Gelawdewos' death, using mercenaries from Adal and Arabia, had built a formidable army and re-established his autonomy. Deprived of the support of Nur, who died in 1567, and his generals in Waj and

Fatagar, whom Serse Dingil won over, Hadya's army was destroyed.[66]

Until 1571 Serse Dingil remained in the Sidama south to consolidate his authority there. He did not attempt, it seems, to reconstruct the *Chewa* infrastructure of the region nor to reintroduce coerced evangelisation in the Sidama principalities, as Gelawdewos had. The monarch even failed to regain control of the peripheral eastern and southeastern provinces and districts lost to the Muslims and Galla, possibly because he may have considered them a barrier against Adal.[67]

Unlike his predecessors, Serse Dingil did not comprehend the crucial strategic and integrative importance of the presence of the royal army in the south. Considering the re-establishment of royal authority his first priority, he decided in 1571 to consolidate his government in the northern provinces and regulate his relations with their powerful governors who ignored him. The monarch was still contemptible of the Galla power, notwithstanding the accelerated advance of the Baraytuma who, after the initiation of the previous *luba* in 1563/4, submerged most of Angot and subsequently began to raid Amhara and Begemder.[68] He did not hesitate, therefore, to entrust the defence of the south to Azmatch Daharagot[69] and the forces under his command, while he took the royal armies and many *Chewa* with him to Dembiya.

While the monarch was away in the south, Harbo of Dembiya and Ishaq of Tigre systematically consolidated their position. They substantially increased their armies, traded with the Turks, obtained from them firearms and could be considered virtually autonomous. On the approach of the emperor Harbo prudently reiterated his allegiance to him and was reconfirmed as governor of Dembiya. Following his example, Ishaq came to Begemder in 1572 to submit to his master. Wishing to honour this powerful vassal and in view of Tigre's special status, the monarch took in marriage the *Bahr Nagash's* sister and piled upon him many honours.[70] Informed of a new Ottoman invasion of Bahr-Midir, Ishaq hastily departed for Tigre, whilst the king turned back to the south when he heard that the Borana had penetrated the Sidama provinces.

As the Baraytuma began their advance into the Harar-Chercher plateau and along the verges of the eastern escarpments in the 1550s they gradually vacated Bali with its excellent grazing lands and left it to their Borana brethren. Invariably, this development relieved the population pressure in the region. But during the coming decades, due to natural growth and the migration of additional Borana clans into Bali, the population pressure increased once again whilst Borana herds rapidly multiplied in the new environments.[71] The Borana's avenue of advance northwards was, however, blocked by the Baraytuma who settled in Dawaro and the Harari plateau. To the west, the provinces adjoining the Rift Valley were defended by local Muslim forces, supported by the mighty Hadyan army with its excellent cavalry.[72]

With the rise to power of a new *luba* in 1571/2 and the rituals related to the initiation into a new *gada*, the Galla, exploiting Serse Dingil's unwise policy, began to invade Ethiopia proper from several directions. The Baraytuma increased the momentum of their migration and the Marawa, followed by the powerful Karayu tribe, raided westwards through Amhara as far as Begemder, Gojjam and northern Showa.[73] The Borana were quick to exploit the power vacuum created by Serse Dingil's activities in the south. The troops of Azmatch Daharagot and the regiments left behind could not compensate for the absence of the royal army from the area. Thus, while the ruler was in Dembiya, the Borana Galla in Bali and Dawaro crossed the Rift Valley into Sidama – populated southern Ethiopia – sending raiding parties as far as Showa.

Showa was considered for a long time the centre of the kingdom[74] and members of the royal family had estates in this province. Ordering *Chewa* and governors from provinces along the way to join his army Serse Dingil rapidly marched southwards and came upon the main Borana camp near Lake Zway. The tribe(s) who spearheaded the Borana migration moved into the southern plateau *en masse* with their dependants and vast herds. Unable to travel quickly they did not succeed in escaping back to Bali and the carnage of the Galla was terrible.[75]

Their setback notwithstanding, the Borana renewed their westward migration immediately after the monarch left the area. However, they prudently adopted thereafter the tactics which had proved successful in the Baraytuma encounters with the Ethiopians along the eastern escarpments.

Refraining from presenting the enemy with a 'hard' target, a raiding party accomplished its limited objectives and quickly retreated to a pre-prepared forward base or to a rear base, where the majority of the tribe and its cattle were located. The terrorised population, conditioned throughout centuries to leave fighting to the professionals, rather preferred to escape to sheltered places than face the Galla.[76] The 'scorched earth' left by the Galla prevented the Ethiopian army, lacking a suitable logistic infrastructure, from following them for more than a few days. Galla disunity and dispersion, moreover, made any Ethiopian attempt to annihilate them in the peripheries of the plateau impractical. A disadvantage when facing strong Ethiopian or Adali forces, the disunity of the Galla was more than compensated for by their ability to attack simultaneously in different areas to the bewilderment of their enemies. Such tactics seldom failing, they demoralised the Ethiopians, eroded the economic framework of the monarchy and facilitated further migration into the plateau.

Be that as it may, as long as the Ethiopian defence system of *Chewa* supported by the iron fist of a strong royal army was still relatively intact, the Galla could not hope to migrate into the Ethiopian-controlled plateau. At this stage the Ethiopian army, vastly superior numerically, was no match for the Galla. If they were to move into Ethiopia, encumbered by their cattle and dependants, they would lose the advantage of surprise and mobility and become an easy prey for the Ethiopians. Even raiding parties in most cases had to retreat quickly beyond the Ethiopian lines in order not to be trapped between the royal army and the *Chewa* stationed near the border. Ethiopia's defences were gravely damaged by the lethargy of its rulers when the Baraytuma overran Angot and parts of Amhara in the 1560s.[77] Indeed, foolishly disregarding the increasing momentum of Galla raids into Ethiopia's heartlands in the 1570s, the monarch, practically abandoning the southern and eastern provinces, continued to carry out his disastrous decision to reorganise the country's military system.

Ethiopia's military system reorganised

Preoccupied in the first years of his reign with re-establishing his predominance in different parts of the country, Serse Dingil, on many occasions, was confronted by the fact that the *Chewa* were undependable and as much a danger to the monarchy and the country as the feudal forces.[78] He became, therefore, convinced of the need to reform the traditional military system and create a 'national' army. Eventually this led to Serse Dingil's decision to dismantle the *Chewa* defence infrastructure in critical provinces just at the time when the Borana and Baraytuma clans simultaneously erupted into Ethiopia. This disastrous decision was the outcome of the king's mistaken sequence of priorities and distorted perception of the Galla migration and the contempt in which he and Ethiopian society in general held these 'uncouth and wild' pastoralists.

The first steps to build a royal army were taken by Serse Dingil between 1564 and 1567. Several *Chewa* in a state of disintegration were enticed by the king to his camp. After 1567, having substantially strengthened his position, Serse Dingil prevented the armies of governors who died or were defeated by him from changing allegiance or disintegrating and formed them into new *Chewa* which he kept with him. As the king's power increased, *Chewa* in provinces which submitted to him were frequently ordered to join his army in its numerous campaigns.[79] Thus the nucleus of a substantial royal army was established.

A revolutionary principle which Serse Dingil attempted to introduce was that fiefs *(gult)* for the maintenance of the *Chewa* did not necessitate their being stationed in the same area nor in peripheral or strategic provinces. Rather the opposite. The monarch believed that he could exercise better control over the regiments and their commanders if they were far from their source of subsistence, in his camp or near it.[80] A permanently mobilised royal army, Serse Dingil demonstrated on several occasions, could march immediately against the enemy and thus dispense with the period of mobilisation, which normally took several weeks. Even when a larger army was required, provincial *Chewa* and governors could join the royal army while it was advancing.

The monarch believed that the rigid defence system, incorporating a line of *Chewa* outposts and the royal army, camped nearby, was no longer suitable in the new situation which Ethiopia faced after Adal's decline. It tied down the monarch and most of his armed forces to peripheral areas, leaving the rest of the country to the treacherous nobility. Disregarding the seriousness of the Galla migration into Ethiopia in the 1570s, Serse Dingil literally stripped many provinces of their *Chewa* garrisons, thus opening the country to Galla migration. In addition, the new royal army created grave logistic and disciplinary problems and, notwithstanding the military ability and personal bravery of the monarch, it rather aggravated the discontent, rapacity and disloyalty of the *Chewa* and contributed to the decline of stability and law and order in the country.[81]

Increasingly disillusioned with the *Chewa*, the monarch began to strengthen systematically his bodyguard battalions. Composed mainly of emancipated slaves or soldiers of non-'Ethiopian' origin, these units, devoted to the king, gradually grew into corps of cavalry, infantry, musketeers and artisans such as the *Querban, Hawash, Aqet Zar* and since 1579 the *Nar* ('Turk Basha').[82] Although he continued to appoint his kinsmen and other nobles from the traditional ruling class as governors of important provinces, Serse Dingil surrounded himself with officials and officers whom he had elevated from the ranks and who reached the highest positions in the army and administration and to whom he gave in marriage his daughters or other royal princesses. On the other hand, because he dispensed with many customs which separated the monarch from his subordinates, some offices of the court, including that of the *Bitwadad,* held by the traditional aristocracy, became superfluous or declined in importance.

In the short run Serse Dingil's attempts to re-establish his authority, even nominally through compromises with the feudal lords or whenever necessary by coercion, more or less succeeded. However, his military reforms completely backfired. The Galla took advantage of the dismantling of the traditional defences, whereas Ethiopia's agricultural population, the majority of whom did not identify with the Solomonic kingdom, were unable and unwilling to defend themselves against the Galla migrants. The reorganisation of the army, moreover, created new tensions among the nobility and the military, rather eroded the stability of the country and produced a new military aristocracy. With no loyalty to Ethiopia's semitised heritage, this aristocracy, after the monarch's death, even challenged the authority of the Solomonic dynasty.

The collapse of Tigrean separatism and the Ottoman threat

Serse Dingil's easy victory over the Borana in 1572 rather contributed to the disregard which the monarch demonstrated concerning the Galla migration and his unwise choice of priorities. Shortly after this episode, he left the south for Damot.[83] In 1572-1574, despite renewed Borana migration into the south, their increasing pressure on Showa and the intensification of Baraytuma raids into Begemder, Dembiya and on the borders of Tigre and Gojjam, the monarch remained in Damot. From thence he raided the Cushitic and other peoples to the west for slaves and booty.[84]

While in Damot, Serse Dingil became aware that Harbo, Ishaq and other nobles were plotting against him. Harbo died, however, in 1574 and the monarch quickly marched into Dembiya to prevent his army, especially a *Chewa* corps placed under his command, from joining Ishaq. In Dembiya he suppressed the rebellion of Muslims and other military elements settled there[85] and established his direct authority over the province. Consequently, the only powerful feudal lord who still defied the monarch and retained a semi-autonomous position in the politically and economically important Tigre was Bahr Nagash Ishaq.

Unreconciled to Serse Dingil's government, Ishaq did not believe that the monarch had truly forgiven him and that he could indefinitely accept his autonomous position. Related to the house of Bora Salawa through his mother, the monarch, Ishaq suspected, was intentionally disregarding his frequent requests for reinforcements in view of increasing Ottoman as well as Galla pressures,[86] in order to erode his power so as to be able to replace him with one of his kinsmen. Bishop Oviedo, moreover, incited the *Bahr Nagash* and the Tigrean nobility against the emperor and encouraged them to apply to Portugal for help.

Until his death in 1577 Oviedo continued to believe in a coerced conversion of Ethiopia to Catholicism and repeatedly wrote to Goa and Rome about this matter. Two small Portuguese boats, arriving in Baylul in 1575, brought letters to the Jesuits which could be interpreted as announcing the departure for Ethiopia in the following year of a Portuguese expeditionary force. Informed of the contents of the letters, Ishaq lost all caution, renounced his allegiance to Serse Dingil and supported the claim to the throne of another member of the royal family.[87]

Despite the huge army at his disposal and the support of the heads of the Ethiopian church, the monarch refrained from attacking Ishaq. Many nobles in his camp warned him against the consequences of challenging the powerful armies of Tigre and recommended prudence;[88] they pointed out that, if pressed, Ishaq might again turn to the Turks, who had considerably reinforced their army in *Habesh* since 1572.

Undoubtedly induced by the traditional delicate relationship between the Solomonic dynasty and the Tigrean nobility, the monarch's cautious handling of Ishaq was also influenced by his ambivalent feeling concerning Portugal and his wish to avoid a clash with it. Admiring and fearing its military-technical ability and imperialist drive, Serse Dingil, although he disliked the Jesuits and rejected their dogmas, like his predecessors desired Portuguese aid, believing it to be an instant antidote for the complex problems which Ethiopia faced,[89] but was apprehensive of the implications of developing relations with the Catholic power. When informed about the contents of the letters received by the Jesuits, he despatched, therefore, a few Dembiyan Portuguese to the coast to assure their countrymen of his friendship for, and toleration of, the Catholics.[90]

In 1576 the monarch learned that the Sultan of Adal, by now co-operating with the Ottomans, had invaded Hadya. Maintaining a traumatic fear of a Jihad which would reunite all the Horn's Muslims and Turks, Serse Dingil quickly settled his differences with Ishaq, marched southwards and defeated the Adali sultan in Bali.[91]

In spite of the increased momentum of Galla raids, the monarch moved his camp back to Damot shortly after he had defeated the Adalis. But informed that Ishaq had allied himself, in the meantime, with the Turks, he stripped Showa and many other provinces of their *Chewa* and in 1577/8 began to march to Tigre. Only the pleadings of his mother and the Showan nobility caused him to turn against the Borana, who had begun to overrun the heart of the kingdom. But once he had defeated the main Borana body, in the southwestern part of Showa, the monarch resumed his campaign against Ishaq.[92]

The emperor's tactics to erode the Tigrean nobility's support for the *Bahr Nagash* were on the whole very successful. Thus, at the end of 1578, when Serse Dingil approached Tigre, the local feudal lords joined his camp and Ishaq was forced to retreat beyond the Mareb. Shortly afterwards, at the beginning of 1579, the monarch soundly defeated the joint army of his enemies and the *Bahr Nagash* and the Turkish Pasha perished on the battlefield.[93]

It has already been pointed out[94] that, although considered the nucleus of the Solomonic kingdom, differences existed between the semitised components of this nucleus. The Amhara provinces were purposely classified as the core area of the kingdom, while Tigre, in the wider sense of the term, constituted the first 'concentric circle' around the core of the kingdom. The variation was not only the outcome of the character of the administration, the language(s) and heritage of the population, but also emanated, to a certain extent, from the stronger links of Tigre with the Muslim-Mediterranean cultural sphere and the sensitivities of an older brother dominated by a younger one, which led to an increasing sense of regionalism in Tigre vis-à-vis the Solomonic kingdom.

Tigre never reconciled itself to the loss of its primacy to the generally Amhara-dominated Solomonic kingdom. Following the holocaust brought by Grañ's Jihad, the Tigrean nobility felt that it, more than anything else, the Portuguese excluded, had saved the Christian semitised kingdom. Consequently, after Gelawdewos' death, when it forfeited its special position and was again reduced to the role of a junior partner in the Ethiopian polity[95,] the feeling of injustice became even more acute in Tigre. It was to be expected, therefore, that when the centre of the kingdom moved to the (relatively) newly Amharised areas around Lake Tana the Tigreans became even more resentful of their inferior position in the Solomonic kingdom. This discontent was to resurface, on numerous occasions, whatever positions Tigrean nobles held at the time in the country's administration, shortly after the death of Bahr Nagash Ishaq and until the 'Zamana Masafint', when Tigrean separatist tendencies reached a peak.[96]

The war of 1576/9 culminated in the most serious Ottoman effort to conquer Ethiopia, and its failure meant the end of the Turkish threat to the Christian kingdom. Nevertheless, Ottoman campaigns in northern Ethiopia in the sixteenth century, and their involvement in its commercial activities, helped strengthen Islam in the Eritrean region and contributed to its development as a special entity following the renewed Turkish invasion of Ethiopia in the nineteenth century.

Economy and expansionism

Ethiopian trade was quick to respond to the increasing demand for its exports resulting from the region's prosperity. Many more indigenous and foreign Muslims, and some non-Muslim merchants, became active in the caravan trade between the coast,

Sudan, western and southwestern Ethiopia, despite the decline of stability and law and order in the plateau. Subsequently, the Funjis of Sennar, but even more so the Turks in Massawa and Sawakin, encouraged this trade which brought them extremely handsome revenues.[97] In fact, Ottoman attempted expansionism from Sawakin and Massawa was economically motivated.

Additional Ottoman eruptions into Bahr Midir in the last decade of his reign notwithstanding, Serse Dingil maintained, on the whole, cordial relations with the Turks and used their good offices to develop his trade, exportation of slaves included.[98] In reality had Serse Dingil wished to rid himself of the Ottoman presence on the coast he could easily have done so, following his victory in 1579. He reconciled himself, moreover, to the traditional *status quo* because of economic considerations. On their part the Ottomans in most cases facilitated commercial activities between the coast and the plateau, which brought the local Pasha enormous revenues until about the middle of the seventeenth century.[99]

Partly motivated by economic considerations, partly by political expediency and consciously or unconsciously because of the Galla migration, the emperor had been devoting most of his time and military resources since 1572 to consolidating his government in the northern and western provinces. This policy led to renewed Ethiopian expansionism in the region and further facilitated the intensified trade relations with Sennar.[100] Following his victory in Tigre, Serse Dingil began to consolidate and expand his government in the northern province. The targets of persistent Solomonic efforts to break their power, the Falasha of Simen, Wogera and Dembiya were among the victims of the monarch's policy. A series of military expeditions which he conducted against them from his camp near Lake Tana greatly reduced their power and number. The enfeeblement of the Falasha facilitated the colonisation of their provinces by Amhara, Amarised elements and Tigreans and the assimilation of the local Agaw, a process which had begun in previous centuries and contributed to the transfer of the centre of gravity of the Solomonic kingdom from Showa to Gojjam and finally to Dembiya.

An Agaw people, with a composite archaic Jewish-Cushitic culture, the Falasha made their appearance on the stage of Ethiopian history in the tenth century (although they must have emerged as a political-cultural entity much earlier), when they dealt the death blow to the Axumite empire. In the following centuries the power of their empire was so formidable that the Zagwe, and especially the Solomonic dynasty, considered them a major rival, if not a threat to their existence.

Unfortunately our knowledge of Falasha history, culture and society is extremely limited. The Falasha-Agaw remained illiterate until modern times. Even if their priests may have mastered the Ethiopic script, used for the translation of the Bible and other religious and prayer books, their physical and cultural destruction by the Amhara kingdom was so complete that no written Falasha sources are known to exist.[101] Notwithstanding contributions of scholars of the old school such as Jacques Feitlowitz, or modern scholars such as Marcel Cohen and Wolf Leslau, the little information about the Falasha comes mainly from biased Ethiopian sources who mention them *en passant*, or from romantic Jewish travellers, who visited nearby countries, or Jewish messianic literature, which is of limited value.[102] Nevertheless, the glimpses of Falasha history, socio-political organisations and religion afforded us by the available sources, only whet one's appetite and excite the imagination.

In its heyday the Falasha kingdom(s) must have been extensive. It was composed of all the territories west of the Takazze as far as, and beyond, Lake Tana (possibly with offshoots among the Gaffat of Damot). It is unclear, however, whether this kingdom(s) had a centralised authority or whether it was a loose confederation of kingdoms and principalities or even tribal groups. A matriarchal society, its queens (Judith) and kings (Gideon) frequently led the Falasha in battle against their neighbours. Yet the extent of the authority of their rulers and their system of government is unknown. In the fifteenth and sixteenth centuries (when Jewish writers and travellers described them as the powerful descendants of the Ten Tribes), these rulers were fighting for survival against Christian Ethiopia. Indeed, although by the sixteenth century the backbone of their power had been broken and they had lost their more fertile territories and been driven to the mountainous parts of their homeland, their resistance was far from crushed. It still took the Ethiopians more than two centuries of merciless wars and enormous efforts to nearly eradicate the Falasha (and subjugate the Agaw).

Disregarding the religious aspect, the struggle between Ethiopia and the Falasha kingdom(s) could be considered a rivalry between the Christian and Judaised semitised-Cushitic political spheres over the supremacy in northern Ethiopia and the control of its Agaw human resources. That the vast Falasha-Agaw enclave was wedged between the Tigrean and newly Amharised-Agaw components of the Ethiopian-Solomonic polity and that it controlled outstandingly important trade routes undoubtedly made Solomonic Ethiopia more determined to destroy the rival entity. It only followed, therefore, that in contradiction to their generally tolerant policy concerning the Sidama of the south, the Solomonic monarchs insisted on the conversion and complete assimilation of the Falasha-Agaw population and that the competition over political hegemony and resources assumed a religious dimension which required the eradication of the politico-cultural framework, representing the 'enemies of Christ'. The continuous campaigns against the Falasha were accompanied, therefore, by their systematic dispossession from their land and their debasement and persecution unless they assimilated completely in the Christian-Ethiopian society.

Be that as it may, the intermittent eruptions of Falasha wars in Simen, Wogera and Welkayt or even in Dembiya (and Agaw uprisings in Wag and Lasta) were considered by the Solomonic monarchs in the sixteenth century an unquestionable priority. Moreover, by the seventeenth century, with Ethiopia's effective borders rapidly shrinking as a result of the Galla migration, it became more imperative than ever to crush the Falasha-Agaw resistance, colonise their territories, assimilate their population and integrate them in the Christian semitised kingdom, in the heart of which they were located.

Ethiopian expansionism in the western-northwestern parts of the plateau, inhabited by Cushitic Agaw and Sidama peasants, 'Arab' and Hamaj pastoralists and negroid cultivators and hunters, differed in character from the process in the northern provinces. The fertile provinces of the west produced vast quantities of agricultural commodities, which served to feed the enormous royal camp and army. Yet the fact that these provinces were a major source of Ethiopia's export products and slaves,[103] some of whom were recruited into the bodyguard battalions, must have been a major incentive. It was also bound to cause increasing tension with the Funjis in Sennar.

Serse Dingil's campaigns west of Lake Tana, in Damot and beyond it, were not accompanied, it is claimed, by the colonisation of these areas and a serious attempt to integrate its population by evangelisation. An important component of the ethnic synthesis of the Ethiopian kingdom, with their decentralised socio-political framework, the western Agaw were ideal material for assimilation. But the monarch rarely encouraged evangelisation and the conversion and integration of the Agaw in the west was spontaneous. Catholic sources, in fact, accuse Serse Dingil of purposely refusing to convert the peoples of the region because he wished to raid and enslave them.[104] Moreover, we are told that the emperor did not have any compunction about the ravages committed by his vast army in these areas, because these territories were not considered an integral part of semitised Ethiopia and their population remained pagan.[105] Nevertheless, a distinction should be made between central Gojjam and Damot, generally Christian and relatively amharised, and the more westerly peripheries of the plateau, which were pagan and less civilised.

Since the first years of his reign Serse Dingil had endeavoured to assert his authority over the rich Sidama kingdoms of the southwest, the terminus of Ethiopia's caravan trade. The economic importance of this region was greatly enhanced by the increasing prosperity of the Red Sea trade and the demand for Ethiopia's luxury products. Hence, notwithstanding the continuous wars and the Galla eruptions in the plateau, Ethiopia's caravan trade continued to intensify. The attraction of the southwestern plateau did not, however, emanate just from the revenue of the trade of the region, but also from the substantial tax in gold paid annually to the Ethiopian monarch, if he was able to show the flag, at least occasionally, in the region.[106]

Muslim sources[107], mainly interested in trade and religion, contribute little to our knowledge of Sidama socio-political organisation and culture. Unfortunately Ethiopian chronicles and other sources tell us even less about the southern Cushites. Modern scholars, mainly linguists and anthropologists, have added somewhat to our understanding of the peoples and history of the Sidama territories. Most of our meagre knowledge about the kingdoms and principalities of the south, their social and political dynamics in the post-mediaeval period, was contributed, however, by the Jesuits who participated in the abortive expedition sent by emperor

Susinyos in 1613 to the coast of the Indian Ocean, strangely enough by way of the southwestern and southern plateaux.

Damot, the most powerful Cushitic polity until the fourteenth century, probably served as a link between the Sidama and Agaw kingdoms and principalities. But when visited by the Jesuits it was already partly overrun by the Galla and partly amharised and governed by Ethiopians. The kingdoms of Enarea and Jinjero in the seventeenth century serve as a prototype of a Sidama monarchy simply because of the source material made available by the Jesuits who visited the region.

The Sidama kingdoms emerged out of a process of social evolution enhanced by their increasing commercial importance and the intensification of caravan trade in the region. Pagan, unless their original culture was influenced by outsiders, the Sidama monarchical institution evolved many elements of divine kingship, probably as a means to induce centralisation and to strengthen their unity. But the population infrastructure being tribal confederacies, the authority of the monarchs of these kingdoms, far from absolute, depended on a council of elders representing the ruling class of the different components and interests of the kingdom. Relatively small, the kingdoms proper served as a core for an additional circle of territories which, to different degrees, recognised the authority of the monarch. This authority was upheld, *inter alia*, by a small army composed of slaves, but in times of need the monarch could call upon the support of the ruling class and its retainers or even mobilise forces from the different affiliated territories.

The economy of the Sidama kingdoms was based on agriculture and cattle-raising. It was dependent on the labour of a large number of slaves obtained through periodic wars with neighbouring territories, or purchased in the markets. But trade was also important because of the revenues accruing from it and because it contributed to the ability of the ruler to reward his supporters, the officers of the court and his soldiers. Most of the trade items, however, were not produced locally but were brought to the markets of the southwest from further west and south. It is evident that control of trade, markets and trade routes were major factors in the rise of the power of Sidama kingdoms such as Hadya (and Damot), whose armies became formidable and their size substantial. In most instances, however, the Sidama kingdoms remained small, weak and disunited. This constant rivalry among them and their internal struggle for power made them an easy prey for aggressive external powers who coveted this rich region.[108]

Superficially implanted in the southwestern kingdoms in previous centuries, Christianity in the Omo-Gibe basin was quickly eradicated by Grañ's conquest. It seems that Gelawdewos led his army into the region on several occasions and in the light of his policy he probably attempted to revive Christianity there.[109] The chronicler of Serse Dingil, however, credits the reintroduction of the faith to Enarea and its sister kingdoms to this monarch, especially in 1586. The Sidama rulers may have welcomed evangelisation because they wished to avoid being pillaged. But the zeal and the use of the national church attributed to the emperor when he revived Christianity in the Omo-Gibe area rather indicates his special interest in the integration of these economically important principalities into his kingdom.[110] Moreover, from Serse Dingil's chronicle it is evident that the monarch was required to negotiate with the southern Sidama and could not dictate to them. Hence he agreed to forego half of the customary tax in gold before Enarea's council of elders agreed to the conversion of their country.[111]

Additional expeditions led by the monarch to the southwest in the 1590s coincided with the migration of the Borana, especially the Mecha group, into Damot and towards Enarea. Supreme efforts were needed in Serse Dingil's last years, therefore, to maintain the road between Gojjam, Damot and the southwest open and to protect Gojjam against Galla attacks.[112]

Galla settlement in the plateau

Until about 1580 Serse Dingil and most of the Ethiopian nobility, not directly affected by the Galla migration, dismissed this phenomenon as a secondary or even a temporary problem. They did not seem to comprehend the unique nature of this migration and its repercussions on their kingdom, institutions and society and considered the Galla another pastoralist people seeking land to settle in, and empty land was plentiful in the plateau. Paradoxically, Ethiopia's rulers were far more concerned with Tigrean separatism, combined with an unrealistic dread of a Portuguese invasion and a traumatic fear of a new Ottoman-Muslim conquest of their country. The relatively easy victories over the Galla in 1572 and 1577 only served to strengthen their contempt for the Galla and justify their assumption that they did not constitute a serious threat to the kingdom. The Ethiopians still did not realise that the organisation of Galla society and its military machine limited the effect of such victories on the momentum of Galla migration. Subsequently between 1572 and 1579 the Galla were able to overrun most of the southern and part of the central plateau.

After his victory over Ishaq and the Turks, with his prestige at its peak and a huge army at his disposal, Serse Dingil could still curb the Galla advance and possibly even force them back to the peripheries of Ethiopia. But instead of a carefully planned campaign, utilising all the resources at his command against the Galla, the monarch preferred to fight the Falasha 'who had shed the blood of Christ'.[113] For this purpose he mobilised *Chewa* from all over the country, including the few which remained in the south. Thus the Galla migration was able to continue to gather momentum and by the 1580s it was inconceivable that the wheel could be turned back.

By 1570, exploiting the topography of Amhara and the character of its government and population, the Baraytuma began to raid westwards into Ethiopia's heartlands, as far as Gojjam and Dembiya. In the 1570s and 1580s, using Angot and Amhara (where the Wollo group began to settle) as their main bases they (mainly the Karayu-Azebu) pillaged Tigre, Begemder, northern Showa and parts of Gojjam. The Borana renewed their westward advance immediately after the departure of Serse Dingil in 1572. No longer hampered by the network of *Chewa* and the presence of the royal army, they submerged the southern provinces and by 1576/7 penetrated Showa. In the coming years the numerous clans of the Mecha group moved west of Showa and began to raid Damot and the nearby territories. Concurrently, their Tulama brothers began to settle in western and northwestern Showa and to raid Gojjam across the Abbay. During the 1580s, while the Abitchu penetrated southern Showa, the Mecha and related groups occupied Bizamo and overran a large part of Damot. From there or from Showa their Sadetcha clans continued to expand toward the Omo-Gibe basin while, at the same time, their Afra-Gudru clans reached the Abbay from the south and increased their pressure northwards on Gojjam and westward on Damot.[114]

The Borana and the Baraytuma unknowingly exploited Serse Dingil's disastrous decision to reorganise Ethiopia's military system in order to penetrate the centre of Ethiopia. Once they had gained a firm foothold in the plateau about 1580, it was next to impossible to check their advance, as each Galla group pragmatically followed a route, dictated by the topography of their new environment, into the different parts of the plateau. Skirting easily defended high grounds and other natural obstacles which nullified their advantages, the Galla continued their advance leaving behind enclaves of unconquered areas. Adapting themselves to the use of horses, weapons and tactics more suitable to fight the Ethiopians, the Galla became more than a match for the individual governors and *Chewa* commanders who attempted to block their way. The complete attrition of the forces of Azmatch Daharagot, who had been posted back to the south in 1579, and the inability of the fierce Maya bowmen to withstand the Galla thrust, were typical of the new situation.[115]

If strategically positioned in the plateau, the royal army could still change the outcome of the struggle between individual governors and *Chewa* and the Galla, or seriously punish migrating Galla clans after their initial success, when retreating to their rear base encumbered with booty. Unfortunately for Solomonic Ethiopia, it was nearly always absent from the heartlands of the kingdom or the crucial provinces attacked by the Galla and was engaged in conquest or pillaging of peripheral Agaw and Sidama territories. To quote the words of the monk Bahrey[116]: 'All this befell because our king ... was absent ... He was victorious wherever he went, but his generals were defeated because he was not with them.' Although Bahrey refers to a Baraytuma raid on Dembiya about 1585, his words can be applied to the unwise shortsighted attitude of the monarch in general.

In the second part of the 1580s, following growing pressure on Damot and Showa and increasing raids on Dembiya, Serse Dingil decided to stem, it seems, a new wave of Galla migration. Repeating the strategy he used in 1572 and 1577, he rapidly advanced to Waj and the Rift Valley lakes district, the key to Showa and the Sidama south. But when he reached his destination, the king did not find any Galla there. Running low on provisions the monarch abandoned the region, again without attempting to deal systematically with the Galla migration, and turned to the southwestern provinces.[117] Subsequently the effective borders of

Ethiopia and the territories controlled by the monarch continued to shrink. When the emperor died in 1597 Showa was progressively separated from the kingdom, whose centre was removed to Dembiya. Moreover, in addition to the provinces submerged until the 1580s, the Galla overran Bizamo, parts of Damot and other areas of the southwest.[118]

The Galla who had penetrated Adal and Ethiopia since about the middle of the sixteenth century, like other pastoralist societies, were egalitarian in the extreme. They did not have an authoritative leadership and obedience to their elected officers was optional. Disunited despite their common socio-political institutions and legendary ancestors, the functional unit when the Galla began to invade Ethiopia was the tribe or the clan. Their expansion over a vast area and the new problems which they faced in the plateau gave rise to the creation of new confederations and alliances, but also polarised traditional grievances and created new rivalries.[119] Finding their political, social and cultural institutions inadequate in their new environment, depending on circumstances and the society with which they were confronted, they were not averse to assimilation. This, however, was a lengthy process, which differed from one area to another. One of the first steps taken in this direction was the employment of Galla auxiliary forces by the Ethiopian ruling class.

The practice of employing Galla contingents began in the 1570s but possibly even earlier. Hence the Galla units which served in the army of Bahr Nagash Ishaq in 1578 are mentioned by the chronicler *en passant*. By 1590 we are told of many Galla warriors deployed by Serse Dingil in various campaigns. When Galla pressure on Damot continued to increase it was only commonsense that friendly Galla were used against their invasion, whereas other Galla clans were deployed to stiffen the line of defence formed around Gojjam and on the borders of Begemder. By the beginning of the next century Galla *Chewa* were already being settled by the Ethiopian rulers in Damot, Begemder and Gojjam.[120]

In view of the limitations imposed by the area which they previously inhabited it is difficult to explain the vast number of Galla who submerged substantial parts of Ethiopia by the turn of the sixteenth century. Writing his monograph about 1593 the monk Bahrey already found it difficult to comprehend how the numerically and culturally inferior Galla were able to overcome the numerous Ethiopians. There is a lot of realism in Bahrey's analysis of the contribution of the stratification of Ethiopian society and the characteristics of its army to the Galla's astounding success.[121] But this theory still does not explain the vast number of the Galla now dominating huge areas of Ethiopia. Bahrey, moreover, ignores the extremely heterogeneous character of Ethiopia's population, a good part of which did not identify with the Solomonic kingdom, and the ambivalent loyalty of the nobility.

Once the Galla had succeeded in breaching the shaky Ethiopian defences, they could be compared to an avalanche, which carried along with it many peoples who were indigenous to the Ethiopian plateau.[122] *Luba Bifole*, probably in the 1550s, is credited with being the first to make the sedentary population of certain areas its serfs rather than annihilating them. At a later stage, the inhabitants of Showa, Amhara, Damot and other areas, spared for the same reason, assimilated the Galla or may have been assimilated into their society.[123] Moreover, many pastoralists and semi-pastoralist peoples who were not integrated, or only partly integrated, in the Ethiopian kingdom were settled on the peripheries of the plateau and in many cases were employed as auxiliary forces or *Chewa* of the Ethiopian kings. In the second stage of the Galla migration such peoples, who at first resisted the Galla, invariably joined them, because they were uprooted from their land or enticed by the prospect of pillaging the sedentary population.[124] Deprived of his estates before coming to power, emperor Susinyos (r. 1607-1632) makes an interesting example. A captive of the Galla in his youth, he joined the latter with his followers in numerous predatory attacks on his countrymen.[125] Such instances and the gradual integration of serfs into Galla society could explain the number of the Galla and their success by the beginning of the seventeenth century.

Serse Dingil's reign – an evaluation

Serse Dingil's decision in 1579 to consolidate his government in the Falasha provinces rather than to confront the Galla could be considered the turning point of his reign, if not a watershed of Ethiopian history. This disastrous decision, part of the emperor's misguided policy, opened the plateau to Galla migration and sparked off a chain reaction which led to the final decline of the Solomonic kingdom.

The acceleration of Galla migration, it seems, enhanced the re-orientation of Ethiopia's expansionism towards the western and northern peripheries of the plateau. Deprived of vast territories and revenues accruing from them, the monarch's ability to reward nobles and warlords whose loyalty and services he needed, or to compensate others whose estates had been overrun by the Galla, was greatly curtailed. Thus, the process of expansion, colonisation and assimilation in the Falasha-Agaw provinces of the north, which had begun in earlier centuries, was now the outcome of necessity.

What seem meaningless, wasteful and cruel campaigns against Sidama, Agaw and other ethnic elements of the western plateau, were in fact a continuation of a strategy adopted by Solomonic monarchs in previous centuries, when integration of peripheral areas into their kingdom by the usual methods was impractical or impossible. It was aimed at annexing territories by the attrition of their inhabitants, and extended the political borders of Ethiopia well beyond the limits of its ability to effectively control such areas by 'showing the flag'. In fact, all the territories considered to belong to the third 'concentric circle' of the Solomonic kingdom were maintained within its political borders only as long as the Ethiopian monarchs were able to show the flag in them.[126]

The transfer of the centre of the kingdom from Showa to the provinces around Lake Tana was a logical consequence of Serse Dingil's policy and the Galla migration. A good part of the third circle in the east and many districts and provinces of the second circle[127] were overrun by the Galla. The growing power of the feudal nobility and warlords, minimising mobility in the government of the remaining provinces of the second circle, gradually eradicated the distinction between the first and second circles. Moreover, progressively 'Gallaised' (Amhara) or partly so (Showa), the previous core of Ethiopia was nearly separated from the territories still within the kingdom.[128]

The many historians who described Serse Dingil as an able, heroic and successful monarch completely distorted the truth. If anything, his long reign, marked by a chain of missed opportunities, should be considered the beginning of the end of Solomonic Ethiopia.

Miraculously surviving the first chaotic years of his reign, while still a minor, Serse Dingil in normal circumstances might have emerged as a passably good monarch. Yet he succeeded to the throne in one of the most critical periods in Ethiopian history, when the increasing power of the centrifugal forces coinciding with Adalite, Turkish and Galla invasions of the plateau necessitated an exceptionally able monarch. Notwithstanding personal bravery and tenacity, Serse Dingil was not endowed with political sophistication, foresight, determination and inspiring leadership, which would mobilise all the country's material and spiritual resources in its hour of need. Despite the grave compound challenges which Ethiopia faced, he was unable to adopt a clear-cut strategy and focus on the priorities dictated by them, and was easily influenced by his supporters. Thus, much of his energy and the resources of the country were consumed by a series of unrelated campaigns to coerce the feudal lords to accept his authority, to raid or conquer Sidama, Agaw-Falasha territories, or to counter the invasions of the Ottomans, Adalites and, as a last priority, to curb the Galla migration into different parts of Ethiopia.

Gran's Jihad threatened the Christian component of Ethiopia and the Solomonic dynasty; the Imam wished to found an Ethiopian sultanate, but his followers were too few (and culturally not very dissimilar to the Ethiopians) to effect a meaningful socio-political change in the plateau. The Galla migration, however, not only diminished the kingdom's political and cultural borders and its economic and population infrastructure and through it the power of the Solomonic dynasty, but in the final analysis caused a revolution in Ethiopia's demographic composition and the rise of Islam in the plateau. Indeed, Serse Dingil, who hardly used evangelisation as an integrative instrument, and Ethiopia's national church – spiritually deficient, elite-oriented, lacking a sense of mission and generally uninterested in proselytising – together with the ruling classes, rejected the 'uncouth Galla' and despised them. Hence, after they had settled in the plateau, a historic opportunity was missed to assimilate the Galla into Ethiopian society, and possibly into the semitised polity.

The effective boundaries of the Solomonic kingdom, which emerged by the turn of the sixteenth century, resemble a semi-circle stretching from Tigre to Damot. It incorporated Tigre and the Amharised or partly Amharised Agaw provinces of the north and Gojjam as well as the Sidama territories around Damot and, to some extent, the Omo-Gibe region. In the coming century Ethiopian rulers strove to consolidate their government in the Agaw-

Falasha territories and the northern and northwestern peripheries of the kingdom, which led to the deterioration of relations with Sennar. The struggle with the Galla focused on the western provinces and its outcome was that the Sidama areas south of the Abbay were gradually relinquished to the Galla, but the Ethiopian monarchs succeeded in retaining Amharised Gojjam within the kingdom, and an ambiguous authority in parts of Showa and an increasingly declining part of Amhara. Theoretically, at least, this remained the political map of Solomonic Ethiopia until its final decline.

NOTES

1. Excluding relatively short campaigns elsewhere in the kingdom.
2. Gelawdewos even conquered Harar about 1550. Conzelman, pp. 145-7, 154-7; 'Documenti Arabi', p. 53; Wendt, K., 'Amharische Geschichte eines Emirs von Harar im XVI Jahrhundert', *Orientalia*, IV, pp. 492-4.
3. Conzelman, pp. 145, 147; Wendt, *Orientalia*, pp. 492-4.
4. 'Documenti Arabi', pp. 55-6; Bahrey, p. 116; Bruce, Vol. III, pp. 224-6; Conzelman, pp. 158-60, 170-5; Yilma Deressa, *Ye Ethiopia Tarik*, Addis Ababa, 1959, E.C. 1967 A.D., pp. 232-4; Beccari, Vol. X, p. 105; Cerulli, *La Lingua*, Vol. I, pp. 36-7. Of artillery and many muskets in Nur's army, possibly from the Turkish Pasha – Conzelman, p. 175; Budge, Vol. II, p. 350; Kammerer (1947), Vol. I, p. 170.
5. As they called themselves.
6. Called so by their neighbours.
7. Bahrey, pp. 112, 136; Beccari, Vol. I, p. 32. Some scholars such as E. von Haberland (*Galla Süd-Athiopiens*, pp. 773-5), claim that they may have been originally sedentary agriculturalists. There is very little evidence to support this claim.
8. According to Yilma Deressa (pp. 219-20) *Abba Korma*. On the purely ritualistic character of this institution – Legesse, A., *Gada*, New York, 1973, pp. 10, 44-9; Bahrey, p. 112.
9. Bahrey, p. 112. On the different Galla groups fighting each other, based on evidence from Jesuit sources – Tellez, pp. 65-6.
10. There seem to have been some variations in the *gada* system.
11. Legesse, *Gada*, pp. 8, 10, chapter 3 (pp. 50-115); Legesse, A., 'Class system based on time', *Journal of Ethiopian Studies*, 1963 (1), pp. 1-19. For a general source: Huntingford, *The Galla;* Salviac, M. de, *Les Galla, grand nation Africaine*, Paris, 1901, pp. 1-2; Asma – a relatively modern source based on oral traditions and unknown Mss. Also: Abir, M., *Ethiopia: The Era of the Princes*, London, 1968, chapter IV; Abir, M., 'The Emergence and Consolidation of the Monarchies of Enarea and Jimma in the First Half of the Nineteenth Century', *Journal of African History*, Vol. VI, No. 2, 1965.
12. Possible relation to the function of the *Abba Muda*.
13. *Lobo*, Le Grand, pp. 22-3; Bahrey, pp. 113-5, 121, fn. 1.
14. Bahrey, p. 122.

15. There is an ambiguity and disagreement in the sources about the exact meaning of *luba*. The most acceptable explanation is that *luba* is the fifth class of the *gada*, which governed the tribe's functions.
16. Conzelman, p. 80; Cerulli, *La Lingua,* Vol. I, p. 36.
17. According to different sources 3000-8000 tribesmen – Paez, Vol. III, p. 98; Tellez, pp. 66-7; Bahrey, p. 120 – Galla overcoming Maya bow-men by using a suitable shield. The column was usually composed of the 'warrior class', but it could incorporate the one in training or the class which preceded them as the 'warrior class'.
18. See above pp. 75-6.
19. Bruce, Vol. IV, p. 96; Tellez, p. 65.
20. Conzelman, pp. 141, 159; Kammerer (1947), Vol. I, p. 165; Wolde Aregay, pp. 170-1. Wolde Aregay's interpretation of events in this period is not properly proved. Gelawdewos rightly considered the Muslims far more dangerous than the Galla, whose raids were no threat to the kingdom.
21. Bahrey, pp. 116-7. The author claims that during the cycle of this *luba* the Galla discontinued the practice of killing the cultivators and made them their serfs. See also Beckingham and Huntingford's remarks on this subject, interpreting Almeida, *Some Records,* p. 139, fn. 1.
22. Beccari, Vol. X, p. 105.
23. Although not always successful. Bahrey, p. 117.
24. Cerulli, *La Lingua,* Vol. I, p. 35; Perruchon, *Sémitique,* 1894, p. 269.
25. 'Documenti Arabi', p. 53; Cerulli, *La Lingua,* Vol. I, pp. 34-6; Bruce, Vol. III, pp. 225, 235.
26. A grandson of an Ethiopian convert who ruled Harar following Nur's death.
27. See below p. 156. Also Rossini, 'Sarsa Dengel', pp. 56-9, 67; 'Documenti Arabi', pp. 54, 60-1, 64, 71; Rossini, 'Turco' (1929), p. 51; Bruce, Vol. III, pp. 248-9; Basset, 'Etudes', p. 111; Beccari, Vol. III, p. 153; Vol. V, p. 488. On Ottoman-Portuguese relations in this period see above, text.
28. 'Documenti Arabi', pp. 54-6.
29. 'Documenti Arabi', pp. 53-4; Basset, 'Etudes', p. 165, note 212.
30. 'Documenti Arabi', pp. 70-1, 80; *Lobo,* Le Grand, pp. 29-30; Bruce, Vol. III, pp. 364-5.
31. On close contacts of the Imam with anti-Catholic party in Susinyos' court (1622-1624) – *Lobo,* Le Grand, pp. 16-7; *Some Records,* p. 199; Pereira, *Sesenyos,* Vol. II, p. 78 – on Imam Umar ad-Din al-Mudaiti's relations with Susinyos and presents to him. The Imam must have been of Dankali origin as the Mudaitu were a branch of the Afar people – 'Documenti Arabi', p. 80. On Ulama in the region – 'Documenti Arabi', pp. 79-80.
32. 'Documenti Arabi', p. 81; *Lobo,* Le Grand, p. 46.
33. Lewis, H., 'The Origins', p. 36; Cerulli, 'La Citta', p. 23.
34. See above, text.
35. Salt, p. 299. See also note 36 below.
36. It is likely that a number of Afar 'sultanates' were in existence. The Afar being nomadic pastoralists, the seat of their most important sultanate may have been situated in different places in different periods. *Purchas, His Pilgrims,* Hakluyt Society, Glasgow, 1905, Vol. III (a collection of reports relating to General Middleton's expedition, 1607-1616, and other sources), pp. 153, 169, 233-4, 243, 397; *Lobo,* Le Grand, pp. 45-69; Salt, pp. 176-7.
37. On relations with Turks in Mukha and trading boats visiting these ports, see: *Purchas,* Vol. III, pp. 153, 169, 233-4.
38. See above, pp. 7-8.
39. 'Documenti Arabi', pp. 80-1; *Lobo,* Le Grand, pp. 45-59; Tellez, pp. 226-30;

Hamilton, Alexander, *A New Account of the East Indies,* Edinburgh, 1727, pp. 23-4; Ludolphus, pp. 230, 337-8; *Purchas,* Vol. III, pp. 153-6, 233-4, 243, 288, 397; Vol. IV, pp. 264-5.

40.   Pereira, F. M. E., *Historia de Minas, Rei de Ethiopia,* Lisbon, 1888, pp. 45-6. Minas was at first a prisoner of Grañ and later was sent to the Pasha of Zabid. Also: Rossini, 'Turco' (1921-2), p. 689; Basset, 'Etudes', pp. 109-10 - hints concerning Minas' severity.

41.   Minas was married to Selus Haile, a woman from a rival noble family in Tigre. 'Annales Iohannis', p. 135.

42.   *Historia de Minas,* pp. 45-6.

43   See above pp. 52, 56-7. Also: *Lobo,* Le Grand, p. 66.

44.   Rossini 'Turco' (1921-2), p. 683; 'Annales Iohannis', p. 35; Bruce, Vol. III, pp. 232-4.

45.   Beccari, Vol. X, p. 105; Bahrey, pp. 116-17; Conti Rossini, C., 'L'autobiografia di Pawlos monaco Abissino del secolo XVI', *Rendiconti della Reale Accademia dei Lincei,* Vol. XXVII, 1918, pp. 286, 293.

46.   Bahrey, pp. 116-18.

47.   In his substantial discussion of Serse Dingil's period, Merid Wolde Aregay (pp. 320-2) dismisses this theory of the author, advanced elsewhere (*Ethiopia: The Era of the Princes,* Introduction, p. xxii). He does not present, however, any convincing alternative explanation for the fact that from the beginning of the 16th century until about 1580 Ethiopian monarchs and their chroniclers ignored, dismissed or misjudged the importance of Galla migration (see comment of Bahrey, pp. 120, 125-8, whose monograph dates to 1593) and continued to consider the Muslims and the rebellious nobility the main threat to 'Christian Ethiopia'. In fact, Wolde Aregay's arguments rather strengthen the impression that the Ethiopian rulers accepted the Galla migration as a relatively common development and not as a threat to their kingdom.

48.   Especially true concerning peoples of negroid origin, commonly called *Shanqalla,* until recently a synonym for slave.

48a. A term used to describe the ruling elements of the Ethiopian kingdom and to differentiate them from the other peoples of the kingdom including the Agaw people who were partly assimilated in the Ethiopian culture or who had not yet undergone the process of cultural assimilation.

49.   The term Gurague, a Sidama people, was a synonym in Ethiopia for a person of low status. See below, attitude to Zasellasie after Serse Dingil's death, p. 181.

50.   Much of the bitterness and dislike of Christian Ethiopians among the Muslims of the eastern escarpment could be attributed to the above rather than to the religious factor.

51.   Perruchon, *Sémitique,* 1893, p. 283; Beccari, Vol. X, p. 105; *Historia de Minas,* pp. 45-6. Of the famine in this period - Conzelman, p. 80; Basset, 'Etudes', p. 336.

52.   Ishaq's 'house' was from the province of Sire, whereas his rivals were led by the house of Bora Salawa. Robel, *Balgada* and *Tigre Makwonen* under Libna Dingil, was Minas' father-in-law - Conti Rossini, C., 'Due squarci inediti di cronaca Etiopica', *Rendiconti della Reale Accademia dei Lincei,* 1893, p. 808. Tekle Yohannis, Robel's son, participated at the side of the monarch in the decisive battle in 1579 against the Turks and Ishaq - Rossini, 'Turco' (1929), p. 55.

53.   Beccari, Vol. X, p. 213; Budge, Vol. II, p. 358.

54.   *Historia de Minas,* p. 46; Paez, Vol. III, p. 70; Beccari, Vol. V, pp. 393-4; Vol. X, pp. 105, 141-6, 151, 160; Basset, 'Etudes', pp. 109-10; Rossini, 'Turco' (1921-2), pp. 687, 689; Bruce, Vol. III, pp. 228-9; Asma, p. 18. See above,

pp. 125-8, on how unrealistic such hopes were. On Barreto's death, Oviedo inherited the title of Bishop of Ethiopia.

55. An outstanding exception was Pero Paez in the first quarter of the 17th century. Jesuit accusations concerning Minas were groundless – Paez, Beccari, Vol. III, p. 57; Vol. X, pp. 151, 171, 184. Suspicions concerning Portuguese intentions existed in Ethiopia since Gelawdewos' reign. See: Ludolphus, p. 320; Tellez, p. 136. The *Ichege*, chief of all the monks in Ethiopia, the leading spiritual position in the national church in the reign of Gelawdewos, was a converted Muslim, a great scholar and of exceptional personality – Trimingham, p. 90, note 2.

56. *Historia de Minas*, p. 46; Rossini, 'Turco' (1921-2), p. 689; Basset, 'Etudes', pp. 109-10; Beccari, Vol. X, p. 105; Asma, p. 18.

57. Beccari, Vol. X, pp. 157, 172; Rossini, 'Turco' (1921-2), pp. 690-1; Tellez, p. 143; Bruce, Vol. III, p. 229; *Historia de Minas*, pp. 49-50.

58. *Historia de Minas*, pp. 50-1; Rossini, 'Turco' (1921-2), pp. 690-1; Basset, 'Etudes', p. 110; Rossini, 'Sarsa Dengel', pp. 30-1; Tellez, p. 143; Bruce, Vol. III, pp. 231-4.

59. Himself a grandson of Libna Dingil through his mother, Hamalmal may have aspired to become king – Rossini, 'Sarsa Dengel', p. 18; Bahrey, p. 16, note 3. On the Karayu advance – Rossini, 'Pawlos', pp. 294-5.

60. See above pp. 125-7.

61. See below, text.

62. See above, pp. 125-7. Two of Ishaq's sons were killed in the war against the Turks – Rossini, 'Pawlos', pp. 294-5; Beccari, Vol. X, pp. 184-5, Oviedo, 1.7.1564.

63. Rossini, 'Sarsa Dengel', p. 41. This attitude was still apparent in 1605. See above, text.

64. Rossini, 'Sarsa Dengel', pp. 5-45; Basset, 'Etudes', p. 110; Rossini, 'Pawlos', pp. 294-6; Beccari, Vol. X, pp. 169 etc. Although some of his soldiers fought at the king's side in 1567/8, Ishaq and his allies continued to plot against Serse Dingil, repeatedly entreating the Portuguese for help – Beccari, Vol. X, pp. 185-238, 344; Tellez, p. 147.

65. See below, text. On Muslims in Damot – Rossini, 'Sarsa Dengel', pp. 42, 52-3; Basset, 'Etudes', p. 111, note 211; Tellez, p. 167. On Muslims in Dembiya – Budge, Vol. II, pp. 362, 364; Coulbeaux, J. B., *Histoire politique et religieuse d'Ethiopie*, Paris, 1838, Vol. II, p. 168.

66. In 1575/6 Harar's sultan invaded Hadya to punish its nobility for submitting to Serse Dingil. See above pp. 137-8.

67. Rossini, 'Sarsa Dengel', pp. 43-4, 47; Basset, 'Etudes', p. 110. The emperor, it seems, did not renew the struggle against the declining sultanate of Adal until 1576.

68. Bahrey, p. 118; Rossini, 'Pawlos', pp. 295-6.

69. Daharagot, a Tigrean noble of the house of Bora Salawa, was related to the king by marriage – Pereira, F. M. E., *Chronica de Susenyos, Rei de Ethiopia*, Lisbon, 1892-1900, Vol. II, pp. 357-8.

70. Rossini, 'Sarsa Dengel', pp. 50-1; Rossini, 'Turco' (1929), p. 50; Basset, 'Etudes', pp. 110-1; Beccari, Vol. II, p. 164; Vol. XI, p. 164.

71. Bahrey, p. 119; Rossini, 'Sarsa Dengel', p. 52 – on the vast number of cattle of the Borana.

72. Rossini, 'Sarsa Dengel', p. 47.

73. In 1571 the Abati (Baraytuma) killed Gojjam's governor in Amhara.

74. Rossini, 'Sarsa Dengel', p. 50.

75. Rossini, 'Sarsa Dengel', p. 51; Bahrey, p. 119.

76. Bahrey, p. 116. This was especially true, it seems, of Amhara, parcelled among monasteries and churches and of Showa, parcelled among the nobility. As Bahrey (p. 127) 'quotes' the Galla: 'Let us not shave our heads when we kill the inhabitants of Shoa and Amhara, for they are like oxen which speak but cannot fight.' Also, Tellez, pp. 66-7.
77. On this attitude of Serse Dingil see Bahrey, p. 120.
78. See above, pp. 47-50.
79. Rossini, 'Sarsa Dengel', pp. 8-9, 16-7, 30-1, 35, 48, 54, 62-3; Beccari, Vol. X, p. 265; Rossini, 'Pawlos', pp. 288, 295.
80. In reality the regiments ceased to have an incentive in defending their respective provinces and learned to live off the land.
81. Wolde Aregay, pp. 291-5; Rossini, 'Sarsa Dengel', pp. 129, 134-5; Paez, Vol. III, pp. 118-19; Almeida, *Some Records*, p. 80; Ludolphus, pp. 217-18.
82. On 'Turk Basha' – Tellez, p. 57; Beccari, *Tigre*, p. 46. They were musketeers, mainly Turks, who became captives in this year, descendants of the Portuguese and others who joined them later on – Kammerer (1947), Vol. I, p. 177. Most of Dembiya's revenues were allotted after 1574 to the maintenance of units of the bodyguard – Ludolphus, p. 206.
83. Gojjam's governor was killed by the Baraytuma in Amhara in 1571 – Rossini, 'Pawlos', p. 296. According to other sources (Basset, 'Etudes', p. 111 and Bahrey, p. 119), he was killed in Gojjam. Another Baraytuma column was annihilated in northwestern Showa by another general in 1573.
84. Rossini, 'Sarsa Dengel', pp. 52-3; Perruchon, J., 'Notes pour l'histoire d'Ethiopie. La règne de Minas ou Admas-Sagad (1559-1563)', *Revue Sémitique*, 1896, p. 276. Writing in 1577 (Tellez, p. 147) the Jesuit Emanuel Fernandez claimed that Serse Dingil was raiding the western Agaw for gold and slaves.
85. On Muslim soldiers in Dembiya – *Futuh*, pp. 343-7; Basset, 'Etudes', p. 111, note 211 (according to Bruce). In Damot – Rossini, 'Sarsa Dengel', p. 42.
86. On Ottoman pressure on Bahr-Midir and Tigre since 1572 – Tellez, p. 147, according to a letter from Emanuel Fernandez in 1572. They renewed their offensive in 1574.
87. Beccari, Vol. X, pp. 186, 235-50, 258, 278-9, 283-4, 286-8, 344; Rossini, 'Turco' (1929), pp. 50-1; Rossini 'Sarsa Dengel', pp. 55-6. The commotion created by the arrival of these letters even affected the Portuguese community in Dembiya – Beccari, Vol. X, pp. 254-5.
88. Rossini, 'Sarsa Dengel', p. 67, on the large amount of firearms which Ishaq acquired from the Turks. The influence of the Empress Maryam Sena, Ishaq's sister, who emerged as extremely influential, especially since 1580 and following her husband's death, should not be overlooked.
89. See below, text.
90. Beccari, Vol. X, pp. 258, 278-9; Ludolphus, p. 176; Coulbeaux, Vol. II, pp. 168-9 – on Serse Dingil requesting in the 1580s from Philip II artisans for the production of firearms. Also Paez (Beccari, Vol. XI, p. 73 from 1605) on Serse Dingil's letter to Goa requesting aid when hard pressed by Galla in the 1590s.
91. See above, p. 138. Beccari, Vol. III, p. 185; Vol. X, pp. 105, 488; Rossini, 'Sarsa Dengel', pp. 56-9; 'Documenti Arabi', pp. 60-1; Basset, 'Etudes', p. 165, note 252; Bruce, Vol. III, pp. 248-9. Muslim amirs from Waj, friendly to Serse Dingil, served as a Trojan Horse in the Adali camp – Rossini, 'Sarsa Dengel', pp. 58-9. If claims of Turkish aid to Nur in 1559 are correct, the emperor's apprehension was justified.
92. Rossini, 'Sarsa Dengel' pp. 62-3; Basset, 'Etudes', p. 111 – Daharagot was among the governors ordered to accompany his master.

93. Rossini, 'Turco' (1929), pp. 51-6; Rossini, 'Sarsa Dengel', pp. 70-93; 'Annales Iohannis', p. 35; Tellez, pp. 148-9. Many of the Turkish captives joined Serse Dingil's army.

94. See above, pp. 52-3.

95. See, for instance, Minas' behaviour during the Falasha campaign in 1560.

96. Abir, *The Era.*

97. Almagia, pp. 45, 48; Paez, Beccari, Vol. IV, p. 31 - on a Venetian in Enarea and a local merchant who had been earlier to Castile and returned by way of India. On *abun* arriving in Dembiya by way of Sennar in 1575 - Rossini, 'Pawlos', p. 296. Also: Almeida, *Some Records*, pp. 85-6, 146; Tellez, pp. 146-7, 173; Suriyano, p. 49. On biannual caravans from Cairo to Dembiya - an Armenian merchant, 'a description of Abyssinia' in *Purchas*, Vol. VI, pp. 418-9; Also: Evilya, Book I, Part I, pp. 85, 89 - on the enormous *khas* of the *beylerbeg* of *Habesh*. Trade by way of the Somali coast rapidly declined. See above, p. 138.

98. In his letter of December 1577 (Tellez, p. 147), the Jesuit E. Fernandez claimed that Serse Dingil raided the Agaw to acquire gold and 'to enslave these pagans, especially those of Damut', acquired by the numerous Muslim merchants living in Ethiopia who sold them on the coast to the 'Turks and moors'. Slaves were the most important trade item, but other Ethiopian products were also in demand - Almagia, pp. 45-7; Beccari, Vol. XI, pp. 94-6; Linschoten, Vol. I, pp. 264-6; *Lobo*, Le Grand, p. 38.

99. Evliya, Book I, Part I, p. 113. On Ottoman involvement in trade - the Italian merchant Cherubini (Almagia, p. 48), who traded in Ethiopia at the last decade of the 16th century. The king is said to have received one half of Massawa's customs.

100. Since the beginning of the 16th century the capital of the Muslim Funj dynasty.

101. Almeida (*Some Records*, p. 55) claims that the Falasha knew corrupt Hebrew, had Hebrew Bibles and sang Hebrew Psalms. There is no substantiation, however, of this claim.

102. On this literature see: Eshcoly, A. Z., *Sefer Hafalashim* (Hebrew), Jerusalem, 1943, pp. 162-72.

103. The 'west' was traditionally considered a hunting ground for the revenue-hungry Solomonic monarchs. Although slaves were an important commodity the acquisition of gold was considered even more important. See Gelawdewos to his Portuguese soldiers - Whiteway, *Castanhoso*, p. 99.

104. Biblioteca de Braga, Ms. 779, document No. 3, Luis de Azevedo, July 8, 1619 (material provided to the author by Dr. Merid Wolde Aregay); Wolde Aregay, pp. 290-6; Oviedo, Beccari, Vol. X, p. 224 (1564); Tellez, pp. 146-7, quoting the Jesuit E. Fernandez, December 1577, on 10,000 slaves from the west sold on the coast. See, nevertheless, for many monks and priests in anti-Catholic rebellion in the west - *Lobo*, Le Grand, pp. 112-13.

105. Rossini, 'Sersa Dengel', pp. 34-5, 94.

106. The gold did not originate in Enarea. Tellez, p. 61; Almeida, *Some Records*, pp. 85-6; Ludolphus, pp. 205-6; Rossini, 'Sarsa Dengel', p. 44.

107. Including the *Futuh al-Habasha;* Al-'Umari; Al-Maqrizi; Ibn Batuta.

108. Almeida, *Some Records*, pp. 149-62. On the 18th and 19th centuries see: Abir, *The Era*, chapter IV. Also: Rossini, 'Sarsa Dengel', pp. 44-5, 136-42; Tellez, pp. 192-200; Biblioteca de Braga, Ms. 779, document No. XLIII (material provided to the author by Dr. Merid Wolde Aregay).

109. For instance, Conzelman, p. 151 and the fact that Serse Dingil was so easily accepted in the Sidama kingdoms in 1567, when still a minor. Also: Gelawdewos' alleged defeat in Enarea - Rossini, 'Sarsa Dengel', p. 44.

110. Rossini, 'Sarsa Dengel', pp. 129-34; Guidi, 'Due Frammenti', p. 593; Basset, 'Etudes', p. 111; Bruce, Vol. II, p. 230; Bahrey, p. 123; Almagia, p. 45; Coulbeaux, Vol. II, pp. 160-1. Only rarely did Serse Dingil attempt to proselytise. Wolde Aregay (pp. 298-300) strongly advocates the theory that the conversion of the Enareans was the outcome of their fear of being pillaged.
111. Rossini, 'Sarsa Dengel', pp. 136-42. On the Sidama kingdoms see above, text.
112. Rossini, 'Sarsa Dengel', pp. 134-5; Ludolphus, p. 205.
113. Rossini, 'Sarsa Dengel', pp. 97-8; Basset, 'Etudes' p. 111.
114. Bahrey, pp. 120-5 – on Gojjam; Bruce, Vol. II, p. 230; Pereira, Susenyos, Vol. II, p. 4; Rossini, 'Sarsa Dengel', pp. 96-7.
115. Bahrey, p. 120. Also: Almeida, Some Records, p. 137; Tellez, pp. 66-7.
116. Bahrey, p. 121.
117. Bahrey, p. 123; Rossini, 'Sarsa Dengel', p. 144.
118. See the descriptions by Jesuits of their travels through the southwest, south and Showa in 1613-14 – Some Records, pp. 143-70; Beccari, Vols. VII, VIII. Also: 'Annales Iohannis', pp. 209-11. See also the provocative question of the ecclesiastic Awsegnyos attempting to depart for Showa to Iyasu I: 'Does not Showa belong to the Emperor?' – 'Annales Iohannis', pp. 128-9.
119. Bahrey, pp. 113-15. Also on clashes between different Galla tribes and clans – Bahrey, p. 113. According to Tellez (p. 65), if it had not been for the incessant fratricide among the different Galla groups, the Galla would have long since overrun the whole empire. On democracy among the Tulama – 'Annales Iohannis', pp. 131-2; Almeida, Some Records, p. 19.
120. Rossini, 'Sarsa Dengel', pp. 79-80, 146; Asma, p. 21; Bahrey, pp. 123-4; Tellez, p. 147.
121. Bahrey, pp. 125-6.
122. Such phenomena were very common in Africa. The Zulu are one example of a 19th century migration.
123. Bahrey, p. 116. On Showa and Amhara – Ibid., p. 127.
124. On this subject see: Nadi, Bekele, 'Adoption among the Oromo of Sawa', Ethnological Society Bulletin, Addis Ababa, 1958, No. 8, pp. 83-91. Also: 'Annales Iohannis', pp. 131-2, 137, 209-13; on Talata peoples among Mecha and on Kordida among Tulama – pp. 202, 212, 267-8; Asma, p. 37; Yilma Deressa, p. 238; Bahrey, pp. 114, 116, note1; Abir, The Era, pp. 43, 164. On Harar see above, pp. 137-8. On the Gaffat of Damot assimilated by the Galla – Almeida, Some Records, p. 136.
125. Pereira, Susenyos, Vol. II, pp. 19, 33, 36; Perruchon, J., 'Notes pour l'histoire d'Ethiopie. Le règne de Susenyos ou Seltan-Sagad (1607-1632)', Revue Sémitique, 1897, pp. 75-6. The example of Susinyos, however, is only one out of many in this hectic period.
126. See above, pp. 55-6. The 'strategy' mentioned above was practised by the enlightened Gelawdewos, who took slaves in such raids – Conzelman, p. 153. See also below, text, on tension with Sennar at the beginning of the 17th century.
127. On this division see above, pp. 54-6.
128. The unique integration and assimilation of the Galla by the local Amhara population of Showa produced by the 19th century the prototype of a new Ethiopia and the new core of the Christian semitised Ethiopian empire, created by Menelik. See: Abir, The Era, chapter VIII.

CHAPTER VIII

A Period of Transition

Ethiopian-European relations: the missionary era

The Solomonic monarchs had attempted since the fourteenth century to develop relations with Christian Europe, not because they sought spiritual guidance but mostly because they admired Europe's cultural-technical development[1] and occasionally because of common anti-Muslim sentiments. Their Red Sea policy might have been related to this inclination, but it was first and foremost motivated by regional politico-economic and religious (pilgrimage) considerations. When contact with Europe was re-established at the beginning of the sixteenth century Ethiopia's rulers were, it seems, somewhat reticent due to traditional cultural differences and suspicion of western Christianity and of Portuguese intentions, enhanced by some ecclesiastics and feudal lords, and by reports brought from India. The performance of da Gama's small force, and the effectiveness of their weapons and technical achievements, greatly increased the admiration for European, Portuguese materialistic culture but, paradoxically, it also awakened fears of Portuguese imperialism.[2]

The theological, dogmatic aggressiveness of Bermudez and the Jesuits and the arrogance of the latter inevitably increased the traditional opposition of the nobility and the church to fostering relations with Catholic Europe. Such relations, it was estimated, could result in the expansion of Rome's influence and the strengthening of the central authority. Playing on fears of foreign domination, exacerbated by reports of Muslim and other merchants about the Portuguese activities in India, the more machiavellian-minded even claimed that the 'spiritual imperialism'

177

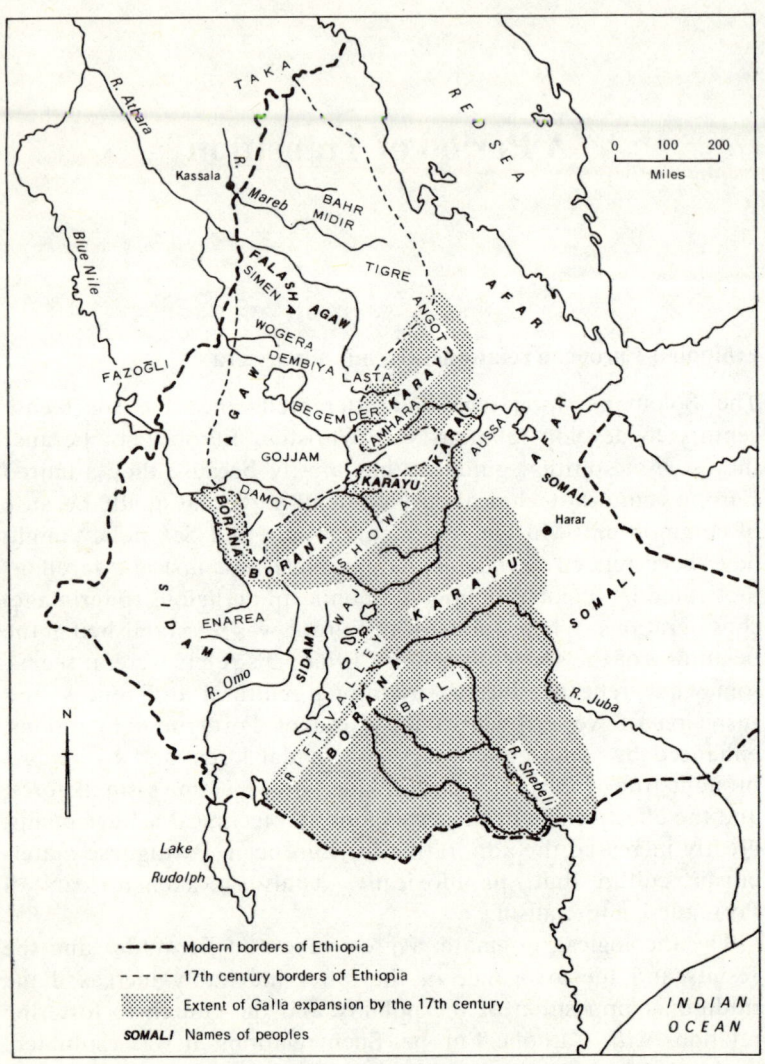

ETHIOPIA AND THE EXTENT OF GALLA MIGRATION
BY THE SEVENTEENTH CENTURY

of the Catholics was but a smokescreen for their political aspirations concerning Ethiopia.[3]

The product of a different cultural evolution, the Portuguese and the Jesuits in Ethiopia could not appreciate the correlation between the ethnic cultural heritage and the social framework of its population and the dogmas and customs sanctified by the traditional church. Disregarding Ethiopian sensitivities, they dismissed the former as barbaric and heretic, being a corruption of the true faith by Judaic and other influences. Shortsightedly, they underestimated the power and influence of the huge infrastructure of the local church[4] and of the feudal nobility which supported it and exacerbated the traditional suspicion concerning Europeans *(Ferenjoch)*.

Having failed in their mission, the Jesuits under Oviedo, probably unaware of the changing balance of power in the Indian Ocean, attempted to win the conversion of Ethiopia to Catholicism by creating a myth about the intention and ability of Portugal-Spain to intervene once again in the affairs of the Horn of Africa. If the Jesuits in Ethiopia in the sixteenth century exploited this myth out of ignorance, the Jesuit Fathers who arrived in the country from the beginning of the seventeenth century were undoubtedly aware of the situation in the Indian Ocean and Europe. Nevertheless, wishing to capitalise on the grave difficulties of the Solomonic monarch, without authorisation, they rekindled hopes of European aid, conditioning it on conversion to Catholicism.

Threatened by Muslim, Galla and other enemies, in addition to the endemic attempts by the nobility to usurp their power, Gelawdewos and his successors encountered even greater difficulties than previous monarchs in maintaining the unity of their heterogeneous feudal kingdom. Their admiration for the materialistic culture and power of Christian Europe and its increasingly centralised system of government (about which they heard from the Portuguese and the Jesuits) may have occasionally led them to contemplate requesting European military-technical aid. But informed by the Jesuits that such aid was conditional on conversion, even though they desired such aid and were aware of the shortcomings of the national church, they could not ignore the historic alliance of the dynasty with it, the repercussions that such a step could have on the country and the suspicions of the colonialist ambitions of the Catholics. Moreover, the theological polemics which the Jesuits initiated caused an immediate upsurge of ecclesiastical controversies within the Ethiopian church[5] and helped undermine unity in the country. Thus, only when convinced of his inability to stop Galla expansion, did Serse Dingil in desperation overcome his reluctance and apply for military aid to the Portuguese in India.[6]

Undoubtedly an exceptional monarch even if the soundness of his judgment is to be questioned,[7] emperor Zadingil (circa September 1603-October 1604) was the first Solomonic monarch who, under extenuating circumstances, abandoned the cautious policy of his forefathers concerning relations with Europe. It was, however, his successor Susinyos (r. 1607-1632) who, for the same reasons and misled by the Jesuits, actually accepted the Jesuits' asserted prerequisite for receiving aid from Spain and, against his better judgment, imposed Catholicism on Ethiopia before receiving the promised aid, after he had become convinced that such conversion would lead to a more meaningful unity in the country and the strengthening of the power of the Solomonic dynasty. The bloody civil wars throughout his reign only proved the wisdom of the prudence of his predecessors. But what happened in Ethiopia is, to a great extent, to be blamed on the Jesuits, who unrealistically exploited the desperation of the Ethiopian monarchs and their admiration for Europe's technical achievements and political organisation, to achieve their goal. The pyrrhic victory of the Jesuits and the backlash which it caused at a time when Europe was undergoing a spiritual, technical and political revolution may have been partly responsible for Ethiopia's stagnation until modern times.

A decade of 'interregnum' – first attempts at modernisation

Maryam Sena bore Serse Dingil three daughters, whom he married off to the leaders of the new military aristocracy. Hence Zadingil, the son of Serse Dingil's brother, was brought up at court as the monarch's heir. Benefitting from excellent formal education and from years of residence in the royal camp and following his uncle in numerous campaigns, Zadingil was considered an ideal candidate for succession. However, in the 1590s the monarch began to support the candidacy of Yaeqob, his infant son by a Falasha princess, whose tender years made him the natural choice of the military aristocracy, courtiers and the powerful *Itege*. When Serse Dingil died the seven-year-old Yaeqob was, therefore, quickly crowned and the twenty-year-old Zadingil was exiled to an island in Lake Tana. Thus, a *status quo* and the regency of Maryam Sena and her sons-in-law were temporarily assured.[8]

By the turn of the sixteenth century Ethiopia no longer functioned as a centralised state but rather as a confederation of feudal principalities voluntarily co-ordinated by a symbolic central authority. The powerful lords, such as Ras Atnatewos of Gojjam, Maryam Sena's son-in-law and co-regent, retained the tribute of their respective governorships, which enabled them to maintain large armies, partly composed of disbanded *Chewa* regiments. Enjoying the revenues of Dembiya, Wogera and parts of Begemder, whose governorships were not conferred upon the nobility and which they garrisoned, the imperial guard emerged as a factor of increasing importance in the kingdom.[9] All this and the Galla migration notwithstanding, Maryam Sena's regency ensured Ethiopia a minimal degree of stability as long as the co-operation between the power factors was maintained. Thus, when Yaeqob's chief steward, Zaselassie, a Gurague who rose from the ranks of the *Querban*, attempted to assume the power of a sole regent he was confronted by a coalition of feudal lords and the guard and was banished from the court.[10]

In mid-1603, barely 14 years old, Yaeqob attempted to terminate the regency and appointed Zaselassie to command his troops. Unscrupulously ambitious, Zaselassie was soon afterwards banished to Enarea when his and Ras Atnatewos' attempt to overthrow the emperor was foiled by the imperial guard. In September, however, the regents executed a swift *coup d'état*, enthroned Zadingil and exiled Yaeqob to Enarea as well.[11] As it came out, Yaeqob's childish attempt to resume power, which mobilised the nobility against him, was inconsequential compared to the far-reaching upheaval in Ethiopia's government and society which Zadingil had been contemplating during the years of meditation and study after his imprisonment.[12]

When he came to power Zadingil took the crown-name of Gelawdewos. But, unlike his able and prudent predecessor, despite his qualities he lacked patience and foresight and disregarded realities. Zadingil considered Ethiopia's feudal military-administrative system part of a syndrome of the deficient Ethiopian social structure, the cause of the monarchy's decline. Hence, disregarding the state of affairs in Ethiopia and before attempting to consolidate his power base, he embarked upon revolutionary reforms of the traditional military-feudal socio-economic system of the kingdom. As if this was not enough, his misguided bid to obtain aid from the Catholic powers caused in 1604 a temporary rupture of the historic alliance between the national church and the Solomonic dynasty.

It has already been pointed out that the Ethiopian class system prohibited the peasantry, the majority of the population, from carrying arms and exempted other classes from participating in their country's defence. Greatly limiting manpower resources for military service, this system afforded the nobility and the soldier-class tremendous leverage vis-à-vis the monarchy. The *gult* system, moreover, intended to provide subsistence for the *Chewa*, nobles, functionaries and ecclesiastics, requiring the peasant-serf to furnish services to the fief-holder(s) in addition to payment of taxation in kind,[13] further strengthened the position of the professional soldiers and the nobility.

Determined to break the power of the feudal lords and the vicious circle by which their power was repeatedly revived, Zadingil decreed at the beginning of 1604 the creation of a 'king's army' – *Malak Hara*.[14] Thereafter all ablebodied males, irrespective of occupation, were to render military service[15] when called to arms. Subsequently it was proclaimed that 'all men are soldiers and the land pays the tribute'.[16] This proclamation eroded the very foundations of the socio-political system. Not only did it threaten the monopoly of professional soldiers and feudal lords on military service but because it emphasised that tribute was levied on land and not on the person of the peasants, it also meant the cessation of serf services (*gabar*) *to gult* owners. This would inevitably have led to a revolution in the power structure of Ethiopia.

With the huge army which he mobilised at the beginning of 1604 Zadingil defeated a three-pronged Galla attack on Gojjam. But, by its very nature the *Malak Hara* was not meant to be a regular army but a militia and once the campaign was over the emperor allowed his peasant soldiers to return to their fields. Evidently, the 'king's army' was not intended to replace the *Chewa* system. Indeed, Zadingil, recognising its importance, strengthened the *Chewa* system by forming on several occasions new regiments out of the armies of warlords composed of *Chewa* which disintegrated.[17] Obviously an additional military framework loyal to the king, the *Malak Hara* was meant to counterbalance the power of the imperial guard and the feudal armies. The creation of the *Malak Hara* and the abolition of serf services were bound, moreover, to increase the imperial guard's dependence on the king and to undermine the power of the nobility. In the short run, in fact, Zadingil's reforms immediately led to armed clashes between peasants and their traditional masters[18] and, excluding the peasants, to universal opposition to the monarch.

In April 1604 the Jesuit Pero Paez was informed by Tigre's governor that the nobility intended to reinstate Yaeqob. But the first to rise openly against Zadingil was the imperial guard commanded by Zaselassie, whom the monarch unwisely brought back from Enarea and appointed governor of Dembiya. Secretly supporting the rebels, the feudal nobility bided a suitable opportunity for joining the uprising.[19]

The Jesuit Pero Paez, an able, scholarly and enlightened person, reached Ethiopia in May 1603, after six years of Muslim captivity. Informed of his arrival and activities in Tigre, Zadingil seriously contemplated the use of Portuguese-Spanish aid to subdue his rebellious army and disloyal feudal lords and to carry out his reforms. Consequently the emperor invited Paez in March 1604 to come to meet him in Dembiya. Arriving in the royal camp in June, Paez found a completely isolated and desperate monarch, who informed him of his wishes when he secretly conferred with him. When the Jesuit offered aid conditional on conversion to Catholicism, he found the ruler not averse to this idea. The monarch dictated to Paez letters for Philip III and to Pope Clement VIII in which he requested soldiers and artisans and declared his willingness to convert. Signed by Zadingil the letters were immediately sent to Goa.[20]

Informed of the letters sent by Zadingil to the Catholic authorities, Abuna Petros absolved the population from their oath of allegiance to the monarch and excommunicated him. The expansion of the rebellion in the following months, however, despite claims of Catholic sources to the contrary, was the outcome of Zadingil's socio-economic and military reforms and the fear of the nobility that foreign aid would completely undermine their power.[21] Unwisely the monarch decided to march against the rebels with a handful of loyal followers, and was killed in Dembiya in October 1604.

It seems that under Zaselassie's influence the victorious nobility decided not to crown a new king. But it took the feudal warlords another century before they were able to usurp completely the authority of the Solomonic dynasty and turn the monarchs into puppets. The imperial guard, still strongly attached to the Solomonic dynasty, their *raison d'être*, supported the succession of Susinyos (r. 1607-1632), Libna Dingil's great-grandson through the male line. Different feudal lords began to press the claims of other princes. The machiavellian Zaselassie, however, fearing that Susinyos, the most likely candidate who had been raiding Ethiopia with his Galla allies, would constitute a worse threat to the power of the nobility, quickly gained general consent to reinstate Yaeqob and messengers were sent to Enarea to bring Yaeqob back to Dembiya.[22]

When a young child Susinyos was taken prisoner by the Borana, who raided Showa in the 1570s. He was adopted, it seems, into the Galla tribe and participated in its westwards migration. After he was indemnified he was brought up by Minas' widow, but only a small portion of his father's estates was returned to him. When Serse Dingil died Susinyos escaped to Walaqa to avoid imprisonment, joined a Karayu band and began to raid Begemder, Dembiya and Gojjam. By 1602 a renowned warrior, when requested to discontinue his devastating attacks[23] he demanded the governorships of Walaqa, Showa and parts of Gojjam, but his demand refused, he continued to raid different parts of Ethiopia.[24]

When Zadingil was killed Susinyos, nearly 35 years old, was the most likely candidate for succession. Determined to undermine what he thought to be a feudal plot to abolish the monarchy, he relentlessly pressed his claim to the throne. By the end of 1604 most of the reluctant nobility agreed to enthrone him and even Zaselassie was coerced by his soldiers to negotiate with him. In March 1605, just before the latter was also about to recognise him, news arrived of Yaeqob's arrival in Damot. Preferring a young and weak king, the feudal lords again swore allegiance to Yaeqob and Susinyos was forced to escape across the Abbay river to Showa.

The two years until Yaeqob's death in March 1607 were marked by a continuous struggle for power between the young king and the aristocracy. Moreover, to bring Susinyos into his camp Yaeqob offered him the governorship of Showa, Amhara and Walaqa which had been partially overrun by the Galla and practically separated from the kingdom. Although a tempting offer in the past, considering himself the legal successor to the throne, Susinyos continued his war against the nobility and Yaeqob. An excellent general and superior tactician, despite the numerical inferiority of his army, he defeated Zaselassie and other generals. Foolishly Yaeqob, at the head of the imperial guard, followed him into an area suitable for Galla warfare. In the battle which ensued the monarch and many of his followers, including Abuna Petros, were killed. Shortly afterwards Susinyos was crowned in Gojjam.[25]

Power politics and Ethiopia at the beginning of the seventeenth century

The arrival of the British and the Dutch in the Indian Ocean in the last decades of the sixteenth century (and in the Red Sea since 1609) completely changed the balance of power and led to the rapid erosion of Portuguese hegemony in the region. The Dutchmen began to attack Portuguese strongholds in Madagascar and Mozambique and the British navies defeated the Lusitanians off the Indian subcontinent in 1610 and 1615. Earlier, unable to apportion sufficient resources to areas with low priority, the Portuguese had lost to local potentates some of the territories which they had previously controlled in the Persian Gulf. The British maritime victories and efforts to break the Portuguese stranglehold over the Persian Gulf led in 1622 to their conquest of Hormuz. Thereafter the Portuguese position in the region continued to deteriorate and it ceased to be a major factor in the Indian Ocean.

The threat to the Portuguese empire in the Indian Ocean became still more ominous at the beginning of the seventeenth century when British and Dutch fleets sailed beyond India to the Far East. In the coming decades the Portuguese lost one territory after another of their East Indian empire to their vigorous Protestant competitors. Thus, constantly on the defensive against their European rivals by the first quarter of the seventeenth century, they could not even contemplate a mission to the Red Sea as the Jesuits in Ethiopia and their allies continually implored them to do.[26]

Turco-Portuguese relations rapidly improved from the turn of the sixteenth century in direct proportion to the decline of Catholic power in the region. Turkish merchants and officials from the Red Sea and the upper Persian Gulf began to trade in the Portuguese possessions while Portuguese subjects frequently visited Yemen and even the coast of Ethiopia, where they may have joined caravans moving between Massawa, Sawakin and the interior.[27] These relations were exploited by the Jesuits, who were able to bring Pero Paez and his companions to Ethiopia in 1603 with the help of Ottoman officials in Sawakin and Massawa, unaware of the impact this seemingly unimportant event would have on the history of the region in future years.

Ottoman power in the Red Sea in the first decades of the seventeenth century was rapidly declining. It was challenged in several provinces of the Fertile Crescent and in the Hijaz, and the Mamluks in Egypt had long since begun to encroach on the authority of the Ottoman Pasha. The rebellion of a new Zaydi Imam in the region of San'a in Yemen quickly gathered momentum and led in 1630 to the termination of Turkish suzerainty in this part of the empire until the nineteenth century. Notwithstanding their growing difficulties in the region and their inability to reinforce their diminishing garrisons in Massawa, Arkiko and Sawakin, the Turks tenaciously held on to these ports (the extent of *Habesh* in the seventeenth century); and they maintained control of parts of the trade with the plateau which provided enormous revenues to local officials. Ironically, the unrest in the Hijaz and the Fertile Crescent caused many more merchants who traded with these areas to divert their activities to the Yemen coast and Ethiopia. The demand for Mukha coffee was constantly growing in the empire and the incessant wars in the Horn of Africa produced a vast number of slaves for whom there was an insatiable market in the Muslim world.[28] Finally, the growing tension between Ethiopia and Sennar in the first decades of the century[29] rediverted part of the trade of the Dembiya-Sennar-Cairo route to the traditional route via the coast of Ethiopia and Sudan.

The arrival of British trading fleets in the Red Sea from 1609, followed by the Dutch in 1616, caused at first some alarm among the Muslims and friction between the Europeans and the local authorities. But realising the purely commercial character of the interests of the Protestant powers and too weak anyway to do anything about it, the Turks reconciled themselves to the new situation and began to co-operate with the newcomers. The latter soon discovered that the Red Sea trade, Ethiopian included, was of marginal importance and practically abandoned it. Nevertheless, European piracy in the Gulf of Aden became a most disturbing factor in the region in the seventeenth century and a nearly permanent European-Protestant presence was established in Mukha.

The Ottomans were completely aware that Portuguese power in the Indian Ocean in the seventeenth century was inconsequential. In a sense they may have considered their old enemies as new allies, because of the highhanded behaviour of the British and Dutch in the Red Sea and their piratical acts in the Indian Ocean. Hence, the Turks continued to develop their commercial relations with the Portuguese and until the 1620s facilitated the passage of Jesuit missionaries through Sawakin and Massawa to the plateau. In fact, the services of the latter were even utilised to overcome differences which sometimes arose between the coastal authorities and the Ethiopian king, by now the patron of the Jesuits. However, the Turks were soon to learn that Susinyos, the Ethiopian emperor, was unwilling to tolerate their occasional eruptions into the Ethiopian plateau, which had gone nearly unnoticed in the past.[30] Moreover, apprehensive about the number of missionaries arriving in their ports since about 1618 and the revolutionary impact of their presence in Ethiopia, the Turks attempted to stop this traffic. But they soon revoked their decision and asked for Jesuit mediation when the emperor took counter-measures against them and in view of their economic dependence on the goodwill of the Ethiopian authorities.[31] Relations with the Portuguese and the Jesuits remained friendly until after the latter were expelled from Ethiopia in 1633/34.

The Galla-controlled plateau at the beginning of the seventeenth century

It would be erroneous to assume that all the vast areas, including the traditional heartland of the Solomonic kingdom, detached from Ethiopia proper by the seventeenth century, had been overrun or were controlled by the Galla. Geographical obstacles not conducive to Galla warfare, such as rivers, rugged mountains and natural fortresses (mainly in the form of flat-topped *ambas*), forced them to leave behind many unconquered enclaves. Some of the larger ones, governed by local potentates or warlords, were either ancient principalities or remnants of provinces. Smaller enclaves, consisting of just an isolated *amba* and the territory around it, were governed by the local commanders or minor governors.

Enumerating the provinces of his empire to his Jesuit mentors, emperor Susinyos claimed that Amhara and part of Showa were under his effective control,[32] even though they had become border provinces constantly suffering from Galla ravages. In reality, the Wollo (Karayu) confederacy and related tribes had already begun to settle most of Amhara. Indeed, even in the parts still under royal authority, adjacent to Begemder and Gojjam, the population was in most cases forced to seek refuge on fortified *amba*s.[33] Showa, however, was practically separated from the empire by the Tulama (Borana) who settled in its western district, and the Warantisha (Baraytuma) in the northwest. Nevertheless, several districts such as Marabeite, Menz, Tegulet, Ifat and parts of Morat, and many isolated *amba*s and the areas around them in the southern and central parts of the province survived Galla attacks and were governed by traditional rulers, local governors and warlords. Although to a great extent autonomous, they maintained lively contact with the Ethiopian court, recognised the overlordship of the emperor, sought re-appointment by him and occasionally paid their tribute.[34]

Somewhat removed from the new heartland of the kingdom and surrounded by Galla, the monastery of Debra Libanos, head-quarters of the Order of Tekla Haymanot, seat of the *Ichege*, and one of the most important spiritual centres of Ethiopia and the area around it was left unharmed and continued to attract ecclesiastics from different parts of the country. Christianity in Showa thus maintained its power in the amharised districts and, in addition to old-established cultural influences, was a major factor in the successful assimilation in the coming centuries of many of the Galla who had settled there.[35] Showa and Amhara nonetheless came to resemble the previous peripheral provinces of the empire where ecclesiastics propagating unconventional dogmas, pretenders to the throne, rebels and brigands of different kinds found refuge from the royal authority.[36] Be that as it may, areas of Showa not overrun by the Galla, although physically separated from the main body of the empire by a nearly continuous belt of Galla settlers, remained to some extent part of the Ethiopian orbit and, depending on circumstances, were involved in its political and cultural dynamics.

Substantial military units displaced from their original territories retreated to Gojjam, Damot and the southwest in the last decades of the sixteenth century and helped the local forces and population to defend themselves against the Galla migrants and their Ethiopian allies. Thus, although Bizamo had been overrun by the Galla as early as the last decades of the sixteenth century, the battle over Damot, or part of it, continued for 200 years. This was related to the prolonged and bitter struggle for the rich principalities of the Omo-Gibe basin terminated only by the beginning of the eighteenth century, when the Sadecha (Mecha) confederation finally overran the region. However, by the turn of the seventeenth century Galla bands were already roaming the areas between these principalities, endangering communications and trade among them and hunting slaves in the districts under their control. Nevertheless, despite the disrupted communications between Gojjam and the southwest and the diminishing tribute intermittently paid from the area,[37] Enarea and its sister kingdoms were considered throughout the seventeenth century Ethiopian territory and its rulers sought appointment by the emperor.

From the reports of the Jesuits who visited southwestern and southern Ethiopia in 1613-1614 it emerges that in addition to the Omo-Gibe cluster, several Sidama principalities survived the Galla invasion in the south. After being separated from the main body of the empire, the Sidama peoples re-established their autonomy and reverted to their original tribal or monarchical socio-political system.[38] They still recognised, to some extent, the shadowy authority of the King of Kings and intermittently maintained communications with the Solomonic court in the north.[39] Hadya once again emerges as the most powerful local power and it was quick to renew its commercial relations with Harar and Zayla despite the Galla and other difficulties.[40] But immediately after the expedition of 1613 the Sidama areas sank into oblivion (until the nineteenth century when they were again visited by Europeans), and hardly anything is known of the development of the south thereafter.

From existing material it appears that the attempts of Ethiopian monarchs, including Gelawdewos, to integrate the south into the empire by conquest and colonisation, and in some instances by evangelisation, was on the whole unsuccessful. The only outcome of the Solomonic period when the south re-emerged in the nineteenth century, in addition to linguistic-cultural influences, was dim memories of Christianity and the claims to Tigrean and Amhara descent among the ruling classes.[41]

The Galla migration following the conquest of Ethiopia by Grañ reversed the process of ethno-political integration of the Cushitic-Sidama parts of the plateau in the semitised Solomonic empire. As the Galla began to settle down in the areas which they conquered, the subjugated Sidama were incorporated into their society as *Gabara* (serfs – slaves) or as subjugated allies, *Talata*.[42] On the other hand, at a later stage, especially when they began to abandon pastoralism for agriculture, the Galla adopted many aspects of Sidama culture and socio-political institutions.[43] They were also quick to appreciate the benefits of trade and the important service rendered by itinerant merchants. The institution of patron (*mogasa*) for travellers, prevalent among the pastoralists and other peoples of the Horn of Africa, may have existed in Galla society before their migration into Ethiopia. But in the seventeenth century this institution facilitated contacts between different parts of the plateau and enabled caravans to travel through Galla territories. This may explain the volume of Ethiopian products and slaves arriving on the Red Sea coast or in Sennar, as long as circumstances in nearby areas were conducive to such activities.[44] By the beginning of the seventeenth century a new era had begun in the relations between the Galla and the other peoples of the Ethiopian plateau.

NOTES

1. See above, pp. 31-9.
2. On Ethiopia's Muslim Mediterranean orientation, see pp. 31-9, 103-4, 142-3.
3. See above, p. 39.
4. See above, pp. 60-1.
5. See below on Gelawdewos, pp. 106-7. On renewal of the controversy about the Sabbath in Serse Dingil's reign – Fernandez (1587), Beccari, Vol. X, p. 342.
6. Beccari, Vol. XI, p. 73.
7. See below, text.
8 Paez, Vol. III, pp. 207-8; Beccari, Vol. VI, pp. 40-3; Pereira, *Susenyos*, Vol. II, pp. 19, 33; Almagia, p. 46; Rossini, 'Due', p. 811; Tellez, p. 163; Ludolphus,

pp. 177-8; Perruchon, J., 'Notes pour l'histoire d'Ethiopie. Les règnes de Ya'qob et Za-Dengel (1595-1607)', *Revue Sémitique*, IV, 1896, pp. 356-7.

9. Pereira, *Susenyos*, Vol. II, p. 46; Ludolphus, p. 105.
10. Pereira, *Susenyos*, Vol. II, pp. 37-9, 86; Rossini, 'Due', pp. 811-12. *Qerban* was a corps of the imperial guard, mainly cavalry, frequently mentioned in Serse Dingil's chronicle.
11. Pereira, *Susenyos*, Vol. II, p. 39; Rossini, 'Due', p. 811; Paez, Vol. III, pp. 225-6.
12. Rossini, 'Due', pp. 812-13; Perruchon, *Sémitique*, 'Ya'qob', pp. 356-8.
13. See above, pp. 47-8.
14. Literally translated 'the king's soldiers'. Wolde Aregay's interpretation (pp. 379-80), based on the translation of *Hara* as 'free men', seems somewhat far-fetched and not in the context of the period.
15. See resemblance in the population classification in this decree (Pereira, *Susenyos*, Vol. II, p. 40-2) to that of Bahrey (pp. 125-6).
16. Rossini, 'Due', pp. 811-12. Conti Rossini translated the text as follows: 'gli uomini tutti sieno soldati e (nel tempo stesso) la terra paghi il tributo.' In note 13 he points out that if the peasants were mastered and had to leave their land, it only stood to reason that they should be exempt from any levies. Merid Wolde Aregay (pp. 379-80) rightly suggests that the second part of the sentence could mean: 'man is free and the land the tributary.' A somewhat inferior translation of the proclamation is suggested by Perruchon, *Sémitique*, 'Ya'qob', p. 362.
17. Paez, Vol. III, p. 227; Pereira, *Susenyos*, Vol. II, p. 46.
18. Pereira, *Susenyos*, Vol. II, p. 42; Rossini, 'Due', p. 812; Paez, Vol. III, p. 254.
19. Rossini, 'Due', p. 812; Pereira, *Susenyos*, Vol. II, p. 42; Beccari, Vol. III, pp. 227, 254.
20. The official reason for the letters was the need for aid to fight the Galla. To show good faith Zadingil banned the observance of the Jewish Sabbath and proclaimed another decree related to theological problems debated in Ethiopia. It is unlikely, however, that the timing of these edicts was a coincidence. The monarch also invited the Spanish king to occupy Ethiopia's northern coast. Beccari, Vol. III, pp. 246, 261, 401. Also: Tellez, p. 168; Budge, Vol. II, p. 378.
21. That Paez, his companions and Zadingil's Portuguese soldiers were not harmed after his death, is also a proof of the above. See also the naive account of Ludolphus (p. 181). Also: Rossini, 'Due', p. 812; Beccari, Vol. III, p. 297; Pereira, *Susenyos*, Vol. II, p. 42. On extensive *gult* of the ecclesiastics, above pp. 61-3.
22. Perruchon, *Sémitique*, 1897, p. 76; Pereira, *Susenyos*, Vol. II, pp. 42-3; Ludolphus, p. 184 – on dissatisfaction of Dembiyan army. Also: Rossini, 'Due', p. 813; Bruce, Vol. III, pp. 269-70 – on Yaeqob's return. On soldiers' pressure to crown a king – p. 272.
23. Pereira, *Susenyos*, Vol. II, pp. 19, 22, 23; Perruchon, *Sémitique*, 1897, pp. 75-6; Papi, Maria R., 'Una Santa Abissinia Anti Cattolica', *Rassegna di Studi Etiopici*, anno III, No. 1, 1943, p. 89, note 1 – in Walaqa Susinyos was given refuge by Dejazmatch Yolyos, its governor, and his future son-in-law.
24. Pereira, *Susenyos*, Vol. II, pp. 32-7. In his role as a soldier of fortune he reached Ifat, fought the Galla together with the Gurague tribes and helped the Galla to conquer many isolated *ambas* in Showa and Amhara.
25. Yaeqob's body was not found, which later gave rise to many pretenders. Pereira, *Susinyos*, Vol. II, pp. 58-61; Ludolphus, pp. 185-7; Tellez, p. 176; Rossini, 'Due', pp. 814-15. Also: p. 814, note 19; Bruce, Vol. III, pp. 274-7.

26. Prestage, Edgar, *Chapters in Anglo-Portuguese Relations*, Watford, 1935, chapter by Boxer, C. R.; *Lobo*, Le Grand, pp. 4, 8-10, 29-30; Beccari, Vol. XIII, p. 361; Danvers, pp. 287-319.

27. Tellez, pp. 161-2, 173-4; Beccari, Vol. XI, pp. 94-6; *Lobo*, Le Grand, p. 38.

28. On the revenues of the Pasha of *Habesh* - Evliya, p. 113. See also: Foster, W., (ed.) *The Journal of J. Jourdain, 1608-17*, Cambridge, 1905, pp. 89-96; *Purchas*, Vol. III, p. 355. Difficulties in the Fertile Crescent and its impact on trade - Foster, *Jourdain*, appendix B, p. 353 Also, p. 103 - on Hijaz.

29. See below, text.

30. See below, text, on the same policy concerning Sennar and Arab and other pastoralists raiding Ethiopia for slaves.

31. Tellez, pp. 174, 211, 216, 221, 235; *Lobo*, Le Grand, pp. 32-4; Morié, Vol. II, pp. 286-8; Wolde Aregay, p. 485, according to Caspar Paez.

32. *Some Records*, pp. 13, 83, 97.

33. Almeida, *Some Records*, pp. 83, 97.

34. On minimal tribute from the provinces cut off by Galla - Tellez, pp. 62-3. See tribute paid by Amha Iyasu and relations between the founder of a new Solomonic dynasty in Showa and the emperor in the 18th century - Abir, *The Era*, pp. 146-7. Also Almeida, *Some Records*, pp. 168-9; 'Annales Iohannis', pp. 128-9, the words of the ecclesiastic Awsegnyos, who wished to retire to Debra Libanos in 1688: 'Does not Showa also belong to the king?'. Also *Ibid.*, pp. 187-90, 209, 213-14. On relations with the Galla - *Ibid.*, p. 131; Basset, 'Etudes', pp. 305, 312. The relationship of the Muslim districts of eastern Showa with the monarch is less clear, as is that of Adal (Aussa) and the Dankali sultanate with Ethiopia. On this see above, pp. 138-42.

35. 'Annales Iohannis', pp. 128-9; Basset, 'Etudes', pp. 307, 312. For obvious reasons the seat of the *Ichege* and the centre of activity of the order of Tekla Haymanot were transferred to the area of Gondar at the beginning of the reign of Fasilidas (r. 1632-1667).

36. The example of Susinyos and later of the rebel Wolde Gabriel (1623-1625) - Perruchon, *Sémitique*, 1897, p. 184. Also: 'Annales Iohannis', pp. 128-9. Similarly the 'new Solomonic dynasty' was able to establish itself in Menz and Ifat in the 18th century.

37. Almeida, *Some Records*, pp. 84-6; Almeida, Beccari, Vol. VI, p. 284; Tellez, pp. 61-2; Ludolphus, p. 205.

38. Probably with some modifications due to Ethiopian and Muslim influences. On the reports of the Jesuits - *Some Records*, pp. 134-71. Also: Beccari, Vols. VII, VIII; Biblioteca de Braga, Ms. 779, document No. XLII (material provided to the author by Dr. Merid Wolde Aregay).

39. It is of interest that the feudal lords, or anti-Catholic party at court, were able to send an important noble to the Muslim rulers in the south to incite them against the ambassadors - *Some Records*, pp. 163-7, 171. On a similar incident in 1624 in Aussa - *Lobo*, Le Grand, pp. 16-17, 45-6.

40. Wolde Aregay, p. 524.

41. Haberland, E. 'The influence of the Christian-Ethiopian Empire on Southern Ethiopia', *Journal of Semitic Studies*, No. 1, 1964 - on the Sidama of the south and their 'Tigrean' origins; Conti Rossini, C., *Etiopia e genti di Etiopia*, Florence, 1937, pp. 55-6, 61, 163-5 - on Tigre origins. See also: d'Abbadie, Antoine, Bibliothèque Nationale, Paris, d'Abbadie Papers. Catalogue France Nouvelle Acquisition, No. 21303, p. 296 and pp. 173-3. According to Paez (Almeida, *Some Records*, pp. 164-6), Emperor Yaeqob married the daughter of the king of Hadya. On Susinyos' relations with the principalities of the south, *ibid*, pp. 164-5.

42. *Talata,* in Amharic: enemy-stranger, was probably a loan word used by the Galla to describe foreign elements who were incorporated in their society but not considered equal nor did they become part of the *gada* system. I am indebted to Prof. Wolf Leslau of UCLA for this possible explanation of *Talata.* See also below, p. 208, n. 16.

43. Abir, *The Era,* chapter IV.

44. On this trade – Bruce, Vol. IV, p. 98. On Galla patrons or *mogasa – Some Records,* pp. 98, 170; 'Annales Iohannis', p. 31. On the problems of patrons in the Horn – Abir, M., 'Brokers and Brokerage in Ethiopia', *Journal of Ethiopian Studies,* Addis Ababa, 1965, pp. 1-6.

CHAPTER IX

The Reign of Susinyos –
A Seventeenth Century Attempt
at Westernisation

The consolidation of Susinyos' government and Galla power

A soldier of fortune for whom the end justified the means, when he came to power Susinyos was determined to reform the whole framework of Ethiopia's monarchy and society. Paradoxically he was guided by the wish to re-establish the emperor's authority, stability and law and order in the country. Described as a scholar with a keen mind and a superior intellect, despising the Ethiopian ecclesiastics for their hypocrisy, shallowness and narrowmindedness, Susinyos considered them a cause of the stagnation of Ethiopia and its decline. Nor could he forgive them the fact that they allied themselves with the nobility, whom he hated, against the Solomonic monarch. On the other hand, he was fascinated by Western power and material culture, but unlike his predecessors he also admired its spiritual qualities. After coming to power, therefore, he became attracted to the Jesuits, their knowledge and teachings and way of life.

Although an excellent tactician and general, with an intimate knowledge of Galla warfare and customs, he often mismanaged operations against his enemies. While in his youth he roamed with his band of highwaymen all over the plateau, after his accession he did not make a serious effort to regain the territories lost to the Galla. With the exception of a few retaliatory expeditions into Galla territory, he followed on the whole a defensive strategy aimed to protect the existing borders of Ethiopia which the Galla migration of the sixteenth century had created. Possibly he thought the task was impossible with the means at his disposal and, therefore, awaited the European aid which he repeatedly requested.

At the same time, clearly recognising the magnitude of the challenges which he faced, he did not hesitate to antagonise all the power elements in the country, including his own supporters, instead of dealing with them piecemeal.

Susinyos' reign is in fact marked by dichotomies. Guided by a strange logic his policy, in the final analysis, was at times too inflexible and to some extent irrational. Too powerful to be overthrown, he drove his country into the most bloody civil wars and his reforms became anathema to all its population – Christian, Muslim and pagan.

Susinyos' victory over Yaeqob made him in theory the master of Ethiopia. His authority was challenged by a score of claimants to the throne in different parts of Ethiopia, who were backed by local governors, nobles and ecclesiastics whose position was threatened by him.

Conquered by the Muslim followers of Grañ who slaughtered all its inmates in 1540, the royal prison of Amba Geshen was not re-established by Gelawdewos, the strong, prestigious and compassionate ruler.[1] Yet some princes chose to live there because they were destitute. Others, like Susinyos' father, resided on estates granted them by the crown, while members of the house of Minas generally lived in the court of Sabla Wengel and co-operated in retaining the succession in their branch of the family. A problem of significance already in the days of Minas, the struggle for succession to the throne was to become a major issue during the seventeenth century.[2]

Due to his background and developments in the first years of his reign Susinyos, more than other monarchs who preceded him, badly needed legitimisation. Considering his coronation in Gojjam insufficient he exploited the first opportunity, when on his way to Tigre in 1609, to have himself crowned in Axum by Abuna Simeon with all the pomp and according to all the ancient traditions of Ethiopia. The ceremony undoubtedly emphasised as well a unity between the Tigrean and Amhara territories under the Solomonic crown.[3]

A pretender who appeared in Tigre shortly after Susinyos' coming to power was probably the most serious challenge to his authority in this period because he was supported by the monks of St. Ewostatewos, whose power in the region was enormous. These suspected Susinyos because of his relations with Debra Libanos

and his sympathy for the anti-Sabbath party.[4] Wearing a veil the
pretender claimed that he was emperor Yaeqob and had escaped
from the battlefield after being wounded in the face. This rebellion
soon became an outlet for Tigrean separatist tendencies and for the
frustration felt by the ancient nobility of the region, whose special
position and rights were threatened by Susinyos' policy, which his
half-brother Si'la Christos tried to impose.[5]

Si'la Christos, Susinyos' tactless and ruthless governor of Tigre,
was removed from this office in 1609. Inevitably when the
governors who followed him resorted to compromises and reverted
to the traditional system of indirect government, the rebellion in
Tigre declined and in 1610 the pretender was killed by nobles from
the house of Bora Salawa. In the meantime the other uprisings in
the country were crushed by the emperor or his governors without
difficulty because the rebels did not co-operate with each other.
Another serious revolt was that of the commanders of the imperial
gurad in Dembiya, Begemder and Wogera, who attempted in 1609
(when Susinyos was in Tigre) to crown a pretender said to be the
grandson of Minas. When finally defeated by Yamana Christos,
the Emperor's brother and governor of Begemder, the leaders of
this insurrection were executed and their lands taken by the
crown.[6]

Administration, army and the Galla

Cognizant of all the ills which befell the country as a result of Serse
Dingil's administrative and military reforms and his *laissez faire*
attitude concerning the nobility, Susinyos was determined not to
repeat the same mistakes.[7] Invariably he based his government, as
other rulers had in the past, on members of his immediate family.[8]
Serse Dingil's military aristocracy was exiled to remote *amba*s and
the traditional nobility was deprived, as much as possible, of its
privileges and power. But in contra-distinction to some outstanding
monarchs in the fourteenth and fifteenth centuries who relied on
their sons and kinsmen – usually in theory only – Susinyos delegated authority to his governors to the extent that he completely
decentralised his administration and, it seems, deprived the
monarchy of much of its power. Thus his eldest half-brother
Yamana Christos was made *Bitwadad*[9] and governor of Begemder,
Dembiya and the central provinces. Another half-brother, Afa

Christos, ruled parts of Lasta and Angot. His younger brother, Si'la Christos, was made governor-general of Tigre and his son-in-law and oldest friend, Yolyos, governed Gojjam.

A powerful and outstanding monarch, Susinyos, notwithstanding the authority entrusted to his governors, could and did rotate them, changed the extent of their governorships or replaced them altogether, as he saw fit.[10] Inevitably this was to become a source of constant friction with his supporters, who interpreted his initial policy and relationship with them as that of *primus inter pares* and envisaged Ethiopia as a federation of feudal estates co-ordinated by the emperor. Indeed, this may have been a major reason for the opposition of most of them to Susinyos' revolutionary concepts and reforms, but their attitude since the second decade of Susinyos' reign also reflected the general discontent in the country with the alien religio-cultural changes and their far-reaching socio-political aspects which the monarch tried to impose in the 1610s and 1620s.

With most provinces simultaneously threatened by the Galla, pretenders to the throne or other rebels, Susinyos realised the impracticability of having an enormous royal army under his command. But unwilling to reinstate the traditional military system and aware of Galla power and tactics, he decided to adopt a defensive strategy based on the ability of each provincial governor to absorb the brunt of Galla attacks. Out of expediency, therefore, he permitted the governors to retain all, or most, of the taxation of their respective provinces to enable them to build their own local forces.[11] A substitute for the *Chewa* and the feudal army, these forces were sufficiently strong to protect their provinces against Galla conquest and suppress any rebellion.[12] The royal army, which the emperor commanded, at first relatively small due to policy as well as financial and practical constraints, served in a sense as a national reserve used in extreme cases. In reality the emperor created new feudal armies at the expense of the central power.

The limited reservoir of people suitable for military service due to the stratification of Ethiopia's society had always proved a major drawback to the attempts of reforming emperors in the past. Susinyos' governors, when building their provincial armies, drew heavily on offspring of *Chewa* soldiers who became gentlemen farmers by usurping lands granted to their ancestors for military services, and on refugee military elements from areas overrun by the Galla and even on Galla warriors. Zadingil's revolutionary attempt to create a national army had proved premature and was not repeated by Susinyos, even though he disbanded the imperial guard, the source of endless troubles in the past, and repossessed the estates allotted for their maintenance in Wogera, Dembiya and Begemder.[13] At the same time, however, Susinyos began to organise a corps of bodyguard battalions, such as the *Kokab* cavalry,[14] composed of Muslim and non-Ethiopian elements, a battalion of Portuguese and Turkish musketeers, and several more of infantry drawn mainly from Gonja, Belaw and Agaw captives and converted Falasha, frequently called *Quayla*.[15]

Undoubtedly an important source of manpower for Susinyos' army were Galla bands who found themselves at odds with their brethren or who through expediency were ready to join the Ethiopian monarch's cause. His intimate knowledge of Galla society enabled Susinyos to exploit and even augment the rivalries between different Galla clans and between the Galla proper and those elements who were incorporated into their society either voluntarily or by coercion. These elements were utilised for two purposes. The majority were excellent material to build the *Chewa* type defence system along Ethiopia's border with the Galla. Another element, probably individuals or renegade bands of Galla proper, was even incorporated into the royal bodyguard battalions.[16] Thus, although relatively small at the beginning, Susinyos' army, a few years after he came to power, numbered some 25,000 men and by the 1620s about 40,000.[17]

By the outset of the seventeenth century the Galla had adapted themselves to the use of the horse and their cavalry was far superior to that of the Ethiopians. They began to fight in large formations strategically placed on the battlefield. The sheer weight of their forces, their mobility and the fear which their dedicated warriors inspired made them nearly invincible as far as the professional-mercenary Ethiopian armies were concerned. The emperor's defensive tactics were based on the assumption that each governor would be able to deal with normal Galla eruptions into his respective territories and prevent their conquest. He also instructed his generals to allow the fury of the Galla onslaught to dissipate before counter-attacking them, especially when they were retreating, tired and encumbered by prisoners and booty, whatever the cost to the population. The provincial armies served, therefore, as a kind of shock absorber redressing the situation after the Galla had achieved their initial goal, or sufficiently delaying them until the arrival of the royal army.

In reality the momentum of the Galla migration in the last quarter of the sixteenth century was nearly spent by the beginning of the seventeenth. After their astounding advance and expansion the Galla undoubtedly needed a period of consolidation and reorganisation; they were now spread over vast territories and their human resources were thinly stretched despite local elements who joined their migration to the plateau. The Galla, moreover, became increasingly engaged in internal struggles over the territories which they had captured and their fratricide, the Jesuits estimated, may have saved Ethiopia from complete conquest.[18] Only this could explain the limited gains of the Galla during the chaotic decade until the rise of Susinyos to power and in the years which followed this event. Despite the advances of several clans of the Karayu and the Marawa in Begemder, Lasta and Amhara, raids by the Azebu on Tigre, and repeated Borana attempts to overrun Damot and Enarea and penetrate Gojjam, Galla gains on the whole were limited. On the other hand, the emperor himself was introducing a Trojan Horse into his realm by settling friendly Galla in different parts of Gojjam and on the borders of Amhara and Begemder.[19]

Insofar as he and his governors were preoccupied with civil wars in most provinces, considering his knowledge of Galla power and motivation and the disregard in which he held the Ethiopian military machine, Susinyos assumed that at best he could block further Galla advances. Indeed despite several half-hearted attempts to penetrate Galla territories, the emperor was convinced that due to the state of Ethiopia and the limited resources he possessed he could not hope to take the offensive and re-establish Solomonic authority in the areas beyond the effective borders of the kingdom which he had inherited from his predecessors. Thus he himself became affected by the psychological impact of the Galla migration and of their strategy, which completely confused the Ethiopians. Yet unlike the apathy of Ethiopia's ruling classes and inhabitants, Susinyos had not given up hope of re-establishing Ethiopia's power in its historic borders. But to achieve that he became increasingly convinced, also due to the reluctance of his soldiers to follow him, that he would need massive European help in the form of soldiers, artisans and instructors. He hoped that the introduction of what he considered the superior European culture, technical and spiritual, would generate a revolution in every aspect of Ethiopian life. Thus, as early as the last months of 1607, we are told, Susinyos had already written to the Pope and the King of Portugal describing the state of Ethiopia, the Galla threat to the country and requesting about a thousand soldiers to help him save the Christian empire.[20]

Ethiopian expansionism, economy and the Funj sultanate

A direct outcome of the contraction of the Ethiopian polity was the pressing need for revenue, which was a factor which led to a more cruel exploitation of the peasantry and was also a factor in accelerating Ethiopian expansionism in the Agaw and Falasha areas in the north and the west and into the peripheral areas of the plateau towards the plains of the Sudan. Inhabited by 'Arab'[21] and other pastoralists and Cushitic and Negroid agriculturalists, these areas, in addition to gold, ivory, wax and slaves, produced enormous quantities of foodstuffs. After Susinyos' authority was relatively secure it became important to show the flag in these areas, where Ethiopian hegemony was no longer recognised.

Densely populated and frequently suffering from drought and locusts as well as from the migration of Beja or coastal pastoralists, Tigre had always served as a reservoir of immigrants which nourished Ethiopian expansionism in the past. Several years of drought, followed by locusts in the beginning of the seventeenth century, caused a new wave of migration from Tigre. Unable to turn southwards the immigrants poured into the newly opened northern provinces.[22] This, at first, had nothing to do with Susinyos' raids on the peripheral areas of his kingdom immediately after coming to power, though it became a factor of increasing importance later on.

Undoubtedly the need of the monarch for revenue to obtain resources necessary to extend his authority in other parts of the country was the immediate cause for the campaigns against the Agaw and other peoples to the west and southwest of Lake Tana in 1607-1608. During the period of interregnum these people did not pay the tribute due from them. Their continuous refusal to pay a greatly reduced tribute to Susinyos served as an excuse for the mass looting of their land and the enslavement of thousands. But such raids also served to show the flag and to re-establish Ethiopian hegemony in areas considered by the emperor to belong to him and which were economically and strategically important.[23]

Susinyos' campaigns to the north and west of Lake Tana resulted in the capture of quantities of ivory, wax, agricultural produce and thousands of slaves, sold immediately to merchants from Sennar and the coast. That these raids were in the context of Ethiopian policy concerning territories in the 'third circle' of the kingdom is evident from the growing tension between Ethiopia and Sennar in the second decade of the century.

The Funj sultanate was established by the beginning of the sixteenth century by Umar dhu Nakhas on the ruins of the Christian kingdom of Alwa. In addition to the more rapid islamisation of their subjects the Funj rulers were instrumental in reviving the caravan trade in the region. Already by the first decades of the sixteenth century Sennar had become an important *entrepôt* of the great caravans travelling between the western Sudan and Sawakin and between Cairo and Ethiopia.[24]

The revival of the Red Sea trade from the middle of the century, accompanied by Ottoman attempts to capture Ethiopia, enhanced the importance of the trade route between the latter and Egypt by way of Sennar. Merchants from all over the Muslim world, sometimes accompanied by Europeans and Armenians (not to mention the Ethiopian Jabartis), exploited the favourable circumstances and travelled beyond Dembiya as far as the Sidama principalities of the southwestern plateau. Even after the Galla had overrun the corridor between Gojjam and Enarea caravans from the north continued to reach the remote markets of the Omo-Gibe basin.[25] The inevitable risk on this route was undoubtedly compensated for by the immense profit made on Ethiopian luxury products and slaves.

The border between Ethiopia and Sudan was never clearly defined. It comprised a wide belt of broken and otherwise difficult terrains where the Ethiopian plateau declines into the plains of Sudan. Ethiopian or Funj authority in different parts of this region depended on the ability of the respective rulers or their governors to show the flag and exact tribute. These areas by their very nature served as a refuge for unruly elements or deposed officials and pretenders with their followers. By the beginning of the seventeenth century the development of trade led to greater co-operation between the Funj and Ethiopian rulers, and the chief of the Arab tribes in the borderland was entrusted with the protection of caravans between the two countries. It seems, however, that political refugees and the pastoralists living in the borderland exploited the weakness of Ethiopia from the end of the sixteenth century to raid Dembiya and Tigre for slaves and Sennar for cattle and horses.[26]

Wishing to suppress the raids into Ethiopian territories and to monopolise the sources of gold, slaves, wax and ivory, Susinyos attempted at an early stage of his reign to strengthen his position beyond the actual frontier of his effective government. His efforts to establish his authority in the rich borderland provoked growing tension with the Funj and with chiefs of the pastoralist peoples who inhabited the region. The gradual advance of the Ethiopians in the direction of the important source of gold in the Fazogli area (centre of gold production), culminating in a major campaign led by Si'la Christos in 1615/1616, was partially the cause of several Funji slave raids on Ethiopian territory[27] (such raids may have been a common phenomenon in the past).

Considered by Susinyos more than just an infringement of his empire because they were directed against Ethiopian populations, these raids caused him to prepare a multi-pronged attack on Sennari territory. The monarch, moreover, conscious of the importance of the colonisation of the northern territories, was determined to protect the new settlers in these areas, as well as to establish once and for all the Ethiopian claim on the peripheral belt around the plateau. Commanded by several governors and by the emperor, columns of Ethiopian troops penetrated (1616-18) beyond the borderland as far as Fazogli in the west and the delta of the Gash and Kassala in the north. The detention and death in Sennar of a new *abun* on his way from Egypt to Ethiopia, although welcomed by Susinyos, served as an excuse for the continuation of his aggressive policy against his former friends. Despite counter-measures by the Funjis and rebellions at home, Ethiopian armies repeatedly penetrated Sennari territory in the west and as far as Dabarki and Taka in the north.[28]

Inevitably the struggle for the mastery of the borderland greatly disturbed commercial activities in the region. Subsequently much of the trade of Ethiopia which had gone by way of Sennar, slaves included, was diverted to Sawakin and Massawa. Thus, despite the decline of their power in the region the revenues of the Turks in *Habesh* were still substantial in the first decades of the seventeenth century. Moreover, with the exception of very short periods, relations between the Ottomans and Susinyos were on the whole cordial, which greatly benefitted the Jesuits who entered Ethiopia. However, when the latter were expelled from the empire the Ottoman authorities on the coast were more than obliging when requested by Fasilidas to prevent Europeans and especially Catholic missionaries from entering the plateau.[29]

The encouragement by Susinyos of Tigrean and Amhara colonisation of Dembiya, Wogera and Simen was bound to affect the Falasha. Susinyos and his generals led a number of major campaigns there, either to suppress rebellions of pretenders who found refuge among the oppressed Falasha or to break their resistance and fully annex to Ethiopia these rugged mountainous provinces. The Falasha were given the option to convert to Christianity and many who chose to do so were assimilated into Amhara culture. Others, who clung to their religion, if they survived the campaigns against them, became serfs of the Ethiopian settlers or were allowed to practise different kinds of handicrafts.[30]

Susinyos' policy concerning the Agaw of the west and of Lasta, the Falasha of the north and the Gonjas, Belaw and Shanqalla of the northwestern slopes of the Ethiopian plateau was not as spontaneous or unplanned as it may have seemed. Even if it was partly motivated by the need for resources, operations in these areas were carefully co-ordinated and their outcome thoroughly analysed. A ruler as intelligent, powerful and determined as Susinyos would not have diverted his limited means from other fronts at critical times merely to conduct slave-raiding in peripheral territories. In contradistinction to Serse Dingil in the 1570s and 1580s, Susinyos had a well conceived plan which he carried out with typical thoroughness. By the first quarter of the seventeenth century Ethiopian territory had been so diminished through the Galla migration that it was essential to consolidate imperial authority in the northern provinces and in the peripheral areas beyond them in order to have a viable empire with the territorial continuity and strategic depth essential for its survival. If he deemed his power inadequate to take the offensive against the Galla, it was definitely sufficient to strengthen what remained of

Ethiopia until the anticipated arrival of Portuguese reinforcements. But as long as the latter did not materialise he limited himself to essential expansionism which his forces could and were willing to carry out.

Reform and Westernisation

By 1610 Susinyos had succeeded in consolidating his authority in what remained of the Ethiopian empire. A strong, intelligent, brave and able ruler and general he could, had he wished to do so, have reorganised the empire on a far stronger foundation through careful and evolutionary reforms of the administrative and military system and the church. This and his knowledge of Galla warfare might have eventually enabled him to re-establish royal authority in Galla-controlled territories.

However, notwithstanding his many talents, Susinyos' reign was unfortunately dominated by an ill-fated attempt to reform the very foundations of Ethiopian society, culture and government through a massive conversion to Catholicism and imposed assimilation of Western (Catholic) culture with the help of foreign instructors. At first Susinyos realistically preconditioned submission to Rome on the arrival in Ethiopia of imperative aid from Europe, but impatient and under Jesuit pressure, he decided not to wait for the means needed to assure the success of his venture. His assumption was that conversion of the Ethiopians to Catholicism would induce the dynamics essential to a more cohesive, stable and culturally advanced Ethiopia, under the leadership of the Solomonic monarchy.

The development of Western technology and especially military techniques since the post-mediaeval period was the object of admiration and jealousy in other parts of the world. As their empire(s) declined in the seventeenth and eighteenth centuries, Muslim scholars and statesmen assumed it was the outcome of the stagnation of material aspects of their culture. Some rulers, therefore, sought to copy the military aspects of Western material culture in order to resist the growing encroachment of Europe. This became quite a common phenomenon by the nineteenth century, when reforming sultans of the Ottoman empire and, more so, Muhammad Ali of Egypt, borrowed Western technology, military innovations and even educational systems.

Along with those who wished to advance the technological development of their countries according to European model, an increasing number of semi-educated people, ignorant of their own heritage and despising their stagnant culture, were ready to accept anything European as automatically superior. Still worse, many who did not understand the substance of Western culture adopted its shell while completely dissociating themselves from their own cultural heritage. Yet a class of 'puritans', frightened by the impact of the West, either rejected everything European and turned back to the root of their own culture or considered any reform as part of Western spiritual imperialism. The happiest, but rare, combination was that of people who, while reviving the foundations of their ancient culture, adapted it to modern times without enslaving themselves to the values of Western society.

It has already been pointed out that Ethiopian rulers admired European material culture as early as the mediaeval period. The arrival of the Portuguese and the Jesuits in Ethiopia demonstrated the superiority of Western Christians, especially in the fields of technology and warcraft. Christian successes against the Muslims in the Red Sea and Indian Ocean gave rise to an exaggerated notion of the power of Catholic nations which was enhanced by Jesuit descriptions of the military strength, government, social systems and wealth of Catholic rulers. The decline of Ottoman-Muslim power in the Red Sea by the beginning of the seventeenth century was emphasized by the arrival there of the British and the Dutch, who easily overcame local resistance to their presence. Protestant powers, uninterested in Ethiopia and disappointed in the trade of the Red Sea, remained an unknown quantity to the highland Christians, but their display of military-maritime might undoubtedly contributed to the respect for European ability, identified with the Portuguese whom the Jesuits ostentatiously represented.

The long but hesitant courtship between Ethiopia and Catholic Europe reached a climax with the rise to power of Zadingil, when the country was involved in a terrible crisis. Too impatient to institute evolutionary reforms while consolidating his base of support, this monarch paid with his life for his rash experiments. Probably the greatest Ethiopian monarch after Zara Yaeqob, Gelawdewos in the mid-sixteenth century was also tempted to reform his country with the help of Westerners and European technical-military aid. Aware, however, of the dangers inherent in such a move, proud of Ethiopia's historical and cultural heritage and the relation between it and his dynasty, Gelawdewos was determined to achieve his objectives by reviving the national church as a major tool for his socio-political reforms and integrative policy. This experiment, unfortunately, was cut short by his premature death.

Unlike Zadingil, Susinyos consolidated his government before attempting to introduce revolutionary reforms. But in contrast with Gelawdewos he despised and rejected the Ethiopian church and culture and systematically destroyed the supportive infrastructure which had been the mainstay of the Solomonic rulers in the past. He was convinced, moreover, that the national church and the traditional socio-cultural organisation was a major reason for Ethiopia's decline and weakness.

Susinyos' attitude to the Ethiopian church should be examined in the context of his period. The church was never strong spiritually and had suffered devastating blows since the time of Grañ. During Serse Dingil's long reign the monarch gave his ecclesiastics a free hand and the controversies in Ethiopian Christianity, especially over the problem of the Sabbath, surfaced again and contributed to the decline of Ethiopia. In the eyes of Susinyos, Abuna Petros, who had allied himself with the hated nobility, was a party to the murder of Zadingil and the abortive attempt of the feudal lords to undermine the monarchical institution. The leaders of the Ethiopian church, including Abuna Simeon, were morally corrupt and relatively ignorant. Just at this time, moreover, Ichege Za Wengel, from his retreat in Debra Libanos, opened a campaign against the church leadership in order to strengthen his own position and possibly that of the house of Tekla Haymanot, which suffered greatly from the fact that most of its centres were conquered or cut away from the kingdom by the Galla. Finally, the ecclesiastics, it was claimed, were in possession of about one third of the land in Ethiopia[31] and of other sources of revenue; they were therefore a natural target for a ruler who badly needed to expand his meagre resources.

The cultural and spiritual stagnation of Ethiopia caused the strong and farsighted Susinyos to become completely hypnotised by what he thought (and was told) European culture could contribute to reform the empire. Observing the ability and way of life of the Jesuits and listening to their seemingly logical theological argumentations and the description of European government, military and social systems, he became fully convinced that to save Ethiopia it was imperative to replace its institutions with a new European-oriented socio-political framework and culture with the help of the Catholic nations. In his attempt to supplant traditional institutions by European, Susinyos rather resembled some of the oriental rulers who sought to do so in the nineteenth century. Yet Susinyos' revolutionary attempt at reforms dated to the beginning of the seventeenth century when the population of his country was still completely unprepared for such upheaval. His rejection of Ethiopian culture and decision to build a new state and society based on European values, moreover, were far more extreme than the feeble efforts at modernisation of many nineteenth century rulers in the Middle East.

Susinyos' long reign was a tragedy to himself and his country. A strong, intelligent and farsighted emperor, a fearless warrior and an able tactician, had he invested his energy in reorganising the Ethiopian polity he might have become, at least temporarily, the saviour of Christian-semitised Ethiopia. Unhappily, however, he chose Catholicism and European culture and, disregarding his own reservations, he undertook Ethiopia's conversion without the means to carry out this revolution, on the premise that it would lead to a more integrated, stable and advanced country. What he and the fanatical Jesuits ignored, or were unable to grasp, was the strong correlation between the Ethiopian church and its ancient customs and traditions and the local socio-political system. The Catholic dogmas, in their rigid Jesuit interpretation, were the outcome of an evolution completely alien to the African Cushitic framework of the semitised Ethiopian society and were unequivocally rejected by it.

NOTES

1. We are told, nevertheless, that even Gelawdewos made an exception of the house of Hezba Nan (1429-1433), known for their violence and disloyalty – Almeida, *Some Records,* pp. 101-2.

2. Fasilidas, Susinyos' son, re-established the royal prison on Amba Wehni (lit. prison) some 25 miles southeast of Gondar. Almeida (Beccari, Vol. VIII, pp. 193-4) and the Yemenite Qadi al-Khaymi (Peiser, F. E., *Zur Geschichte Abessiniens im 17 Jahrhundert,* Berlin, 1898, p. 52) claim that this happened

shortly after Fasilidas' coming to power. There he imprisoned his many brothers (with the exception of Gelawdewos) and subsequently had them murdered. There are indications, however, that the royal prison at Amba Wehni was established at a later date, as Si'la Christos was interned on a mountain in Simen in 1633 before his execution (Béguinot, F. (ed. and trans.), *La Cronaca Abbreviata d'Abissinia*, Roma, 1901, p. 48; Basset, 'Etudes', p. 133) and others were sent to islands in Lake Tana. The establishment of the royal prison probably took place after Fasilidas overcame the Lasta rebellion in 1635 and before al-Khaymi's visit in 1647.

3. It is evident that the emperor came to Axum determined to be crowned there despite the seeming disrespect shown by him to tradition, according to the Jesuits. There is an exaggeration in the claims that he was contemptuous of customs relating to the Ethiopian monarchy and that he dispensed with all the ancient barriers which separated him from his subjects and especially from the Jesuits. The tendency to lower the barriers between monarch and subjects had already emerged during the reign of Serse Dingil, who wished to jettison the mediating services of the nobility and directly control his officers and army. But both Serse Dingil and Susinyos were careful not to dispense altogether with the dignity of royalty. On distance maintained between the emperor and the Jesuits – *Lobo*, Le Grand, pp. 254-5; Almeida, *Some Records*, p. 81; Tellez, p. 54. See Ludolphus (p. 208) on Susinyos' insistence on being crowned in Axum according to all the ancient traditions. Also: Tellez, p. 185; Bruce, Vol. III, p. 299.

4. Beccari, Vol. XI, p. 166; Pereira, *Susenyos*, Vol. II, p. 78 – on expropriation of church funds to the emperor.

5. Beccari, Vol. XI, pp. 223-4 – on the nobility. On different pretenders – Paez, Vol. III, pp. 409-10. Also: Tellez, pp. 182-3.

6. Perruchon, *Sémitique*, 1897, pp. 181-3; Beccari, Vol. III, pp. 409-19; Vol. XI, pp. 223-5; *Lobo*, Le Grand, p. 300; Pereira, *Susenyos*, Vol. II, pp. 98-9; Bruce, Vol. III, pp. 229-301.

7. On his attitude to the nobility – Almeida, Beccari, Vol. V, pp. 66-7.

8. Mainly his half-brothers, nephews, cousins and sons-in-law, who were old comrades-in-arms.

9. The title fell out of use in the 16th century and was bestowed upon Susinyos' elder brother. The emperor, moreover, directly commanded his army. *Bitwadad* became just an honorific title no longer attached to the court and command of the army – *Lobo*, Le Grand, pp. 254-5.

10. Yolyos was rotated three times, first to Gojjam, then to Tigre and in 1614 to Wogera, Begemder and parts of Tigre.

11. Paez, Vol. III, p. 284.

12. Susinyos gave up a tribute of 3000 (?) horses due from Gojjam because this province was under constant Galla pressure from several directions – Tellez, p. 62; Ludolphus, p. 205.

13. Mainly the *Qerban* cavalry composed, it seems, of large elements of Muslims. Paez, Vol. II, p. 136.

14. Literally star, which was to play an important role in the history of Ethiopia in the future. It had many Muslims in its ranks.

15. 'Annales Iohannis', pp. 8, 18, 46. Such units are already mentioned in the time of Fasilidas.

16. Pereira, *Susenyos*, Vol. II, pp. 147, 219-20. The *Talata*, frequently mentioned in the chronicle of Susinyos and of later rulers, were probably non-Galla elements incorporated into Galla society but not into the *gada*. See above, p. 192, note 42. On internal struggle among the Galla – *Some Records*, p. 135;

'Annales Iohannis', pp. 254-5. On *Qalagand* – Basset, 'Etudes', pp. 303-4. ' ... Galla to whom the emperor himself has given much land in Gojjam and Dambea so that they should help him against other hostile Galla tribes' – Almeida, *Some Records*, p. 54. Also: Tellez, p. 38; Pereira, *Susenyos*, Vol. II, pp. 110-13.

17. Paez, Vol. II, p. 136; *Some Records*, p. 77.

18. Almeida, *Some Records*, p. 135.

19. Basset, 'Etudes', p. 121; Perruchon, *Sémitique*, 1897, pp. 182-3; Pereira, *Susenyos*, Vol. II, pp. 82-4. The rise of the next *luba* was due 1611.

20. Bruce, Vol. III, p. 284; Wansleben, p. 18; Tellez, p. 189. Even if Paez wrote to King Philip of Spain about Susinyos' alleged inclination to Catholicism and his special regard for the Portuguese, it is unlikely that at this early stage Susinyos was sufficiently aware of the meaning of Catholicism and, notwithstanding his admiration for European material culture, he did not consider conversion to Catholicism at this time.

21. 'Arab' – a general term used to describe Hamitic pastoralist tribes in Sudan, living in areas adjacent to Ethiopia's northern and northwestern border. They may have incorporated, at some time, Arab-nomad elements in their ranks. However their claim to being Arab in origin is nearly always fabricated.

22. On difficulties in the past – Alvarez, Vol. I, pp. 133-4; Whiteway, *Castanhoso*, p. 8; Conzelman, p. 138. On droughts, locusts and migration from Tigre in Susinyos' period – Tellez, pp. 234-5; *Lobo*, Le Grand, p. 81; Morié, Vol. II, p. 234.

23. Paez, Vol. III, pp. 444-5; Beccari, Vol. II, p. 267; Pereira, *Susenyos*, Vol. II, pp. 81-5; Perruchon, *Sémitique*, 1897, pp. 182-3. Following his theory that Ethiopian kings were only interested in enslaving the Agaw, Wolde Aregay (pp. 477-9) rejects the claim of the sources that the Agaw were attacked because they were unwilling to accept the authority of the emperor and to pay the reduced tribute demanded from them. Forced out of their original homeland they were unable to pay even the reduced taxation and the raids on them were the outcome of the need for resources to maintain the royal army. He overlooks, however, the fact that this army was still very small and that although the monarch granted his governors nearly all the revenues accruing from the territories under their command they still paid him the *mashumya* (payment on appointment to office) in gold on their appointment (Beccari, *Tigre*, pp. 68-9), that the king repossessed most of the territories previously under the imperial guard and that one of the most important revenues of the realm was the tribute on cattle introduced in the 16th century – Almeida, *Some Records*, p. 88; Ludolphus, p. 206; Beccari, *Tigre*, p. 69.

24. Shibeika, Mekki (ed.), *Ta'rikh Muluk al-Sudan*, Khartoum, 1947/1247 H. p. 26; Eschcoly, *Hareuveni*, pp. 7-12. See above, p. 8.

25. Almagia, p. 45; Paez, Beccari, Vol. IV, p. 31 – on a Jewish merchant from Vienna active in Ethiopia at the beginning of the 17th century. Vitteleschi, Muric, *Lettre annue dell' Etiopia dell' anno 1626*, Roma, 1629, pp. 8-9.

26. Crawford, O. G. S., *The Fung Kingdom of Sennar*, Gloucester, 1951, pp. 329-30; *Futuh*, p. 321; Bruce, Vol. III, p. 314. See the story of Yaeqob's son seeking refuge with the Funj sultan in 1607/1608 – Morié, Vol. II, pp. 278-9; Pereira, *Susenyos*, Vol. II, pp. 125, 163-4.

27. Susinyos adopted a similar attitude regarding Ottoman raids, see below note 29. Pereira, *Susenyos*, Vol. II, pp. 82, 108, 125, 163-4, 450-1; Bruce, Vol. III, pp. 312-14; Paez, Vol. III, pp. 499-500; Almeida, Beccari, Vol. VI, pp. 327-8. A correlation may have existed between Si'la Christos' campaign and the Enarean king's attack on the Galla which brought him as far as the Abbay – Almeida, Beccari, Vol. V, pp. 78-9.

28. Pereira, *Susenyos,* Vol. II, pp. 157-9, 161-4; Bruce, Vol. III, pp. 314-18. Of special interest is the claim of the queen of the 'shepherds' (Bruce, Vol. III, p. 317) that she discontinued the payment of tribute to the Ethiopians because they could no longer protect the Belaw against the 'Arabs' and the Funj. In his answer Susinyos claimed (p. 318) that he intended to hold all the area from Fazogli to Sawakin previously belonging to Ethiopia.

29. British sources concerning the limited trade of the Somali coast and Zayla – *Purchas,* Vols. III, IV. See Bruce, Vol. III, pp. 312-18, Vol. IV, p. 119, on the concept of Susinyos' campaigns. On Turkish raids on Eritrean provinces and the punitive action by Susinyos which led to the complete capitulation of the Turkish authorities and their undertaking to buy only 'legal' slaves – Beccari, *Tigre,* pp. 46-7; Wolde Aregay, p. 485, according to Caspar Paez, Goa 39(II), Archive of the Society of Jesus, Roma. The governor of Sawakin used Mendez' good offices to reach an agreement with Susinyos in 1624 – *Lobo,* Le Grand, pp. 31-3. On the thriving trade between Ethiopia and the Ottoman coast – *ibid.,* p. 36; Tellez, pp. 265-6.

30. Tellez, p. 38; Almeida, *Some Records,* p. 54; Bruce, Vol. III, pp. 303-4, 307-8. It is suggestive that the new converts were forced to work on the Sabbath. See also Morié, Vol. II, p. 290; Perruchon, *Sémitique,* 1897, pp. 181-3; Pereira, *Susenyos,* Vol. II, pp. 116-17.

31. Almeida, Beccari, Vol. V, p. 81; *Some Records,* p. 35; Bruce, Vol. III, pp. 365-7. According to the different Jesuit sources up to one third of the cultivable land belonged to the church and the monasteries when Susinyos came to power.

CHAPTER X

Imposed Conversion and the Triumph
of the National Church

In 1607 Susinyos wrote to King Philip of Spain and Pope Paul V and solicited aid. His letters reflecting his own difficult position and the Galla threat to Ethiopia were probably written on the advice of the captain of the Portuguese or Pero Paez.[1] But his close relations with the Jesuits and the increasing influence of Pero Paez over him began in 1610, when back in Dembiya with his camp near the Jesuit centre in Gorgora he frequently met with the missionaries.[2]

Susinyos not only enjoyed listening to the Jesuits' theological discussions but was greatly impressed by their description of European nations, their material and spiritual culture and their socio-political and military organisation. The confrontations which he arranged in his court between the Jesuits and the local ecclesiastics only strengthened his contempt for the latter's ignorance and the shallowness of their argumentation.

The emperor had, it seems, already opted for Catholicism by 1612. He came to believe that Catholic Christianity was not only by far superior to the Ethiopian, but could also serve as a means of reforming the foundations of the Ethiopian polity, society and culture. Yet he prudently disregarded the persuasion of the Jesuits to convert because he realised that Ethiopia was still unprepared for such a revolutionary step and that he was insufficiently strong to undertake it by himself. He encouraged, however, his kinsmen and closest supporters to follow the teachings of the Jesuits and himself supported their anti-Sabbath campaign, careful, however, not to show favour to their polemics concerning diophysitism.[3]

It was only to be expected that the national church became increasingly apprehensive about the growing Catholic influence in the court.[4] Yet the anti-Catholic party drew its strength not from the ecclesiastics nor from the powerless and frustrated nobility but rather from members of the royal family, friends and sons-in-law of the emperor and court stewards. Undoubtedly the special relations between Susinyos and the Jesuits and the latter's growing influence on the monarch evoked resentment. However, the high-handed behaviour of the emperor, once he had established his authority, and his tactless treatment of his closest subordinates, were also major factors to be considered.

The xenophobic feelings towards the Jesuits were at first restricted to elements within the church and ruling classes and were, as pointed out above, also the outcome of frustrated ambitions, which in many cases had nothing to do with theological matters. The more machiavellian among the ruling classes feared that once Susinyos received aid from the Catholic powers, he would become so strong that their influence would be completely eroded. But many important officers, close to the emperor, believed his policy a tragic mistake that might undermine the fragile infrastructure upon which the monarchy rested. Moreover, Susinyos' attempts to ally himself with the Catholic powers through the Jesuits awakened the apprehension that spiritual domination was a means for imperialist aspirations of the Europeans.

The embassy which Susinyos had sent in 1613 to Goa carried secret letters to the Spanish king and to the Pope requesting soldiers, artisans and priests so that the monarch would be able to declare for Catholicism. The secrecy surrounding the mission, its strange itinerary and the difficulties it met bear evidence of the opposition which the emperor already encountered in implementing his policy and his concern lest his plans became prematurely known. Although he was ready to convert to Catholicism Susinyos was still cautious enough to make an open declaration for Rome conditional upon the arrival in Ethiopia of a substantial Portuguese force.[5] The attempts of the anti-Catholic faction to frustrate the Jesuit efforts indicate how justified the monarch's apprehension was.

The failure of his embassy and the opposition which his plan met did not deter Susinyos from pursuing his plans. His military successes between 1613 and 1617 strengthened his confidence and determination to carry out his plans. Convinced by Paez that Catholicism and the help of the Catholic powers would enable him to reform the foundations of the Ethiopian society and state and overcome the Galla, Susinyos was rapidly drifting away from the national church. In the heated court polemics over 'Judaic' influences in the Ethiopian church and diophysitism the monarch covertly came out on the side of the Jesuits.

The opposition to the monarch's policy at this stage seemed, at least on the surface, weak and lacking in leadership. The Ethiopian church had still not recuperated from the devastating blows which it had suffered in the past. Immediately after his victory, the monarch had shown his preference for the order of Tekla Haymanot, possibly because many monks of the rival order, with Abuna Petros, were in the camp of his enemies. Thus the house of Tekla Haymanot continued to maintain an ambivalent attitude concerning the emperor's pro-Catholic stance as long as this related to coercion of anti-Sabbath edicts and opposition to 'Judaic' influences in the church[5a] and to the erosion of the power of their St. Ewostatewos rivals. The nobility, stripped of authority, privileges and power, was impotent as far as active opposition to the monarch was concerned. The semitised population remained as lethargic as ever because it was still not directly affected by what was happening at court. Even rumours about Susinyos' conversion to Catholicism did not seem to hurt his prestige or affect his authority as long as he did not enforce a meaningful religio-cultural revolution. Indeed, in a country as indifferent to church affiliation as Ethiopia, where conversion from one religion to another was a most common phenomenon, the favour shown by the emperor to one sect or another could not ignite popular opposition beyond clerical circles and their immediate supporters.

The most serious reaction to the monarch's pro-Catholic policy continued to grow in Susinyos' own family and the orbit of his original followers. These were infuriated by the disregard shown them by Susinyos compared to the many privileges which he bestowed upon his younger brother Si'la Christos, a fanatical Catholic who tirelessly worked for Ethiopia's conversion to Rome. The cause of the national church thus served as a most convenient channel for their dissatisfaction and enabled them to attempt to gain power and fight the primacy of Si'la Christos by opposing the increasing influence of Catholicism in the country.

Having converted to Catholicism in 1612 Si'la Christos replaced Yolyos as governor of Gojjam. With Damot, parts of Amhara and Showa also under his command he ruled a substantial part of the empire and enjoyed enormous revenues. On the other hand Yolyos, dismissed in 1614 from the governorship of Tigre, was given that of Begemder and several other provinces and districts around the Takazze. What disturbed him most, it seems, was the lack of consideration and respect shown him by his father-in-law and old friend, whose decision to dismiss him from the vice-regency of Tigre was partly influenced by the complaints of the Jesuits against him. The emperor's brother, Yamana Christos, was also shifted from one governorship to another and in 1616 lost to Si'la Christos the honorific title of *Bitwadad,* ostensibly because his soldiers refused to follow him into Galla territory. Other imperial kinsmen and trusted generals were also rotated in their positions or lost their governorships altogether in occasional administrative reshuffles.[6] In addition to their personal grievances none could tolerate the special position reserved to the Jesuits. Although ecclesiastics were respected in Ethiopia, very rarely had they been preferred so markedly to royal princes and officers; they were, moreover, *ferenjoch.*

Paez' influence over Susinyos had grown substantially by 1616. Under his influence the King of Kings strictly forbade observance of the Sabbath. Capitulating to Paez' coercion, just before he led another campaign against the western Agaw, Susinyos ordered the people to accept the diophysitist dogma. This decree more than anything else caused a substantial uproar among the ecclesiastics, nobility and many of the followers of the emperor because it subverted monophysitism, one of the most sacred pillars of the Ethiopian church.

Every lay clergyman, not to mention monks and hermits, felt that national heritage and religion were at stake and incited their parishioners to ignore this edict. Abuna Simeon excommunicated whoever obeyed the royal decree and accepted diophysitism, but under pressure he temporarily retracted the excommunication. Still, the emperor's departure from his cautious policy caused the opposition to his pro-Catholic stance to penetrate even beyond Ethiopia's ruling classes and ecclesiastics.

The immediate outcome was a secret alliance between Yolyos, the governor of Begemder and Lasta; Yamana Christos, the emperor's older brother and governor of Wogera and Dembiya; Beletengeta Keflo,[7] one of the most powerful personalities in the court administration; the ecclesiastics, led by the *abun*; and the traditional nobility. Each for his own reason was determined to break the stranglehold of the *ferenjis* over the emperor to do away with Roman influence in Ethiopia or gain power.[8] When he returned in 1617 from his war in the west, the breach between Susinyos, the national church and his frustrated officers was still not irreparable. Yet Susinyos refused to listen to the pleadings of his mother, friends and kinsmen. So convinced was he of the virtue of his belief and so certain of his power that he dismissed all complaints and warnings and himself led an all-out attack against the Funj sultanate. But the opposition to the monarch's religious policy continued to spread and the anti-Catholic party bided the opportunity to overthrow Susinyos or at least bring him back to his senses.

Abuna Simeon emerged as an arch-villain in the rebellion of 1618. He renewed the excommunication of all those who would betray monophysitism, encouraged leaders of the opposition to rebel against their master in the name of true Christianity, released them from their sacred vows to the emperor, and called upon the populace to join the revolt. In reality he was a mere tool in the hands of the lords behind the plot,[9] and the nobility which wished to capitalise on it. The official cause of the rebellion was the arbitrary dismissal of Yamana Christos from his position as *Bitwadad*. Indeed, the latter employed his two sons and their armies to capture strategic objectives and negotiated a military alliance with the Galla of Begemder, Amhara and Showa.[10]

When informed of the rebellion in 1618 Susinyos was in the area of the Atbara. But even before he reached the heart of the empire[11] the coalition quickly collapsed. Only Yolyos with the powerless *abun* and some ecclesiastics was determined to fight to the end. Yolyos' army was still formidable, but the battle concluded with the complete victory of the monarch and the death of Yolyos, Abuna Simeon and many of the ecclesiastics and monks who accompanied him. This victory, however, was in a way a milestone in Susinyos' reign and the beginning of the decline of his power. The bloodshed only served to embitter further the opposition to his anti-Ethiopian policy. But so convinced was the emperor of the righteousness of his cause and so hopeful still of Catholic aid that he pressed on with his policy on the premise that Catholicism would create the momentum necessary for the implementation of his reforms.[12]

The date given to Susinyos' official conversion to Catholicism is 1625, even though he publicly professed the faith twice in 1622. Yet the national church and its supporters already considered him a renegade in 1618.[13] From that year onwards opposition to Susinyos' pro-Catholic policy became open, more violent and rapidly spread from one province to another. In reality, traditional or new grievances against the monarch or the Solomonic dynasty now assumed, in the different parts of the country, a religious ideology with xenophobic undertones relating to the Jesuits and the alien dogmas which the emperor enabled them to impose upon Ethiopia. The enemies of the monarch drew heart, moreover, from the expansion of the opposition to his reign.

The shocking experience of the rebellion of 1618 did not deter Susinyos, nor did it persuade him to adopt a more balanced or cautious policy. If anything, it accelerated the process of complete alienation from the national church. Shortly after his victory Susinyos published a number of edicts, meant to erode the foundations of the church and to bring about Ethiopia's conversion to Catholicism. These were to be enforced with the help of a handful of Jesuits and thousands of fanatical Ethiopian converts, above all Si'la Christos.

A primary target of the emperor and the Jesuits were customs, traditions and dogmas of the Ethiopian church and society, considered by then a Jewish-pagan corruption of Christianity. What the dogmatic Jesuits ignored, or were incapable of understanding, was that these constituted much of Ethiopia's cultural heritage and way of life, probably a product of an ancient synthesis between the semitised and Cushitic cultures, undoubtedly unique yet an integral part of the Ethiopian environment. The monarch and his Jesuit mentors were challenging, therefore, the very foundations of Ethiopia's society – popular customs and manners regulating everyday life rather than being part of a religion. Their struggle with the national church was foolishly turned into a confrontation with the Ethiopian people.

The Jesuits were attempting to supplant flexible African-Mediterranean mores with an alien religious culture which grew out of very different environments and conditions. Their dogmatism was such that they ignored realities and were unwilling to compromise. In similar circumstances, Islam avoided such a grave mistake. Extremely pliable, patient and egalitarian, it adapted itself to local particularism, sure that a purer form of the Faith would eventually emerge through evolution. With such an approach it easily penetrated developing societies and had no difficulty in overcoming the dogmatic European-oriented Christianity.

Determined to carry out his policy at all cost and disillusioned with many of his veteran friends and kinsmen, the monarch became more dependent on the Jesuits and his Catholic Ethiopian supporters. Governors and officials considered disloyal to Catholicism were dismissed from their position and punished if they did not follow his religious policy. Ecclesiastics unwilling to co-operate with Susinyos' pro-Catholic edicts were banished from their parishes and monasteries and in some cases cruelly punished. In an effort to re-educate the Ethiopians the Jesuits (reinforced in the meantime by several Fathers from India) instructed the population in the new belief, supervised their conversion and intervened in the affairs of the state on every level. Inevitably, the frustration of all classes grew to such an extent that in the coming years one religiously motivated revolt followed another.[14]

The rebellion of Yonael (1620), the new governor of Begemder and one of Susinyos' trusted officers, was supported by ecclesiastics, the nobility, the people of Begemder, Wogera and Amhara and the local Galla. Baraytuma clans actually fought in the ranks of Yonael's army and when he was defeated he was taken in by his Galla friends. Constantly harassed by Susinyos and Si'la Christos and bewildered by the new religious edicts, a general uprising broke out among the Agaw of the west nearly simultaneously with that of Yonael. Led by monks, hermits and nobles who found refuge among them, the Agaw demanded, *inter alia*, that the Catholics be expelled and their books burnt. Both rebellions were crushed with the help of Si'la Christos, and thousands of clergymen and monks were killed fighting for their faith. Yonael and other officials were murdered in 1622 by a Galla chief at the instigation of Susinyos.[15]

The abortive rebellions of Yolyos and Yonael signalled the final alienation between the Solomonic monarch and the national church. The latter lost its predominant position in the country and a good part of its infrastructure was wiped out in the civil wars. Its churches and monasteries were closed, their property confiscated and the monks and clergy dispersed or fled to remote areas. Nevertheless, fighting for survival, the Church establishment and monks, no longer lethargic and submissive, were now in the forefront of resistance to Susinyos' attempt to impose on Ethiopia the religion of the *ferenji*s and their culture. Inevitably, as their suffering grew, the Catholics, and especially the Jesuits, became the target of intense hatred.

Until 1618 the attitude of the order of Tekla Haymanot to Susinyos' policy was somewhat ambiguous, if not ambivalent. If its leaders occasionally censured the emperor's innovations, their criticism was muted. In addition to the preference shown to this order from the beginning of his reign it had always supported the anti-Sabbath cause. Compared to the order of St. Ewostatewos, which drew its power from the northern and western provinces, that of Tekla Haymanot had lost much of its own due to the Galla migration. Consequently, its leaders may even have watched with delight the calamities which befell their rivals in the first decade of Susinyos' reign.

But once the emperor attempted to coerce the population to accept diophysitism and persecuted those loyal to the dogmas of the national church, the leaders of Tekla Haymanot could no longer remain neutral. Thus the *Ichege* arrived in the royal camp in 1622, reprimanded the King of Kings for persecuting those loyal to the national church and demanded that he stop his support of diophysitism. Alarmed by the general elation which swept the country, Susinyos considered revoking, at least temporarily, the measures taken against the national church. However, the pro-Catholic party, led by Si'la Christos and the Jesuits, expressed such strong opposition to any concessions to the loyalists that he quickly abandoned the idea of appeasement.

The early conversion of Si'la Christos to Catholicism and his relations with the Jesuits played a major role in developments in Ethiopia during Susinyos' reign. Si'la Christos exercised an immense influence on his brother and greatly encouraged his revolutionary plans. Once appointed governor of Gojjam, Dembiya and the other territories, he utilised his vast revenues to build a substantial private army from refugee and local military elements who became as devoted to Catholicism as himself and who received substantial estates previously allotted to the church and the nobility.[16] Inevitably, Si'la Christos' fanatical opposition to any change in the pro-Catholic policy in 1621/1622 and his special relations with the Jesuits and Rome began to frighten the monarch somewhat. The latter, it seems, came to realise the extent of his brother's power and of his dependence on him; also that his brother, rather than himself, was the favourite of the Catholics. This was the watershed in relations between them. Indeed, shortly afterwards the emperor began to undermine his brother's nearly absolute powers. On the other hand, to win the support of the Jesuits and Ethiopian Catholics he now openly declared for Rome.[17] His attempts to disgrace Si'la Christos, however, coincided with the new and most dangerous wave of rebellions, possibly sparked off by his impolitic declaration of 1622. Susinyos was repeatedly forced to call upon Si'la Christos' aid and temporarily restore him to some of his governorships. Unfortunately for Susinyos, Pero Paez died just at this time (1622).

A complete departure from his prudent policy in the first decades of his reign, Susinyos' public submission to Rome only confirmed what was generally believed by the Ethiopians since 1618/1619 and even earlier. This united most Ethiopians not, as the Jesuits promised, behind their ruler, but rather against him. At most it gained the emperor the approval of the handful of Jesuits, a few hundred Portuguese soldiers and the Ethiopian converts to Catholicism. Even the traditional centre of the Solomonic dynasty in Showa and Amhara showed its disapproval by erupting in 1623 into a general rebellion led by the pretender Wolde Gabriel. Supported, it seems, by the order of Tekla Haymanot, and probably with the sanction of the Abbot of Debra Libanos,[18] this revolt ignited the central and eastern plateaux with Muslim and Galla elements actively participating in it.

Ethiopia's vast Muslim population became increasingly apprehensive over the religious-oriented civil wars caused by the *ferenjis*. The Jabartis feared their religious zeal and fanaticism and the socio-political reforms which the monarch wished to institute. This attitude influenced neighbouring Muslim rulers previously friendly to Susinyos. Worried about the possibility of an Ethiopian-European alliance, they still did not differentiate, it seems, between the aggressive Protestant powers whose navies arrived in the Red Sea and the Portuguese. The Sultan of Aussa, possibly a tributary of Susinyos, corresponded with Wolde Gabriel and sent him presents, while the Turks may have even developed closer relations with him. The Jesuits who reached Aussa in 1624 were murdered and their colleagues who landed in Sawakin were prevented for a time from proceeding to the plateau.[19] Things returned to normal when the rebel was defeated and killed by Si'la Christos, again recalled from partial retirement.[20]

Even before the death of Paez the emperor had become fully aware that his policy greatly increased dissent in Ethiopia and that the religious-oriented civil wars were sapping its resources. The promise of military and technical aid from the Catholic powers did not materialise and Susinyos already doubted if it would ever arrive. Fearing the power of his brother, who was completely devoted to the triumph of Catholicism in Ethiopia, Susinyos considerably limited the extent of his governorships and resources. He still insisted, moreover, that his official declaration for Rome be conditional upon the arrival of a Catholic expeditionary force, which would help him withstand the opposition such a step would arouse and the Galla threat.[21]

In 1624 the emperor nominated his son Fasilidas as heir designate and made all his kinsmen, governors and officers swear an oath of allegiance to him. Although he paid lip-service to Catholicism and maintained correct relations with the Jesuits, Fasilidas was critical of his father's policy, which caused so much bloodshed, undermined the foundations of the monarchy and forfeited his dominant position to *ferenji* missionaries. Wooed by the loyalist party, Fasilidas remained, nevertheless, loyal to his father and avoided all contacts with his enemies.

Cognizant of the heir designate's lukewarm attitude to Catholicism, the zealous, arrogant and possibly envious Si'la Christos publicly made his allegiance to Fasilidas conditional upon the latter's loyalty to the Roman church. The undiplomatic threat in Si'la Christos' words did not escape the monarch. Having planned for some time to reduce his brother's power, he now deprived him of many of his appointments and command of the army. Even though he was reinstated shortly afterwards, when the Wolde Gabriel rebellion seemed to get out of hand, it was evident that Si'la Christos was out of favour. Susinyos carefully calculated his steps before challenging his able and powerful brother. But it seems that the proud feudal lord acquiesced in the emperor's decision only because of the influence of the Jesuits, who were apprehensive lest a struggle between the two brothers completely undid their achievements in Ethiopia.[22]

There are indications that Susinyos contemplated the mending of his fences with the national church after Paez' death in 1622. The King of Kings was not unaware of the increasingly bitter opposition to his religious policy. As late as 1623 he still made full recognition of Rome conditional upon the arrival of the promised Portuguese soldiers and artisans.[23] Despite his friendship with the Jesuits and his admiration of Catholicism he did not permit the missionaries to manipulate him and on several occasions rejected demands which seemed to him illogical and excessive.[24] Realising, moreover, that his new edicts were utterly incompatible with the customs and way of life of his partially assimilated Agaw subjects, Susinyos exempted them from several edicts issued in the 1620s. All this notwithstanding, in 1624, even before the arrival of Bishop Mendez who was to replace Paez, Susinyos publicly declared for Catholicism and made it the official faith of Ethiopia.

Despite his faith in Catholicism it is curious that Susinyos decided to commit himself fully to the Roman faith at a time when he had given up hope of receiving aid from Spain and when he realised that Catholicism divided rather than united Ethiopia. The explanation for this seeming enigma is to be found in the internal situation in the country. The number of Catholic converts by 1624 probably surpassed a hundred thousand. Whether adventurers or true believers, these converts were united by vested interests and fear of an anti-Catholic reaction. They owed their appointments to their affiliation to the Roman church and all were in possession of *gult* and other sources of revenue, previously taken from the Ethiopian church, monasteries, rebels or nobles. A victory for the anti-Catholic party, they realised, would result in the restitution of this property to its previous owners and a substantial socio-political upheaval, if not physical danger to themselves.

The emperor was not unaware that in addition to his large and superior army Si'la Christos could rely on the support of the many thousands of Catholics in the administration who considered his brother's devotion to Rome the best guarantee of their position, property and safety. To confess Catholicism publicly was an important step toward gaining the confidence of the pro-Catholic party and dispelling its fears and suspicion about his loyalty to Rome. Indeed, so intent was he to please the Jesuits and their followers that after the arrival of Alphonso Mendez he even accepted in 1625 the latter's demand that he, his kinsmen and stewards should undergo a humiliating (in the eyes of the Ethiopian people) public ceremony of baptism.[25]

It is doubtful whether anything could have prevented the inevitable collapse of Susinyos' revolutionary experiment to modernise his country through a religio-cultural upheaval. Nevertheless, left to himself and convinced of failure he might have found it prudent to reconcile himself with the national church and his previous supporters.[26] The arrival of the zealous and arrogant Alphonso Mendez, who was ignorant of Ethiopia but determined to convert it at all cost, intensified the religious wars and accelerated Susinyos' fall and the debacle of Catholicism there.

A true disciple of the Holy Inquisition, Mendez was responsible, from 1625, for the most cruel and humiliating persecution of all 'sinners' and 'non-believers', which shocked even the hardened Ethiopians. His absurd demands on Susinyos and his impolitic treatment of the King of Kings, the royal family, nobility and officials were undoubtedly responsible for the escalation of the civil war in Ethiopia and the rapid growth of power of the anti-Catholic party after 1625. Even the tens of thousands of Ethiopian Catholics of consequence were also under continuous scrutiny. Moreover, their leaders, as well as the local Catholic clergy, were not treated as equals and none was allowed to share in the responsibility, position and honour reserved for the Jesuits and other European Catholics.

The persecution which accompanied the persistent campaigns between 1625 and 1632 to implant Catholicism and to uproot the 'heathen-Jewish' customs of Ethiopia, so repugnant to the dogmatic Jesuits, drove the Ethiopian people to rebel against the emperor, his *ferenji* mentors and their local supporters. Although time and again defeated by Susinyos' armies, the Christian-semitised population, led by ecclesiastics, nobles and pretenders of different kinds, continued the struggle against foreign spiritual-cultural domination with increasing tenacity and bitterness. Thus each victory which Susinyos won became pyrrhic.

Immediately after the death of Wolde Gabriel in Showa another pretender[27] led a rebellion supported by the Falasha of Simen. When this uprising was crushed[28] another broke out in 1628 in Tigre led by its viceroy Tekla Giorgis, Susinyos' old friend and son-in-law. Relatively tranquil since about 1610, Tigre was intermittently disturbed by the eruptions of the Azebu Galla who had conquered the lowland of Doba. By 1625, however, Tekla Giorgis succeeded in pacifying the Galla and incorporated many of them into his army. Yet due to personal grievances and the fanaticism of Mendez, which affected Tigre through the Jesuits' centre in Fremona, Tekla Giorgis rebelled in 1628 against his master. Although he was defeated and killed the Tigrean nobility, it seems, was reluctant to accept Susinyos' rule and again maintained relations with a pretender, Malkea Christos, who appeared in Lasta.[29]

Malkea Christos' rebellion, which may have begun even before 1629, served as an outlet for the frustration of the Agaw of Wag, Lasta and Begemder. The imposition of a strict Catholic code of personal behaviour and the suppression of their ancient customs greatly aggravated the situation. Amhara imperialism had been strongly resisted among the Agaw in the past, but never as bitterly as in the time of Susinyos.[30]

The revolt in Lasta quickly attracted many of the opponents of Susinyos' government. A loose coalition even emerged between rebels in Amhara, the Lastans under Malkea Christos, Tigrean nobles and Galla tribes. Although defeated on several occasions the Lastan rebellion was the final factor which led to Susinyos' downfall. At first a purely ethnical-cultural protest movement, it became the nucleus of a popular revolution against the emperor, rejecting alien religio-cultural changes which he wished to impose upon the Agaw with the help of foreigners.[31]

The uprising of Malkea Christos surpassed anything which Susinyos had encountered in the past. The pretender survived repeated defeats inflicted upon him. By 1631/1632 he even succeeded in eliminating several armies sent against him. With his army swollen by many volunteers Malkea Christos conquered Begemder in 1632 and marched into Dembiya. The heart of his empire at stake, Susinyos took command of the royal army and emerged triumphant from a most bitter battle. But the cost in human life was terrible. Everyone, including the king, was horrified by the sight of the thousands of dead warriors lying on the battlefield.[32]

Susinyos had been reconciled for some time to the fact that his attempt to reform the country through conversion to Catholicism was a failure, if not a tragic mistake. Hence when implored by a delegation led by Fasilidas to discontinue the bloodshed in the country, he agreed to revoke all the edicts aimed at imposing

Catholicism by coercion. Soon afterwards, bitter and disappointed, he appointed Fasilidas his regent and retired from active government. Inevitably the Ethiopian church was again recognised by Fasilidas as the national church though Susinyos, who died broken-hearted in September 1632, remained a loyal Catholic.[33] Thus ended a revolutionary attempt to Westernise-modernise Ethiopia in the first decades of the seventeenth century.

We have already pointed out that coming from another cultural orbit Europeans, and especially the dogmatic Jesuits, were incapable of understanding the correlation between church and culture in Ethiopia and the significance of the practices and customs which had become part of the beliefs of the national church. Although an elitist institution, the latter was still the product of a synthesis between semitised influences and the native Cushitic culture and had its roots in the African soil of the Horn of Africa. European Catholicism was not only the product of an alien cultural evolution, but at this time and under Jesuit supervision, it did not tolerate any aspect of Ethiopian Christianity, usually an outcome of local cultural evolution, which did not conform with accepted Catholic dogmas and practices.

The struggle between Catholicism and the Ethiopian church in the first decades of the seventeenth century became, in a sense, a *Kulturkampf* in which an alien religious culture tried to superimpose itself upon reluctant people determined to preserve their ancient indigenous mores. Always oriented to the Muslim-Mediterranean cultural sphere, Ethiopians regarded Western Christians *(ferenjoch)* with suspicion and from the sixteenth century with some fear. The covert xenophobia which existed to a degree with regard to Western Christianity in the past became nearly universal in Ethiopia as a result of the Jesuit attempt during Susinyos' reign to uproot the local culture and supplant it by their own through a regime of terror and persecution. The victory of the national church in 1632 was, therefore, considered not as much a religious as a cultural-political triumph over the hated Westerners. The feeling of exhilaration in Ethiopia following this event was best expressed by the unknown poet, quoted by Gregory, the informant of Ludolphus.[34]

> At length the sheep of Ethiopia freed
> From the bold lyons of the west

Securely in their pastures fed
St. Mark and Cyril's of Rome.
Rejoice, rejoice, sing Hallelujah all,
No more the western wolves
Our Ethiopia shall enthrall.

With their strict dogmatism the Jesuits were least suitable to implant Catholicism in Ethiopia. They completely ignored the correlation in Ethiopia between belief, customs and local culture and dismissed the latter as being inferior in every aspect to their own. They had shown complete lack of understanding, tact and commonsense in their relations with the Ethiopians, and in their attempt to replace a way of life, which had its roots in a native socio-economic evolution, with the European-Catholic values of the period. For this reason, as well as on religious grounds, they rejected ancient Ethiopian-African institutions such as, for instance, polygamy, concubinage, divorce and circumcision, as well as matters of belief, universally practised in Ethiopia (and most of Africa). Hence they antagonised not only the ruling classes but also the usually passive masses of agriculturalists and completely compromised Susinyos' attempt at modernisation.

Considering the past attitude of Ethiopians to their church and their general indifference at first to the Jesuits' initial gains, it is even possible that, if more tolerant, patient and pragmatic toward local culture and realities, they could have eventually succeeded in their undertaking. But this is only a hypothesis. In fact, European missionaries and churches, Protestants included, came to appreciate African values and practices only in the twentieth century and only then re-evaluated their attitude to African culture, especially to African churches and their liturgy.

The loyalist party considered Fasilidas its champion even before he became heir-designate. Prudently avoiding the pitfall of plotting against his father, he allowed his powerful uncle to undermine his own position and thus opened the way for his accession to the throne. Despite his loyalty to his father there was no question, however, of Fasilidas' sentiments and no love spent between him and Mendez. Already when he was his father's regent, in 1632, it was evident that the era of the Jesuits was over. The hatred for the latter was so intense and universal that there was a danger that the population would attempt to seek retribution by harming them concurrently with the widespread and cruel persecution of their local converts.

Still respecting the mythical power of Portugal and fearing the Catholic party, Fasilidas expelled the Jesuits from Ethiopia shortly after he succeeded to the throne. The Ethiopians who chose to remain loyal to their new religion were constantly harassed, while Si'la Christos was imprisoned on an *amba* in Simen and later killed.[35] The Turks on the coast were only too glad to oblige when Fasilidas officially requested them in 1634 not to allow any Catholic missionary or layman to enter Ethiopia. In fact for a time they prevented all Europeans from reaching the plateau.

Apprehensive of Portuguese intervention and the revival of Catholicism in his country, Fasilidas attempted to create an anti-Portuguese alliance with the Ottomans and the new Zaydi imams of Yemen.[36] Such an alliance, he hoped, would be able to repulse any European attempt to intervene in the affairs of his country. Obviously mistaken in the political field, his policy, however, was also economically motivated and aimed at expanding Ethiopia's foreign trade. But the strengthening of its traditional Mediterranean-Muslim cultural orientation, coinciding with the beginning of the accelerated decline of the latter sphere, was bound to affect the development of Ethiopia.

In addition to fighting the many Catholic converts Fasilidas still faced numerous pretenders, including Malkea Christos in Lasta. It took him some time to comprehend that the resistance to his father's attempt to convert Ethiopia to Catholicism was not just the outcome of loyalty to the national church nor merely a rejection of *ferenji* (Western) culture, but rather a synthesis of these factors with personal and regional interests. Only after the first decade of his reign did he overcome regional rebellions which in Susinyos' time seemed to emanate from resistance to European culture and religion superimposed by the Jesuits. However, tension was progressively building up in the country due to the intensity of theological disputes.

Controversies inspired by Catholic dogmas broke out in the national church even during Susinyos' reign. As expected, they focused on the problem of the nature(s) of Christ.[37] While supporters of Tekla Haymanot, although loyal to monophysitism, evolved theories based on a logical explanation of the Scriptures that would stand up to Catholic polemics, the supporters of St.

Ewostatewos stood by a pure monophysitism and rejected all attempts at compromise. These controversies were to become a major factor undermining Ethiopian unity and political-spiritual development throughout Fasilidas' reign and in the coming two centuries. Indeed, Ethiopia since the rise of Fasilidas to power entered a new era.

NOTES

1. The claim of Catholic sources that Susinyos was inclined to Catholicism a few months after his accession is absurd. Tellez, p. 189; Bruce, Vol. III, p. 284; Wansleben, p. 18. Catholic sources mention land grants to the Jesuits. According to Susinyos' chronicler (Pereira, *Susenyos*, Vol. II, p. 78) he dedicated his crown to Debra Libanos and ordered that the emblem of Tekla Haymanot be put on his flag immediately after coming to power.

2. Tellez, pp. 356-7. In 1609 he left the allegedly morally corrupt Abuna Simeon with the Jesuits in Tigre for instruction.

3. Paez, Vol. II, p. 480.

4. Shortly after coming to power Susinyos expropriated funds paid to clergymen who were considered morally corrupt, possibly because he needed the resources – Pereira, *Susenyos*, Vol. II, p. 78.

5. Perruchon, *Sémitique*, 1897, pp. 181-2; Tellez, pp. 189-90; Paez, Vol. II, pp. 478-80. The monastic order of Tekla Haymanot, centred on Amhara and Showa, suffered greatly from the Galla migration. Gojjam, Damot and the northern provinces, now the centre of the empire, were the traditional strongholds of the rival house of St. Ewostatewos.

5a. While some customs and beliefs in Ethiopia are undoubtedly of Judaic origin, many others which seem to be the outcome of Judaic influences could have been the result of south Arabian and other influences which affected the Ethiopian culture as well as a local development.

6. Paez, Vol. II, pp. 480-1; Pereira, *Susenyos*, Vol. II, pp. 122-30; Beccari, Vol. XI, pp. 421-6; Ludolphus, p. 330; Bruce, Vol. III, pp. 340-1; Papi, p. 89 and note 1.

7. *De facto* minister of the interior, responsible for all governors and sometimes commander of the royal army, in this period.

8. Tellez, pp. 206-8; Papi, p. 89, note 1.

9. There are signs that he was encouraged by the See of Alexandria to take this strong stand.

10. Pereira, *Susenyos*, Vol. II, pp. 130-2; Ludolphus pp. 330-3; Tellez, pp. 205-8.

11. Significantly Yolyos expelled all the Catholics from Wogera and confiscated their property – Bruce, Vol. III, pp. 341-3.

12. Beccari, Vol. XI, pp. 426-8; Paez, Vol. III, pp. 430-5; Ludolphus, pp. 330-2; Tellez, pp. 205-9; Perruchon, *Sémitique*, 1897, p. 182; Bruce, Vol. III, pp. 341-9.

13. This is stated by the Ethiopian chronicles. See: Perruchon, *Sémitique*, 1897, p. 182; Basset, 'Etudes', pp. 292-4; Bruce, Vol. III, pp. 348-9; Ludolphus, p. 333.

14. Tragically, a civil war in Ethiopia erupted just about the time a new *luba* came to power among the Galla and began to attack the Ethiopian provinces in

1619. Perruchon, *Sémitique*, 1897, p.184; Bruce, Vol.III, p.320; Pereira, *Susenyos*, Vol.II, pp.172-3.

15. Pereira, *Susenyos*, Vol.II, pp.172-3; Beccari, Vol.II, pp.425-8; Ludolphus, pp.333-5; Bruce, Vol.III, pp.349-53.

16. Paez, Vol.III, pp.432-42.

17. He strongly condemned the mistaken dogmas of the national church and the ignorance and the immorality of its clergy and its *abuns*. Tellez, p.212; Bruce, Vol.III, pp.56 8; Budge, Vol.II, p.389. To become monogamous he divorced all his wives with the exception of the *Itege*.

18. Biblioteca de Braga, Ms. 779, document 20, 10 May 1624 – material provided to the author by Dr. Merid Wolde Aregay.

19. On Aussa's sultan's relations with Susinyos and the anti-Catholic party in his court, the execution of the Jesuits and a letter from the sultan to Susinyos denouncing him for betraying the religion of his ancestors, and on presents to Wolde Gabriel, see: *Lobo*, Le Grand, pp.16-17, 116; *Some Records*, p.199; Tellez, p.39; Bruce, Vol.III, pp.364-5. On the Turkish authorities' reaction to Susinyos' conversion, fear of Portuguese intervention and the influence of the See of Alexandria on Ottoman officials at Sawakin – Ludolphus p.354. In a land charter Susinyos granted to Si'la Christos for suppression of the rebellion, Wolde Gabriel is called 'the imposter, the slave of the Turks' – *Land Charters*, pp.60-1.

20. Perruchon, *Sémitique*, 1897, p.184. This strongly anti-Catholic source blames the death of the rebel as well as other calamities on the Franks, i.e., the Catholics. See also: Bruce, Vol.III, pp.558-9; Almeida, *Some Records*, p.199; Beccari, Vol.XI, p.488.

21. Ludolphus, p.328, according to a letter to Pope Paul V, January 1623.

22. Ludolphus, p.345; Tellez, pp.230-4.

23. Ludolphus, p.328, according to a letter from the Jesuits to Pope Paul V, January 1623.

24. He rejected repeated requests to punish a Jewish rabbi from Vienna who has been preaching for some time in northern Ethiopia. An exceptional scholar with superb knowledge of the Scriptures, the rabbi repeatedly embarrassed the Jesuits. Susinyos appreciated, it seems, his knowledge, modesty and dedication and only after Mendez' intervention agreed to deport him. Vitteleschi, pp.8-9; Mendez, Beccari, Vol.VIII, pp.231-45.

25. Tellez, pp.212-13; Bruce, Vol.III, pp.353-6; Paez, Vol.III, pp.434-43; Wolde Aregay, p.467.

26. Susinyos' complete isolation and ability to alienate or antagonise all the power factors in the country simultaneously should be compared to a similar situation during the reign of another 'moderniser', Tewodros in the 1860s.

27. The son of Abeto Arzo, the pretender killed with the commander of the imperial guard in 1609. See above, p.196.

28. Perruchon, *Sémitique*, 1897, pp.181-3; Morié, Vol.II, p.290.

29. Tellez, pp.235-6; *Lobo*, Le Grand, pp.103-4; Bruce, Vol.III, pp.376-8; Ludolphus, pp.342-4.

30. The Agaw found a common denominator with Tigrean separatism and hence the relations between the rebellion of Malkea Christos and the Tigrean nobility. The special character of the Lastan revolt explains its continuation after the debacle of the Jesuits.

31. Among the Amhara rebels was the son of Zaselassie. In his attempted attack on Tigre he was accompanied by three provincial governors and several lesser rulers who together mastered 32 *negarits* (cattle drums), representing district governorships – Tellez, p.237. On relations between Malkea Christos and the

Tigrean nobility – Ludolphus, p. 347. Further on this rebellion – Tellez, pp. 235-7; Bruce, Vol. III, pp. 379-400; Papi, pp. 89-90.

32. Beccari, Vol. VII, pp. 159-62; Almeida, Beccari, Vol. VII, pp. 150-64; Tellez, pp. 239-41; Ludolphus, pp. 349-54; Bruce, Vol. III, pp. 396-401; Pereira, *Susenyos*, Vol. II, pp. 258-9.

33. Beccari, Vol. VII, pp. 175-6, 180-9; Almeida, Beccari, Vol. VII, pp. 155-64; Tellez, pp. 239-41; Ludolphus, pp. 349-54; Pereira, *Susenyos*, Vol. II, pp. 259-61.

34. Ludolphus, pp. 357-8.

35. Basset, 'Etudes', p. 133; Béguinot, p. 48.

36. His ,embassies to San'a and Istanbul and the arrival in Gondar of the Yemeni Qadi al-Khaymi should be understood against this background. See: Abir, M, 'Ethiopia and the Horn of Africa', Chapter 8 of *The Cambridge History of Africa*, 1975, p. 551.

37. Tellez, p. 242. Also Conclusion below.

Conclusion

The endemic weakness of the Ethiopian empire emanated from the fact that throughout the Solomonic period it remained in a mediaeval-feudal state. Its semitised 'core', moreover, was not fully united and its rapid expansion contributed to its heterogeneous character. The contradictory interests of the central authority and the military-feudal system of government were the cause of an endless struggle for power between the two. These struggles were polarised by attempts of strong emperors to introduce administrative and military reforms which would undermine the power and jurisdiction of the regional nobility and warlords.

The incessant war with Adal, followed by the Galla invasion of the plateau, sapped Ethiopia's resources and demanded the constant attention of its rulers. This and the succession system of the Ethiopian dynasty deprived the more powerful and enterprising monarchs of the minimal time-span necessary for their reforms to take root. Even when successful such reforms, moreover, proved self-defeating because, lacking the necessary social structure, a wider base of support or the drive of a cultural-religious ideology, they inevitably produced a new aristocracy which joined the centrifugal forces in the country. This was, to some extent, the outcome of socio-cultural stagnation enhanced by an elitist church lacking spiritual inspiration, which left most of Ethiopia a conglomeration of conquered peoples. Hence the emperor, ruling an empire but not a nation which identified with him, could not hope to mobilise popular support and army and dispense with the professional-mercenary forces which were a major cause of the constant instability of Ethiopia.

The military and technical ability of the Portuguese expeditionary force in Ethiopia, the discipline of its soldiers and exaggerated descriptions of European achievement in the administrative, material and cultural fields, had fired the imagination of Ethiopian monarchs ever since the sixteenth century. Nevertheless, they refrained from requesting aid from Catholic Europe until driven to do so by desperation. Their hesitation was probably the outcome of historical suspicions of *ferenjoch* exacerbated by the behaviour of the Jesuits in Ethiopia and by Muslim propaganda, supported by local ecclesiastics, about European imperialism and its aspirations concerning their country.

Susinyos' revolutionary attempt to modernise and unite his country through Westernisation and Catholicism has no equivalent in the history of the period. Only at the turn of the eighteenth century did some Muslim rulers make halfhearted experiments to copy Western military technology. Unfortunately Susinyos was too impatient, his Jesuit mentors too zealous and shortsighted and Ethiopia far from prepared for such a step. Indeed, the coerced conversion of Ethiopia proved counter-productive. It further undermined the foundations of the country and caused it to turn its back on evolutionary reforms, in a most crucial period of its history.

Whatever the claim of Jesuit sources, Fasilidas did not cause the isolation of Ethiopia. His commercial agents traded with many countries and he corresponded with or despatched ambassadors to the Dutch in Batavia and the British in India. Several Europeans who were not missionaries were even allowed into Ethiopia during his reign. The 'Jesuit period' and Ethiopian reaction to it, however, resulted in Ethiopia's cultural alienation from European Christianity. To some extent, this was responsible for Ethiopia being left out of the mainstream of the social, spiritual, technical and artistic revolution which Christian Europe underwent in the coming period.

The transfer of Ethiopia's centre of gravity from Showa to the area of Lake Tana culminated when Fasilidas established Gondar as a permanent capital. A logical sequence of the contraction of the empire to its northern and northwestern provinces, Fasilidas' decision signified a final acceptance of the new realities in the plateau. The establishment of a permanent capital in fact terminated an era in the history of the Solomonic dynasty and opened a new one. In this new era, the empire was directed from Gondar and the country's politics were mainly focused on nearby territories.

Consequently, the Abbay, the plains of Amhara (to some extent parts of Showa as well) and part of Angot as far as the verges of the eastern escarpments became the accepted borders of the Gondarine kingdom. The Gondarine rulers, with one or two exceptions, showed, moreover, no aptitude for regaining areas beyond this line and were anyway involved in constant struggles to preserve their diminishing territories and authority.

The advantage of a mobile royal camp had been not only military and strategic; it had also had an important integrative value. The arrival of the emperor and his court in remote provinces had had the effect of 'showing the flag' and had enhanced the unification of the country. Now that the King of Kings remained in Gondar, except for short military expeditions, that process of integration was more difficult. This was especially true of areas with strong traditional regional sentiments such as Tigre, Bahr-Midir and Lasta.

With the imperial centre now in the Falasha-Agaw heartland, the process of incorporation of these areas into the Ethiopian polity and the assimilation of their population was accelerated. However, these new central provinces were very different from Ethiopia's old 'core'. Here the process of cultural assimilation of the population by the semitised society, initiated in the fourteenth century, was incomplete and at best superficial. The Falasha and Agaw steadfastly resisted the Ethiopian submersion, and campaigns against 'Lasta rebels' were a common feature during the reigns of most of the Gondarine rulers.

Deprived of grass root support which they had enjoyed in Amhara and Showa, and with control of the territories around the capital gradually reverting to the increasingly foreign military-administrative superstructure of their government, the monarchs became progressively dependent on them. In the final analysis, this evolution enabled elements whose affinity to the cultural heritage of Ethiopia was minimal gradually to usurp the power of the King of Kings and, by the eighteenth century, to make him their puppet. Such a state of affairs affected the character of the empire and limited the central government's ability to impose its authority on warlords and the feudal rulers of the provinces.

One of Fasilidas' early acts was to transfer the seat of the *Ichege* and many monks from Debra Libanos to Azazo near Gondar. Undoubtedly this was meant, *inter alia*, to demonstrate the renewal of the traditional alliance between the monarchy and the national church. But it also proved his bias towards the order of Tekla Haymanot, supported by the Amhara elements of the empire which maintained in most periods a special relationship with the Solomonic dynasty. However, by transplanting the headquarters of monasticism, the church and the centre of the order of Tekla Haymanot to the environs of the capital, the emperor unintentionally caused theological polemics to assume a major role in the politics of his court. Encouraged by the victory of the national church over Susinyos, the many thousands of monks and clergymen who settled in the area of Gondar became progressively more militant and frequently attempted to force their wishes upon the monarch. The Gondarine period of Solomonic Ethiopia was increasingly plagued by the intensity of Christological debates and their increasing impact on the country's politics.

Fasilidas realised that the endemic civil wars were not just religiously motivated, but were also an outlet for regional or personal dissatisfaction which conveniently adopted religious ideology. Notwithstanding the neutral position which he attempted to maintain in matters of faith, the emperor mercilessly punished the more extremist elements among the ecclesiastics in order to preserve some semblance of unity in the church and in the country. However, the growing aggressiveness of the house of Tekla Haymanot by the last decade of his reign drove Fasilidas into the arms of their opponents who, it seems, were the strongest element among the Christian population away from the capital. His successors, who lacked his ability, gradually lost control of the ecclesiastics and their intervention in these controversies only contributed to a further deterioration in the situation.

The introduction of Catholic dogmas into the country from the sixteenth century greatly exacerbated the traditional theological disputes. In addition to Judaic influences in the Ethiopian church – already a source of controversies between the monastic orders – the Catholics attacked the very foundations of monophysitism. As supporters of diophysitism, the Catholics easily explained the incompatibility between the human character of Christ mentioned in the Scriptures and his divine nature. The monophysites, however, found it far more difficult to explain this distinction.

The roots of the dispute around the nature(s) of Christ were to be found already in church councils of the fourth and fifth centuries.

The Ethiopian church traditionally maintained that the two natures of Christ were perfectly united, as at· the moment of Christ's conception the Divine had sanctified the human nature, made it perfect and thus the two natures became one and inseparable. This original *tawahdu* (united) theory was generally accepted by the moderates in the different camps of the Ethiopian church until the seventeenth century.

Already during Susinyos' reign, due to Jesuit polemics, but especially after Fasilidas came to power, the followers of the order of St. Ewostatewos, mainly of the Gojjamite branch, no longer satisfied with *tawahdu*, maintained that the union between the two natures of Christ was brought about through unction *(qibat)*. The followers of this theory acquired the name of *qibatoch* – 'unctionists'. This theory and others, more extreme, sparked off a most bitter new controversy with the loyal supporters of *tawahdu* – 'unionists' – mainly the house of Tekla Haymanot, which dominated Ethiopia's spiritual life and politics until the final decline of the Solomonic dynasty.

The controversy between the *qibatoch* and the *tawahdu*, which repeatedly shook the very foundations of the national church from the seventeenth century onwards, became a major issue in the political history of Ethiopia in the Gondarine period. In addition to the harm caused to the church, it undermined the belief of Ethiopian Christians and aggravated the disunity among the Christian-semitised population of the country. Tragically, it may have also affected the ability of the Ethiopian church to exploit the opportunity to assimilate the Galla masses, a fact which has proved a disaster for Ethiopia until recently.

The momentum of Galla migration and expansionism had already begun to dissipate at the turn of the sixteenth century. No longer hungry for land, different Galla groups, even more disunited than before, began to undergo a process of settlement which necessitated the transformation of their socio-political institutions and the adoption of cultural influences suitable for their new style of life. The Galla, moreover, became increasingly involved in the affairs of Ethiopian society and state, still the most important and developed entity in the Horn. Indeed, from being a marginal element since the struggle for power in the Horn, they gradually emerged as a predominant one, while the Solomonic empire and the sultanate of Harar continued to decline. In fact, the increasing deployment of Galla forces by Ethiopian and Muslim rulers and their participation in internal Ethiopian and Harari conflicts, not to mention lesser Cushitic principalities, signal the beginning of the Galla era in the history of the Horn of Africa, Ethiopia included. This process culminated at the turn of the eighteenth century when Galla warlords became the regents of the puppet Solomonic kings, intermarried with the amirs of Harar and established their own kingdoms in the southwestern plateau.

The character of the Ethiopian church and its spiritual shortcomings have been discussed elsewhere in this book. Despite its being an indigenous church with its roots in the African soil, it was unable and unwilling to dedicate itself to evangelisation and cultural assimilation of the heterogeneous population of the plateau. Rebuffed by the Ethiopian church and the semito-Cushitic society as a whole, the Galla became progressively more alienated from the empire and its cultural-religious components. Thus they were easily attracted by Islam which was anxious to proselytise, egalitarian and considered prestigious.

No longer threatened by Muslim power since the turn of the sixteenth century, Ethiopia's relations with its neighbours were normally friendly. Despite the rapid decline of the Ottoman empire (Egypt included) and its economy, the transit trade of the Red Sea continued to flourish (until about the middle of the eighteenth century). Although the Muslim empire had little to offer to the merchants of the Far East other than gold and silver coins from their depleting treasuries, the market for Ethiopian products, especially slaves, was nearly insatiable. Moreover, notwithstanding the constant instability in Yemen, the demand for 'Mukha' coffee rapidly increased after the introduction of this beverage into Europe during the seventeenth century. Subsequently, caravans dominated by Muslim merchants intensified their activities in the plateau and, finding an accommodation with its new Galla inhabitants, penetrated deeper and deeper into the interior. Thus a slow process of islamisation of the Galla had begun already in the seventeenth century and was accelerated as an outcome of the revival of Islam in Arabia about the middle of the eighteenth century.

The fusion between the growing Galla power in the Ethiopian empire and the expansion of Islam while the Christian-semitised society and polity were disintegrating nearly led, once again, to the extinction of Christian Ethiopia. Resembling the last-minute rescue of Christian Ethiopia by the Portuguese in the sixteenth century, the active intervention of Western powers in the affairs of the Red Sea basin since the turn of the eighteenth century helped prevent the submersion of Christian Ethiopia by Muslim forces, supported by Egypt.

By the middle of the nineteenth century the desperate masses of semitised Christians produced a leader who took the mythical throne-name Tewodros, re-established their kingdom, revived their cultural heritage and reconquered most of the territories lost in the sixteenth century. Later on in the century the new Solomonic dynasty of Showa continued to expand the borders of the empire and defeated an Italian attempt to conquer it in 1896. Thus Christian-semitised Ethiopia entered the twentieth century as the only independent African country which preserved its ancient heritage intact, but with nearly the same grave problems as those which had affected its stability in the past.

Bibliography

In this book abbreviated to

Archives and Manuscripts

d'Abbadie, Antoine, Bibliothèque Nationale, Paris. d'Abbadie
   Papers, Catalogue France Nouvelle Acquisition.
Abir, M., 'Trade and Christian – Muslim relations in post-
   medieval Ethiopia'. A paper submitted to the International   Abir, International
   Conference of Ethiopian Studies, Chicago, April 1978.   Conference
Archive of the Society of Jesus, Roma. Ms. Goa 39 (II). *
Asma-Giyorgis Gabra Masih, *Ya Galla Tarik.* Ms. Institute
   of Ethiopian Studies, Addis Ababa.   Asma
Biblioteca Publica de Braga, Braga (Portugal). Ms. 779. *   Biblioteca de Braga
Ozbaran, Salih, *The Ottoman Turks and the Portuguese in
   the Persian Gulf,* an unpublished Ph.D. thesis, University
   of London, 1969.   Ozbaran
Wolde Aregay, Merid, *Southern Ethiopia and the Christian
   Kingdom 1508-1708,* an unpublished Ph.D. thesis, Uni-
   versity of London, 1971.   Wolde Aregay
* Courtesy of Dr. Merid Wolde Aregay.

Books

Abir, M., *Ethiopia: The Era of the Princes,* London, 1968.   Abir, *The Era*
Abir, M., 'Ethiopia and the Horn of Africa', chapter 8 of
   The Cambridge History of Africa, Cambridge, 1975.
Abu Salih, *The Churches and Monasteries of Egypt and
   Some Neighbouring Countries* (trans. Evetts, B. T. A.
   and Butler, A. J.), Oxford, 1895.
Adler, E. N., *Jewish Travellers,* London, 1930   Adler, *Jewish
                                                                 Travellers*
Almagia, R., *Contributi alla storia della conoscenza dell'
   Etiopia,* Padua, 1941   Almagia
Al-Maqrizi, Ahmad ibn 'Ali ibn 'Abd al-Kadir, *Historia
   regnum Islamicum in Abyssinia* (ed. Rinck, F. T. – Arabic
   text), Leiden, 1790   Maqrizi
Almeida, M. de., *The History of High Ethiopia or Abassia*
   (ed. Beckingham, C. F. and Huntingford, G. W. B.),
   London, 1954.   Almeida

Al-Sakhawi, *At-Tibr al-Masbuq* (Arabic), Cairo, 1896.
Al-Umari, ibn Fadl Allah, *Masalik el-Absar fi Mamalik
al-Amsar* (Arabic), Paris, 1927.   Al-Umari
Alvarez, F., *The Prester John of the Indies* (ed. Beckingham,
C. F. and Huntingford, G. W. B.), The Hakluyt Society,
Cambridge, 1961.   Alvarez
Bahrey, *History of the Galla,* in Beckingham, C. F. and Hunt-
ingford, G. W. B. (trans.), *Some Records of Ethiopia,
1596-1646,* London, 1954.   Bahrey
Baratti, G., *The Later Travels of S. Giacomo Baratti,*
London, 1670.   Baratti
Beccari, C., *Rerum Aetiopicarum scriptores occidentales
inediti a saeculo XVI ad XIX,* Roma, 1903-1917.   Beccari
Beccari, C., *Il Tigre del secolo XVII,* Roma, 1909.   Beccari, *Tigre*
Beckingham, C. F. and Huntingford, G. W. B., *Some Records
of Ethiopia, 1596-1646,* London, 1954.   *Some Records*
Béguinot, F. (trans and ed.), *La Cronaca Abbreviata
d'Abissinia,* Roma, 1901.   Béguinot
Boxer, C. R., *The Portuguese Seaborne Empire,* London, 1969.   Boxer
Britton, S., *The Rise of the Imams of Sanaa,* Oxford, 1925.
Bruce, J., *Travels to Discover the Source of the Nile in the
Years 1768, 1769, 1770, 1771, 1772 and 1773,*
Edinburgh, 1790.   Bruce
Budge, E. A. W., *A History of Ethiopia, Nubia and Abyssinia,*
London, 1928.   Budge
Celebi (Shelebi), Evliya, *Narrative of Travels in Europe, Asia
and Africa in the 17th Century* (trans. Joseph
von Hammer), London, 1834.   Evliya
Cerulli, E., *La Lingua e la Storia de Harar,* Vol. I of *Studi
Etiopici,* Roma, 1936.   Cerulli, *La Lingua*
Cerulli, E., *La Lingua e la Storia dei Sidama,* Vol. II of *Studi
Etiopici,* Roma, 1938.
Cerulli, E., *Somalia, Scritti Vari Editi ed Inediti,* Roma, 1957.
Chiab ed Din Ahmed Ben Abd el-Qader. See Shihab
ad-Din Ahmad b. 'Abd al-Kadir.
Conti Rossini, C., *Storia d'Etiopia,* Milan, 1928.
Conti Rossini, C., *Etiopia e genti di Etiopia,* Florence, 1937.
Conzelman, W. E., *Chronique de Galâwdêwos,* Paris, 1895.   Conzelman
Correa, C., *Lendas da India* (ed. R. J. de Lima Felner),
Lisbon, 1858-64.   Correa
Coulbeaux, J. B., *Histoire politique et religieuse d'Ethiopie,*
Paris, 1838.   Coulbeaux
Crawford, O. G. S., *The Fung Kingdom of Sennar,* Gloucester,
1951.
Crichton, A., *History of Arabia and its People,* London, 1852.
Danvers, F. C., *The Portuguese in India,* London, 1894.   Danvers
Deressa, Yilma, *Ye Ethiopia Tarik,* Addis Ababa, 1959
E.C. 1967 A.D.   Yilma Deressa
Eshcoly, A. Z., *Sipur David Hareuveni* (Hebrew),
Jerusalem, 1940.   Eshcoly, *Hareuveni*
Eshcoly, A. Z., *Sefer Hafalashim* (Hebrew), Jerusalem, 1943.
Freeth, Z. and Winstone, V., *Kuwait Prospect and Reality,*
London, 1972.

Foster, W. (ed.), *The Journal of J. Jourdain 1608-17*,
    Cambridge, 1905.
Guillain, C., *Documents sur l'histoire, la géographie et le
    commerce de l'Afrique Orientale*, Paris, 1856.   Guillain
Haberland, E. von, *Galla Sud Athiopiens*, Stuttgart, 1963.
Haji Khalifeh, *The History of the Maritime Wars of the Turks*
    (trans. Mitchell, J.), London, 1831.   *The Maritime Wars*
Hamilton, A., *A New Account of the East Indies*, Edinburgh,
    1727.   Hamilton
Hasan, Yusuf Fadl, *The Arabs and the Sudan*, Edinburgh,
    1967.   Yusuf Fadl Hasan
Heyd, W., *Histoire de commerce du Levant au Moyen Age*,
    Leipzig, 1865.   .   Heyd
Huntingford, G. W. B., *The Galla of Ethiopia*, London, 1953.   Huntingford,
                                                                     The Galla
Huntingford, G. W. B., *The Glorious Victories of Amda Seyon
    King of Ethiopia*, Oxford, 1965.
Huntingford, G. W. B., *The Land Charters of Northern
    Ethiopia*, Addis Ababa – Nairobi, 1965.   *Land Charters*
Ibn Batuta, *Rihla* (Arabic), Cairo, 1939.
Johanssen, *Historia Yemenae*, Bonn, 1828.
Kahle, P. (ed.), *Die Chronik des Ibn Ijas*, Leipzig, 1932.
Kammerer, A., *La Mer Rouge, l'Abyssinie et l'Arabie
    depuis l'Antiquité*, Cairo, 1935.   Kammerer (1935)
Kammerer, A., *La Mer Rouge, l'Abyssinie et l'Arabie aux
    XVI et XVII siècles*, Cairo, 1947.   Kammerer (1947)
Kammerer, A., *La Mer Rouge, l'Abyssinie et l'Arabie*, etc.
    Cairo, 1952.   Kammerer (1952)
Kammerer, A., *Routier de Dom Joam de Castro, L'exploration
    de la Mer Rouge par les Portugais en 1541*, Paris, 1936.   *Routier*
Kolmodin, J., *Traditions de Tsazzega et Hazzega*, Upsala,
    1915.   Kolmodin
Kerr, R., *Collection of Voyages*, Edinburgh, 1812.
Legesse, A., *Gada*, New York, 1973.   Legesse, *Gada*
Le Grand, J., *Voyages historiques d'Abyssinie du R.P. Jérôme
    Lobo*, Paris, 1728.   *Lobo*, Le Grand
Linschoten, J. H. Van, *The Voyage of John Huyghen Van
    Linschoten*, Hakluyt Society, London, 1885.   Linschoten
Ludolphus, J. (trans. Gent, J. P.) *A History of Ethiopia*,
    London, 1864.   Ludolphus
Morié, L. J., *Histoire de l'Ethiopie*, Paris, 1904.   Morié
Neushtadt (Ayalon), D. and Goitein, S. D., 'Negidei Eretz
    Teyman', chapter 2 of *Boyi Teyman* (Hebrew, ed.
    Ratsahbi, Y.), Tel-Aviv, tav sheen kaf vav, (5726 J.C.).
Paez, Pero, *Historia de Ethiopia*, Vols. II and III of Beccari,
    C., *Rerum Aetiopicarum scriptores occidentales inediti a
    saeculo XVI ad XIX*, Roma, 1905-1906.   Paez
Pankhurst, R., *An Introduction to the Economic History of
    Ethiopia*, London, 1961.
Peiser, F. E., *Zur Geschichte Abessiniens im 17 Jahrhundert*,
    Berlin, 1898.
Periplus of the Erythrean Sea (trans. and ed. Schoff, W. H.),
    New York, 1912.

Pereira, F. M. E., *Historia de Minas, Rei de Ethiopia*,
Lisbon, 1888.   *Historia de Minas*
Pereira, F. M. E., *Chronica de Susenyos, Rei de Ethiopia*,
Lisbon, 1892-1900.   Pereira, *Susenyos*
Perruchon, J., *Les chroniques de Zar'a Ya'eqob, et de Ba'eda*   *Les chroniques de*
Maryam, rois d'Ethiopie de 1434 à 1478. Paris, 1893.   *Zar'a Ya'eqob*
Prestage, E., *Chapters in Anglo-Portuguese Relations*,
Watford, 1935.
Purchas, S., *Purchas, His Pilgrims*, The Hakluyt Society,
Glasgow, 1905-1907.   *Purchas*
Quatremère, E., *Mémoires géographiques et historiques sur*
l'Egypte et sur quelques contrées voisines, Paris, 1811.   Quatremère
Ramusio, G. B., *Delle navigationi et viaggi*, Venice, 1563.   Ramusio
Renneville, Constantin de, *Recueil des Voyages de la*
Compagnie des Indes, Amsterdam, 1763.
Roncière, C. G. B. de la, *La découverte de l'Afrique au moyen*
age, Cartographes et explorateurs, Cairo, 1925-27.   de la Roncière
Ruppell, E., *Reise in Abyssinien*, Frankfurt, 1838, 1840.
Ryley, J. H., *Ralph Fitch, England's Pioneer to India*, London,
1899.
Salt, H., *A Voyage to Abyssinia in the Years 1809 and 1810*,
London, 1814.   Salt
Salviac, M. de, *Les Galla, grand nation Africaine*, Paris, 1901.
Schefer, C., *Le voyage d'outre mer de Bertrandon de la*
Brocquière, Paris, 1892.
Scholem, G., *Kiryat Seffer* (Hebrew), shana zain (7th year),
Jerusalem.
Serjeant, R. B., The *Portuguese off the South Arabian Coast*,
Oxford, 1963.   Serjeant
Shihab ad-Din Ahmad b. 'Abd al-Kadir (Arab Faqih),
Futuh al-Habasha – Histoire de la conquête de l'Abyssinie
(trans. and ed. Basset, R.), Paris, 1897.   *Futuh*
Shibeika, Mekki (ed.), *Ta'rikh Muluk al-Sudan* (Arabic),
Khartoum, 1947/1247 H.
Sousa, F. Y., *The Portuguese Asia* (trans. Stevens, J), London,
1696.   Sousa
Stanford Shaw, J., *The Financial Administrative Organisation*
and Development of Ottoman Egypt, 1517-1789,
Princeton, 1958.
Stripling, G. W. F., *The Ottoman Turks and the Arabs*
1511-1574, Urbana, 1942.   Stripling
Suriano, F., *II trattato di Terra Santa e dell' Oriente* (ed.
Golubovich, G.), Milano, 1900.   Suriano
Sylvester de Sacy, A. I., *Christomatie Arabe* (collection of
Arab texts), Paris, 1826-27.
Sylvester de Sacy, A. I., *Le Foudre de l'Yémen*, Paris, 1897-98
(Arab texts).
Taddesse Tamrat, *Church and State in Ethiopia*, Oxford, 1972. Tamrat
Tellez, F. B., *A View of the Universe or a New Collection of*
Voyages. The Travels of the Jesuits in Ethiopia,
London, 1710.   Tellez
Thévenot, Jean de. *Voyages de M. de Thévenot tant en*
Europe qu'en Asie & en Afrique, Paris, 1689.   Thévenot

Trimingham, J. S., *Islam in Ethiopia,* London, 1965.   Trimingham
Vambéry, A. (ed.), *The Travels and Adventures of Sidi Ali Reis,* Vambéry, *Sidi Ali*
   London, 1899.   *Reis*
Vitteleschi, M., *Lettre annue dell' Etiopia dell' anno 1626,*
   Roma, 1629.   Vitteleschi
Wansleben, J. M., *A Brief Account of the Rebellions and*
   Bloodshed Occasioned by the Anti-Christian Practices of
   the Jesuits and the Popish Emissaries in the Empire of
   Ethiopia, London, 1679.   Wansleben
Winter Johns, J., *The Travels of Ludovico Di Varthema*
   1503-1508, London, 1863.   *Varthema*
Whiteway, R. S., *The Portuguese Expedition to Abyssinia in*   Whiteway –
   1541-1543, as Narrated by Castanhoso with Some Con-   *Castanhoso*
   temporary Letters, the Short Account of Bermudez, and   Whiteway –
   Certain Extracts from Correa, London, 1902.   *Bermudez*
Wiet, G., *L'Egypte Arabe 624-1517,* Paris, 1937.

Articles

Abir, M., 'Brokers and Brokerage in Ethiopia'. *Journal of*
   Ethiopian Studies, Vol. III, No. 1, Addis Ababa, 1965.
Abir, M., 'The Emergence and Consolidation of the
   Monarchies of Enarea and Jimma in the First Half of the
   Nineteenth Century', *Journal of African History,* Vol. VI,
   No. 2, 1965.   Abir, *JAH*
Abir, M., 'Salt, Trade and Politics in Ethiopia in the
   "Zamana Masafent" ', *Journal of Ethiopian Studies,*   Abir, 'Salt, Trade
   Vol. IV, No. 2, 1966.   and Politics'
Avanchers, L. des, *Bulletin de la Société de Géographie,* Paris,
   1866.
Basset, R., 'Etudes sur l'histoire d'Ethiopie', *Journal Asiatique,*
   Vol. XVII and XVIII, 1881.   Basset, 'Etudes'
Bombaci, Alessio, 'Notizie Sull' Abyssinia in Fonti Turche',
   Rassegna di Studi Etiopici, anno III, No. 1.   Bombaci, 'Notizie'
Cerulli, E., 'Documenti Arabi per la storia dell' Etiopia',
   Rendiconti della Reale Accademia dei Lincei, Vol. IV,   Cerulli, 'Documenti
   1931.   Arabi'
Cerulli, E., 'Il sultanato dello Schioa nel secolo XIII',   Cerulli, 'Il
   Rassegna di Studi Etiopici, Vol. I, 1941.   sultanato'
Cerulli, E., 'La Città de Merca e tre sue inscrizioni Arabe',
   Oriento Moderno, 1943.   Cerulli, 'La Città'
Conti Rossini, C., 'Due squarci inediti di cronaca Etiopica',
   Rendiconti della Reale Accademia dei Lincei, Vol. II, 1893.   Rossini, 'Due'
Conti Rossini, C., 'Historia regis Sarsa Dengel (Malak
   Sagad)', *Corpus Scriptorum Christianorum Orientalium,*   Rossini, 'Sarsa
   Vol. III, 1907.   Dengel'
Conti Rossini, C., 'L'autobiografia de Pawlos monaco
   Abissino del secolo XVI', *Rendiconti della Reale*
   Accademia dei Lincei, Vol. XXVII, 1918.   Rossini, 'Pawlos'
Conti Rossini, C., 'La Guerra Turco-Abissina del 1578',
   Oriento Moderno, 1921-1922, 1929.   Rossini, 'Turco'

Curles, A. Y., 'The Ruined Cities of Somaliland', *Antiquity*, X, 1936.

Dames, L., 'The Portuguese and the Turks in the Indian Ocean', *Journal of the Royal Asiatic Society*, London, 1921.   Dames, 'The Portuguese'

Gallina, F., 'I Portughezi a Massaua nei secoli XVI, XVII', Bollettino di Società Geografica Italiana, Serie III, Vol. III, 1890.   'I Portughezi a 'Massaua'.

Guidi, I., 'Di due frammenti relativi alla storia d'Abissinia', *Rendiconti della Reale Accademia dei Lincei*, Vol. II, 1893.   'Due Frammenti'

Guidi, I., 'Le liste dei metropoliti d'Abissinia', *Bessarione*, VI, 1899.

Guidi, I., 'Annales Iohannis I, Iyasu I et Bakafa', *Corpus Scriptorum Christianorum Orientalium: Scriptores Aethiopici*, V, 1903.   'Annales Iohannis'

Haberland, E. von, 'The Influence of the Christian-Ethiopian Empire on Southern Ethiopia', *Journal of Semitic Studies*, No. 1, 1964.

Lane, F. C., 'The Mediterranean Spice Trade', *American Historical Review*, 1839-1840.   Lane

Legesse, A., 'Class system based on time', *Journal of Ethiopian Studies*, No. 1, 1963.

Lewis, B., 'The Ottoman archives as a source for the history of the Arab lands', *Journal of the Royal Asiatic Society*, 1951.

Lewis, H. S., 'The Origins of the Galla and Somali', *Journal of African History*, Vol. VII, 1966.

Lewis, I. M., 'The Galla in Northern Somaliland', *Rassegna di Studi Etiopici*, Vol. XV, 1959.

Lewis, I. M., 'The Somali Conquest of the Horn of Africa', *Journal of African History*, Vol. I, 1969.

Nadi, Bekele, 'Adoption among the Oromo of Sawa', *Ethnological Society Bulletin*, Addis Ababa, 1958.

Neushtadt (Ayalon), D., 'Kavim letoldot hakalkala shel hayehudim veyishuvam bemitsrayim biyemei habenayim', *Zion* (Hebrew), 1937.   Neushtadt, 'Kavim'

Newbold, D., 'The Crusaders in the Red Sea and Sudan', *Sudan Notes and Records*, Vol. 26, 1945.

Orhonlu, C., 'Seydi Ali Reis', *Journal of the Regional Cultural Institute Iran, Pakistan and Turkey*, Teheran, 1967.

Papi, Maria R., 'Una Santa Abissinia anti Cattolica', *Rassegna di Studi Etiopici*, anno 1, No. 1, 1943.   Papi

Perruchon, J., 'Notes pour l'histoire d'Ethiopie. Le règne de Lebna Dengel', *Revue Sémitique*, I, 1893.   Perruchon, *Sémitique*, 1893

Perruchon, J., 'Histoire d'Eskender, d'Amda Seyon II et de Na'od, rois d'Ethiopie', *Journal Asiatique*, 1894.

Perruchon, J., 'Notes pour l'histoire d'Ethiopie. Le règne de Gelawdewos ou Asnaf-Sagad', *Revue Sémitique*, II, 1894.   Perruchon, *Sémitique*, 1894.

Perruchon, J., 'Notes pour l'histoire d'Ethiopie. Le règne de Minas ou Admas-Sagad (1559-1563)', *Revue Sémitique*, IV, 1896.   Perruchon, *Sémitique*, 1896

Perruchon, J., 'Notes pour l'histoire d'Ethiopie. Les règnes de Ya'qob et Za-Dengel (1597-1607)', *Revue Sémitique*, IV, 1896.   Perruchon, *Sémitique*, 'Ya'qob'

Perruchon, J., 'Notes pour l'histoire d'Ethiopie. Le règne de
  Susenyos ou Seltan-Sagad (1607-1632)', *Revue*   Perruchon,
  Sémitique, V, 1897.   *Sémitique*, 1897
Wiet, G., 'Les relations Egypto-Abyssines sous les sultans
  Mamlouks', *Bulletin de l'Association des Amis des
  Eglises et de l'Art Coptes*, Cairo, 1938.   Wiet, 'Les Relations'
Wiet, G., 'Les marchands d'épices sous les sultans Mamlouks',
  Cahiers d'histoire d'Egypte, 1955.
Wendt, K., 'Amharische Geschichte eines Emirs von Harar
  im XVI Jahrhundert', *Orientalia*, IV, Roma, 1935.   Wendt, *Orientalia*

Ethiopian chronicles quoted in this book were used in their annotated European
translations and not in their Amharic originals.

Index